To Save My Race from Abuse

RELIGION AND AMERICAN CULTURE

Series Editors
David Edwin Harrell Jr.
Wayne Flynt
Edith L. Blumhofer

To Save My Race from Abuse

The Life of Samuel Robert Cassius

EDWARD J. ROBINSON

THE UNIVERSITY OF ALABAMA PRESS

Tuscaloosa

Typeface is AGaramond

∞

The paper on which this book is printed meets the minimum requirements of American
National Standard for Information Sciences-Permanence of Paper for Printed Library
Materials, ANSI Z39.48–1984.

Robinson, Edward J., 1967–
    To save my race from abuse : the life of Samuel Robert Cassius / Edward J. Robinson.
        p.   cm. — (Religion and American culture)
    Includes bibliographical references and index.
    ISBN-13: 978-0-8173-1555-9 (cloth : alk. paper)
    ISBN-10: 0-8173-1555-1 (cloth : alk. paper)
    1. Cassius, Samuel Robert, 1853–1931. 2. African American evangelists—Biography.
3. Restoration movement (Christianity)—History. 4. Racism—Religious aspects—
Christianity—History. 5. Race relations—Religious aspects—Christianity—History.
6. African Americans—Religion. I. Title.
    BV3785.C37R63 2007
    286.6092—dc22
    [B]
                                                                    2006024303

To Toni

Contents

Acknowledgments

This book would have been impossible without the encouragement and assistance of the following people: John L. Robinson; Fred Bailey; Calvin Bowers; Michael W. Casey; Bob Chada; Doug Foster; E. Stanly Godbold, Jr.; David Edwin Harrell, Jr.; Don Haymes; David Holmes; Richard Hughes; Rick Hunter; Robert Jenkins; Connie Lester; Greta Leverett; John F. Marszalek; Tom Olbricht; William E. Parrish; Jack Reese; Hans Rollmann; Jerry Rushford; Ellen Schoenrock; Lady Vowell Smith; Jerry Taylor; Bobby Valentine; and David Wray. I especially thank my wife, Toni, and our three daughters, Clarice, Ashley, and Erika, who have endured my preoccupation with this important project. I affectionately dedicate this book to my greatest supporter.

Chronology of Samuel Robert Cassius

1853	Born in Gainesville, Virginia (Prince William County), son of Jane, a slave, and James W. F. Macrae
1860	Sold along with mother to an unknown buyer
1863–64	Relocates to Washington, D.C., and attends public schools
1874	Marries Effie Festus-Basil
1883	Converts to Disciples of Christ (Restoration Movement) in Brazil, Indiana
1885	Begins preaching in Indiana and Illinois
1889	Relocates and preaches in Sigourney, Iowa
	Publishes first known extant article in *Christian Evangelist*
1895	First wife dies
1897	Becomes postmaster of Tohee, Oklahoma Territory
	Starts paper *Industrial Christian*
1898	Publishes *Negro Evangelization and the Tohee Industrial School*
	Suspends paper *Industrial Christian*
	Marries second wife, Selina Daisy Flenoid
1899	Opens Tohee Industrial School

Introduction

Samuel Robert Cassius (1853–1931), an ardent black evangelist and a scrupulous race man[1] in Churches of Christ, straddled two complex worlds. In the world of religion, Cassius toiled as a passionate preacher in the Stone-Campbell Movement,[2] relying on white believers for financial support as he advanced the "pure Gospel"[3] among African Americans. Cassius constantly pled with white Christians for monetary assistance, even as he vigorously protested and detested the paternalism and racism he faced in his chosen religious community. In the world of race, Cassius, an ex-slave, worked to elevate his people in an anti-black society that discounted black Americans and portrayed them as intellectually inept, habitually immoral, and naturally demonic. Cassius angrily rejected those stereotypes in sermons, writings, and deeds. Cassius's preoccupation with the evangelization of black people in America merged with his thinking about race so seamlessly that his racial thought and his religious behavior became virtually indistinguishable.

A telling illustration of Cassius's fusion of race and religion emerged in 1920 when Thomas H. Kirkman, a white preacher for Churches of Christ along the Ohio–West Virginia border, invited Cassius to proclaim the Gospel to blacks in the Ohio Valley. Kirkman, confident in Cassius's preaching ability, arranged two evangelistic appointments for him. "We have the offer of the colored Baptist meeting house in Point Pleasant, W. Va., for a meeting at that place. We have a place in Gallipolis, Ohio, where he can preach the Gospel to his own race," Kirkman wrote.[4]

Cassius enthusiastically accepted Kirkman's proposal, planning his Gallipolis arrival for June 12. "I am making my way to this point, without the promise of a cent, and I hope that it will result in much good to the cause of Christ. Brethren, don't forget my family while I am out in the field." Two white Christians, A. Allinder from West Virginia and Rena Carpenter from California, gave Kirkman three dollars for the Gallipolis meeting and helped make it possible for Cassius to travel from Oklahoma in order to preach in the Ohio Valley.[5]

A week after beginning the preaching campaign in Gallipolis, Cassius confessed to mixed emotions about his efforts. He expressed disappointment that there had been no baptisms, "no visible results," but he was optimistic to be preaching in a "very promising field." Cassius reported that Pentecostal groups sought to destroy his evangelistic meeting: "The Holy Rollers, the Jesus Only, and three and four other white bands are doing all they can to kill our meeting." Yet he rejoiced that the Ohio Valley was "one of the greatest fields of labor I have seen for many years, just think of it!" Attempting to forestall any questions about his presence in Ohio, he remarked that he was "doing what every other preacher ought to do, 'preaching the Gospel.'" Equally impressed with the collaboration and camaraderie of Christians of Ohio and with Kirkman's efforts to have the Word of God "preached to all people, regardless of race or color," Cassius hoped "to make this the greatest trip of my life."[6]

Disappointment dogged Cassius, however, through the seven-week preaching tour in Gallipolis, because he had not "won a single soul." Returning from Ohio to his Guthrie, Oklahoma, home, Cassius reflected on his experiences in the Ohio Valley and attributed his lack of success to unpleasant "weather conditions," lamenting, "I have been hindered by rain during the past seven weeks. Therefore, I feel sure that the weather was the cause of our seeming failure." Indeed, the *Gallipolis Daily Tribune* reported that on June 12, the day Cassius arrived in Gallipolis, the region experienced a "severe rain and hail storm." On July 15, lightning struck and killed a horse in the area, and nine days later the paper reported "one of the worst storms they ever saw," marked by "hail and a tremendous downpour of rain."[7]

Even the thousand-mile journey home offered the black evangelist no respite; weather might moderate, but the era's racism held distressingly stable. Traveling through Ohio, a weary, hungry, and penniless Cassius approached the house of a white preacher for the Disciples of Christ, "whose house of worship and parsonage covered a half a block." Cassius knocked on the door and explained to the minister his deplorable condition. "The man treated me," Cassius grumbled, "just like some mean people treat tramps. I was tired and rest broken, but he told me that if I would clean the water out of his cistern he would help me out of my cramp." Initially reluctant and indecisive, Cassius consented to do the job to earn money for travel fare to Oklahoma; but more importantly, he compromised with the minister in order to save African Americans from verbal abuse and racial stereotypes. "At any other time I would not have done it, but I thought I saw where that man would have used my refusal to work as a text to abuse the rest of the Negro race as being lazy brutes."[8] In the mind of Cassius, many white Americans were prone to attach derogatory labels to all African Americans because of the misdeeds of one black man. "If one low-down, drunken negro does a despicable act," Cassius had earlier written, "it is charged up to the entire race."[9]

After performing what he deemed a humiliating task, Cassius admitted proudly, "I did his work and did it well," even though "I had to ruin my clothes to save my race from abuse." Feeling cheated, however, because he received a mere "one dollar for five dollars' worth of work," he acknowledged the white preacher "got the best of me, made me do his dirty work for nothing, but he will not be able to say that all negroes are worthless brutes." Cassius felt the white clergyman, who preached for the "richest church in the city," had debased and degraded him, but Cassius preferred personal humiliation over group disgrace; he sacrificed clothing, body, and pride to rescue black Americans from the verbal damnation of white America.[10]

For Cassius, the phrase "to save my race from abuse" carried not merely theological importance; it also bore racial and social significance. Despite the dehumanizing experience of cleaning out a white preacher's cistern for a meager one dollar, Cassius exhibited a sense of relief, knowing "that man will not have the chance to curse the rest of the negro race through me."[11] Cassius's racial consciousness was as strong as his religious convictions; saving the souls of black folk from the wrath of God went hand in hand with rescuing their names and reputations from the condemnation of white America. Cassius crafted words and actions to the same end, elevating African Americans both spiritually and socially.

Cassius's life as a dynamic man of faith confirms W. E. B. Du Bois's assessment of the black American's double consciousness. Du Bois felt that

"One ever feels his twoness,—an American, a Negro; two souls, two thoughts, two unreconciled strivings; two warring ideals in one dark body, whose dogged strength alone keeps it from being torn asunder."[12] Du Bois's insight into the emotional turmoil roiling within black Americans was equally true for Cassius particularly and the African American religious community generally.

Church historians C. Eric Lincoln and Lawrence H. Mamiya, expanding on Du Bois's metaphor of double consciousness, have discerned a dialectic at work in America's black church and have identified six polarities in the black religious community. The first dialectic is between priestly and prophetic functions, the former stressing the spiritual life of black parishioners with the latter emphasizing the community involvement of its members. The second dialectic, that between otherworldly and this-worldly, focuses first on heavenly matters even while accentuating social and political involvement in the present. The third dialectic, universalism and particularism, acknowledges an all-encompassing Gospel which endorses "black consciousness" while recognizing "particularistic racial views." The fourth dialectic underscores both the communal and the privatistic. On the one hand, the black church seeks to address the economic, educational, social, and political concerns of its members even as it concentrates on religious and spiritual needs. The fifth dialectic manifests charismatic and bureaucratic emotional traits and characteristics in worship and produces organizational forms with financial and membership records. The final dialectic contrasts accommodation with resistance. In some respects, white churches influence black congregations, yet at the same time African American leaders resist the hegemony of white clergymen.[13]

Cassius lived out these six dialectical polarities, and each elucidates his complexity and intricacy as both a racial reformer and a racial theologian. The plight of black people in postbellum America compelled Cassius to tightrope between two worlds. As a black preacher in a predominantly white religious fellowship, Cassius violated traditional evangelistic roles in order to uplift his race by working as a political and social activist. Cassius, first and foremost a passionate evangelist, displayed priestly and prophetic traits as both a church and community leader. He sought a better life in the other world, but he also labored to improve life for himself and black Americans in this world, as a farmer, entrepreneur, and educator. A proclaimer of a universal Gospel, Cassius expressed concern for all men, but his priority was the evangelization of black people in this country. Working to evangelize African Americans, Cassius had to fight his way through the apathetic societal attitudes and racist mentalities of white Christians who seemingly cared more about foreign than domestic sinners. Cassius, therefore, often challenged the racial views of the very white believers he relied on for monetary support. These were the two complicated and contradictory worlds in which Cassius lived and moved.

However, the divergent worlds in which Cassius functioned led to his divided mind. Like many contemporary African Americans in the age of Booker T. Washington, Cassius possessed what historian August Meier has called a "divided mind."[14] As an evangelist in the Stone-Campbell Movement, Cassius felt the doctrinal tug-of-war between the "loyals" and "progressives." The former opposed instrumental music and evangelism through missionary societies; the latter endorsed them. Even though Cassius sided with the loyals, he often appealed to the progressives for monetary support. As a black man in politically Progressive America, Cassius became entangled in the tension between the Bookerites and anti-Bookerites. Certainly a disciple of Booker T. Washington, Cassius yet incorporated the racial militancy of Frederick Douglass, Ida B. Wells, and W. E. B. Du Bois.[15] Like Washington, Cassius pursued moral and economic uplift, but unlike the Tuskegee Wizard, Cassius unabashedly demanded immediate civil and political rights for fellow black Americans, as attested by his involvement in the Negro Protective League in Oklahoma. The dichotomy of religious preoccupation and social activism shaped Cassius's complex and contradictory mind.

A thoroughgoing study of Cassius's life reveals the paradoxes of the America of his times and the variegated ways in which any black preacher of integrity was obliged to navigate those troubled waters. An analysis of his religious career and his racial thought further discloses the context of his life both in the Stone-Campbell Movement and in Progressive America as well. J. E. Choate, professor emeritus of philosophy at David Lipscomb University, comments on Cassius in a biography of black cleric Marshall Keeble, the premier evangelist in twentieth-century Churches of Christ: "Never at a loss for words, S. R. Cassius was given to speaking his mind in a very plain fashion." Church historian Earl I. West notes Cassius's preoccupation with the race problem in American society and his frustration with white Christians' indifference to the predicament of blacks in the

United States: Cassius "thought long about his race, hoping to convince the white man of his people's character and potential. If he failed, it was because he was toying with an idea whose time had not yet come." More recently, Calvin Bowers, author of a history of black Churches of Christ in southern California, has argued that Cassius was "the first of a long line of California dreamers who would work in preaching the gospel and developing churches among the black people of Los Angeles."[16] Cassius relocated from Minneapolis, Minnesota, to California in 1924 to help his son Amos Lincoln Cassius establish a Church of Christ in Los Angeles. But aside from these brief references, Cassius has been generally ignored in Restoration Movement historiography.

Most of Cassius's writings, however, appeared in two popular religious journals, the *Christian Leader* and the *Gospel Advocate,* and remain available. Of the many journals issued by members of the Stone-Campbell community, Cassius considered these two papers the only ones "worth reading."[17] He penned the majority of his descriptions of his evangelistic endeavors and his addresses on race in the *Christian Leader,* an important and influential paper which Christians in Cincinnati, Ohio, published from 1886 until 1960. The bulk of Cassius's voluminous discussions on race and experiences in religion lie in the pages of the *Christian Leader,* which many members of Churches of Christ in the South have since forgotten. In 1904, Cassius praised the journal as the "only church paper that gives to the negro an unrestricted welcome."[18] Cassius seized this open-door opportunity to become the most recognized black preacher in Churches of Christ. "In this great mass of colored people," he wrote, "I presume we have about one hundred thousand members, and perhaps two hundred and fifty preachers, of which number I am sure that I am the most widely known, and I think I can say that I have done as much to call the attention of the white Christians to the needs of my race as any man living in my time."[19]

Appropriating a mixture of biographical, historical, chronological, and thematic methods to capture the essence of his religious life and his racial thought, this book offers the first detailed study of Samuel Robert Cassius's life and intellect. After an assessment of Cassius's transition from slavery in Virginia to a study of his residence in the nation's capital, the narrative examines his conversion to the Stone-Campbell Movement and that entity's white leaders who contributed to his religious development as well as the literature that molded his intellect. Next, the study compares and contrasts Cassius's biblical hermeneutics in the context of his chosen fellowship, followed by an exploration of the racial and racist mentalities Cassius encountered and challenged in Churches of Christ. Then his three-decade experience as a preacher, farmer, postmaster, educator, and family man in the state of Oklahoma are probed, leading to an analysis of his 1925 publication, *The Third Birth of a Nation*, in which Cassius delineated his racial and religious ideology. The book closes with an assessment of Cassius's evangelistic activities in his declining years.

While Marshall Keeble's fame surpassed that of Cassius by the 1930s, Cassius stood unchallenged as the most vocal and visible African American preacher in Churches of Christ during the Progressive Era, 1890–1920. And while scholars have focused on such illuminating figures as Frederick Douglass, Booker T. Washington, Ida B. Wells, Marcus Garvey, and W. E. B. Du Bois, Cassius represents a black search for truth rather closer to the hopes, aspirations, and disappointments of the black common folk. When explaining the mission of his life, Cassius declared, "It is my purpose to try, as far as in me lies the power, to make the Church of Christ see its duty to the Negro of the United States."[20] In doing so, "I got it fixed in my head that my race had need of me, and even when I could not provide food, I gave more thought to the needs of my race than to the needs of my family."[21] These words epitomize the essence of Cassius's life. He committed himself wholly to solving the race issue in American society, designing everything he did and said to uplift black Americans. He at times neglected his family and his health for the "needs" of his race, convinced that "God would take care of me and mine, and say, brethren, I have not been mistaken."[22] This book, then, represents an attempt to understand the American past more fully while rescuing an important, imperfect, and complex black evangelist and race man from undeserved obscurity.

I
The Education of a Black Man

I
"I Am What I Am"
The Formative Years

> But by the grace of God I am what I am: and his grace which was
> bestowed upon me was not in vain; but I labored more abundantly
> than they all: yet not I, but the grace of God which was with me.
>
> —1 Corinthians 15:10[1]

Meadow Farm, a nine-hundred-acre verdant and luxurious estate, lay a few miles outside Gainesville in Prince William County, Virginia. Consisting of well-watered fields, sprawling meadows, bluegrass, and plentiful fruit trees, this plantation with its country stores nourished a comfortable and convenient life for the estate's white owner and his family. Twenty-three black slaves maintained the property, cultivating the crops, grooming the livestock, manicuring the lawn, caring for the owner's children, cleaning the Big House, and cooking for both the white owners and for fellow black bondsmen. A local newspaper praised Meadow Farm as "unsurpassed by any in the State for health, and affords the Best Society."[2]

In the fall of 1852, James W. F. Macrae, Meadow Farm's owner, a powerful politician, an influential physician, and a chronic alcoholic, cornered one of his young, vibrant, and intelligent house slaves, Jane, and raped her.[3] Nine months later this illicit union, altogether typical of life in the Old South, produced a mulatto baby boy, Samuel, one of the half-million "new people" in the United States. The infant's first name reflected his mother's religious piety and devotion to God, while his middle and last names, Robert and Cassius, were probably self-bestowed after emancipation.[4] An active toddler on Macrae's plantation, precocious Samuel felt the rumblings that the publication of *Uncle Tom's Cabin,* the Kansas-Nebraska Act, the Brooks-Sumner affair, the *Dred Scott* case, and John Brown's raid stirred in the 1850s. These events dramatically impacted Cassius's life and symbolically presaged the turmoil which engulfed his adult career.

Because of his debauchery and the impending Civil War, the brutal Macrae sold Cassius and his mother. According to Cassius's description, "It hurt [Macrae] so much to think that there was a possibility of losing his slaves, 'he got on a drunk,' and made such a debt that my mother and myself had to be sold ahead of the time of sending slaves South." Cassius claimed that Macrae's relative Gen. Robert E. Lee, "not wanting my mother and myself sold to an outsider, bought us in on the day of the sale. We were sold from the block at the Court House in Warrenton, Virginia in the summer of 1860." Cassius's assertion is difficult to verify, since Lee never owned slaves until his father-in-law, George Washington Parke Custis, died in 1857, bequeathing him an estate that included 196 slaves and instructing him to free them within five years. Lee fulfilled Custis's wishes and manumitted his slaves in the winter of 1862–63, and neither Cassius nor his mother was named among the slaves Lee inherited and freed.[5]

Despite the ambiguity and mystery surrounding Cassius's claim, his literate mother gave him emotional strength and a sound intellectual foundation in his formative years. Unlike many slaves who never knew their birth date, Cassius was certain of his own, confidently stating, "I was born a slave, in Prince William Co., Virginia, May 8, 1853."[6] Knowing when he entered the world endowed Cassius with a sense of pride throughout his life, especially in his declining years. In 1926, he proffered the following poem in honor of his birthday:

I AM THE QUEEN OF MAY
Now sit down dear brother.
And listen to what I say.
I am going to have a birthday
On Saturday, the eighth of May.

Don't ask how old I am, brother.
For that I don't recall.
But I was born when folks say
The stars were going to fall.

Now listen to my story, brother:
I look forward to the day
That I have lived in this world
To see the eighth of May.[7]

The staunchly anti-Catholic Cassius perhaps unknowingly embraced a tradition of Catholicism which extolled the Queen of England in the month of May. Knowledge of his birthday gave Cassius a sense of strength and pride, yet his excessive, Catholic-like emphasis on his special day in May was one of many paradoxes that would mark his life.

From his house-servant mother, Cassius learned how to read. Even though an 1831 Virginia law forbade white Virginians from instructing slaves, mistresses in the Macrae household, Amanda the wife and Susan the daughter, displayed courage, defiance, and humanity in tutoring Cassius's mother, who, Cassius later wrote, "in turn taught me to read in a John Comly Speller." Comly, a Philadelphia teacher, compiled this popular textbook for a Pennsylvania boarding school. His *English Grammar,* replete with moral advice and biblical references, enjoyed numerous editions and furnished Cassius with a ready command of the English language and English prose as well as a working knowledge of Scripture. Cassius credited his mother for his training, his knowledge, and his confidence. "I am what I am," he averred, "because of my mother, and for her sake I have tried to make good."[8] Cassius honored his mother and his blackness, but rejected his debased father and his whiteness. Indeed, much of Cassius's aversion to racial and sexual mixing in his adult life stemmed from his racially mixed childhood in the Old South.

2

The Three Emancipators

Encounters in the Nation's Capital

> And Moses stretched out his hand over the sea; and the Lord caused
> the sea to go back by a strong east wind all that night, and made the
> sea dry land, and the waters were divided.
>
> —Exodus 14:21

When Abraham Lincoln issued the Emancipation Proclamation in 1863,
ten-year-old Cassius and his mother joined scores of "hungry, naked and
sick" ex-slaves who crossed the long bridge over the Potomac River, flock-
ing from Virginia to Washington, D.C.[1] From 1860 to 1863, the black
population in the nation's capital increased by ten thousand. By 1865, approximately forty thousand black newcomers had taken up residence in
Washington.[2] Cassius and his mother numbered among the black "contra-
bands," former slaves whom Union forces divided into family groups, using
the men as ditchdiggers and road and bridge builders and the women as
cooks and laundresses. These black refugees received regular soldiers' food
with a half ration for each family member. While acknowledging that he
was a contraband during the Civil War, Cassius never specified the tasks,
if any, he carried out.[3]

Notwithstanding Cassius's silence about his work in the District of Columbia, three important people and events there forever changed his life.
First, Cassius encountered a white female educator who profoundly shaped
his intellect. "It was a white Christian woman who molded my young mind
into what it is to-day. I came in contact with her in the first public school
opened for negro children in the District of Columbia."[4] Young Cassius
probably attended the tax-supported school at Ebenezer Church on Capitol
Hill, which the Board of Trustees of Public Schools opened on March 1,
1864, for African Americans. Its lead teacher was Emma V. Brown, a black
woman, assisted by Frances W. Perkins, a white woman supported by the
New England Freedmen's Aid Society.[5] Miss Perkins was evidently the
white teacher who made an indelible imprint on Cassius's formative mind.

Frances W. Perkins, a native of Middlefield, Connecticut, received monetary support from the New England Freedmen's Aid Society to teach black students in Washington, D.C. Her father, George W. Perkins, a "fiery advocate of immediate emancipation,"[6] pastored a Congregational church. As an adolescent, Frances recalled her father helping runaway slaves escape to freedom on the Underground Railroad. At age twenty-five in 1864, Frances Perkins obviously imbibed her father's abolitionist fervor and worked to liberate the minds of young black scholars. Emma V. Brown valued Perkins as a "faithful friend and an excellent teacher." In a letter to a colleague named Miss Stevenson, Brown expressed her delight over Perkins's arrival in Washington. "Perhaps you have struggled alone, month after month, hoping that you were doing good; perhaps after looking for a time, you received aid; if this is your experience, you know something of the joy I felt at the arrival of Miss Perkins. I had no friend in Georgetown; Miss Perkins came, and I was no longer alone and friendless."[7]

Perkins not only brought joy to Brown, but she also gladdened the hearts of her black pupils. On the first day of school, Perkins reported teaching "thirty-two scholars," and within three days attendance had increased to almost one hundred. "To-day, in a pouring rain," Perkins explained, "we had ninety; others want to come, but we doubt about receiving them, lest we should have more than we can do justice to. I have in the primary department already nearly seventy,—as many as I can well manage; but I cannot find it in my heart to refuse any that are anxious to come."[8] The population surge in the nation's capital affected the rapid increase in the student-body matriculation.

Furthermore, students often increased a school's enrollment by recruiting children from their neighborhoods. Perkins singled out one student, "a thoroughly wicked fellow and very hard to control," who moved into a neighborhood where children were without schools. The student, acting as a "decoy duck," brought a "new pupil nearly every day, for whose reception he pleads in such a manner that I have hitherto been weak-minded enough to yield, though I have made very good resolutions for tomorrow in case he appears with another." The teacher found humor, however, in the pupil's chicanery. "I cannot help laughing, when he is seen advancing upon us with his train each morning."[9] The mischievous boy could well have been young Cassius, who in later years displayed an indomitable will to educate other black youth. Perkins's story reveals how determined some black children were to acquire an education, and it further attests to the difficulty many teachers had controlling overcrowded classes with limited resources. Thus, by 1866, Perkins's "arduous labors" had emotionally exhausted her, and she returned temporarily to Connecticut to recuperate.[10]

Even though Cassius failed to remember his teacher's name, he believed that she belonged to the Stone-Campbell Movement. "I am sure she was one of the early disciples of Christ, brought in through A. Campbell's reformation movement, because she came into my life with the New Testament in one hand and the school books in the other, and while she taught me the three R's, she also led me into paths of righteousness for his name's sake by ever keeping before me what the will of the Lord was."[11] Frances Perkins indeed instructed her students in "reading the Testament,"[12] although she apparently gained her religious heritage outside the Restoration Movement.

Cassius lauded her for the secular knowledge she dispensed, but he valued even more the religious guidance she provided. "So far did she shape my religious thoughts that when I came to myself I naturally entered the Church of Christ as my only home." Cassius also credited Perkins with steering him toward spiritual rather than political and material pursuits. "The early training of that Christian woman," Cassius later reflected, "turned my mind in the trend of religious work instead of along the lines of political and worldly paths." The young white instructor helped move Cassius into spiritual realms, unlike the path taken by his much-admired co-laborer Booker T. Washington. "Therefore, under the training of that Christian woman I have done as much for my race in a gospel way as Booker T. Washington has done in a worldly way. I am doing what spiritual knowledge has taught me to do."[13] Cassius believed that the public school system of the District of Columbia providentially steered him toward the ministry and into the Stone-Campbell Movement.

While living in the capital Cassius also met President Abraham Lincoln. After Lincoln's 1864 reelection, crowds thronged the streets of the city to congratulate the Emancipator, Cassius and his mother among them. The president opened his receptions to ex-slaves, and Cassius recalled "my mother taking me by the hand and going to the White House to see the negroes' Moses. I shook hands with Mr. Lincoln, and remember the scene as though it was yesterday. I saw old, gray-headed men and women not only shake hands with President Lincoln, and weep tears of joy as they kissed his hand."[14] This brief encounter with the sixteenth president of the United States indelibly impressed Cassius, and he installed Lincoln in his pantheon of heroes.

If Lincoln's life of courage and heroism inspired African Americans, his assassination stunned them into "voiceless sorrow."[15] For most black freedmen, Lincoln's death was unforgettable. James Lucas, a Mississippi slave, recalled, "I never knowed Marse Lincoln, but I heard he was a powerful good man. I 'members plain as yesterday when he got kilt and how all de flags hung at half mast." Similarly, Wylie Nealy, a South Carolina bondsman, reflected, "I remembers when Lincoln was made the President both times and when he was killed. I recollects all that like yesterday."[16] Although Cassius lived in Washington when John Wilkes Booth murdered the president, he never mentioned the tragic event. Rather than dwell on Lincoln's death, Cassius honored the slain Emancipator by naming one of his sons after him. Amos Lincoln Cassius (1889–1982) worked as a reputable evangelist in twentieth-century Churches of Christ.

Cassius met four other presidents while in Washington: Andrew Johnson, Ulysses S. Grant, Rutherford B. Hayes, and James A. Garfield. Cassius wrote that "Even Andrew Johnson received colored people at his reception. I shook hands with him, and Grant, and Hayes, and Garfield. Every one of those men have made no distinction in color, and the only comment ever made on it was one of commendation."[17] Cassius later pointed to his brief meetings with these chief executives to argue for societal equality and inclusion for African Americans. Throughout his life Cassius stayed abreast of America's political currents, viewing political and racial issues as inseparable. His merging of politics and religion prompted conflict with many white leaders in the Stone-Campbell Movement who tended to be antipolitical. From Cassius's perspective, however, the treatment of black Americans was the best measure of any politician's quality.

Prominent black politicians also worked in the capital while Cassius lived there. Frederick Douglass served as U.S. marshal for the District of Columbia, and ex-slaves Hiram Revels and Blanche K. Bruce, both preacher-politicians and both United States senators from Mississippi, worked in Washington. John M. Langston, as professor, dean, vice president, and president of Howard University, represented blacks in the educational field. Cassius recognized such men as role models and mentors since he "lived contemporaneous with such men of my race as Fred Douglass, Revels, B. K. Bruce, John M. Langston and many others, with all of whom I have been on intimate terms. The above men were my ideals of negro statesmanship." These African Americans instilled in Cassius a sense of pride as he looked to them as symbols of black promise and black advancement. Writing several decades later, he expressed that their rise from slavery to freedom, from bondage to statesmanship, from obscurity to prominence presaged an "optimistic future" for himself and other young black Americans.[18]

Cassius clearly identified with the four legislators because they all were former slaves who transitioned from black bondage to leadership roles. Douglass, Revels, Bruce, and Langston collaborated in the nation's capital and often attended the same public functions. When these men addressed audiences in black Washington, Cassius was likely a curious spectator. Of the four statesmen, Cassius held the highest regard for Douglass, who "was born a slave; made his escape from slavery; picked up an education, and finally became the greatest negro in America, if not the world."[19] This assessment gains even greater significance since Douglass was an integrationist while Cassius was a separatist. In fact, even though Cassius never mentioned Douglass's controversial marriage to a white woman, Helen Pitts, he firmly opposed on biblical grounds such racial and sexual mixing. Despite Douglass's transgression, Cassius still admired him.

Cassius found more reason for optimism in Washington, D.C., when he reportedly became the "first colored boy to finish high school." Perhaps Cassius attended the Preparatory High School which opened in 1870 and graduated its first class in 1875. Since the school did not hold its first commencement until 1877, it is difficult to substantiate the assertion that Cassius was the first African American male to complete high school in the nation's capital.[20] Furthermore, in 1874 Cassius married his first wife, Effie Festus-Basil of Columbus, Ohio. Virtually nothing is known about Effie other than the bare family facts. Her marriage to Cassius engendered eleven children, beginning with a daughter, Julian, born in 1875 in Washington, but details concerning Cassius's other children remain nebulous.[21]

Cassius's early years in the District of Columbia were formative times for him. Frances W. Perkins helped him develop reading and writing skills in a Washington public school, stirring in Cassius a love for poetic literature and inspiring him to become an educator in later years. Cassius's encounter with Abraham Lincoln, the "negroes' Moses," instilled in him a sense of hope and optimism for African Americans. Political leaders from Johnson to Garfield raised his expectations of the federal government, teaching him to look to politicians for protection of civil rights as well as social elevation. Black statesmen also gave him a sense of race pride.

Cassius actually met three emancipators: Abraham Lincoln, Frances W. Perkins, and Frederick Douglass. The legal assistance Cassius received from Lincoln's Emancipation Proclamation taught him to look to white benefactors to finance his evangelistic endeavors in later years, the intellectual skill he learned from Perkins whetted his thirst for knowledge and inspired him to educate others, while the verbal inspiration he garnered from Douglass spurred him to do all he could to elevate fellow black Americans socially and spiritually.

But of the many different people who helped shape Cassius, none was more potent than Frances W. Perkins. In 1919 Cassius, then sixty-six years old, recalled the influence the young white woman exerted on his unformed intellect: "The teacher that faced us was a Christian white woman, who met us colored children with a New Testament in her hand. Nor did that Testament cease to be part of our education; it was that that fixed it in my mind that the Bible was God's revealed will to man, and made it impossible for me to ever be anything [but] 'a Christian only.'"[22] She was in truth a Moses who led young Cassius from the slavery of ignorance to the Promised Land of knowledge.

Cassius's encounter with Perkins led him to imbibe an assortment of both secular and religious literature which contributed to his complex and combative racial thought. This intellectual foundation launched him on a lifelong quest, and by age fifty-two, he had amassed a library of 250 books in pursuit of his goals, no small accumulation for a poor black in Gilded Age America. These sources, which Cassius read and which comprised his impressive literary collection, formed the nexus of his learning. Beyond these volumes, certain key individuals also contributed to Cassius's development of mind and soul. The following chapter explores these springs of Cassius's spiritual and intellectual maturation.

3
The Molding of a Mind
Personal Influences and Literary Sources

> Therefore if any man be in Christ, he is a new creature: old things are
> passed away; behold, all things are become new.
>
> —2 Corinthians 5:17

Withering economic opportunities and heightening racial discrimination
squeezed Cassius and his family out of the nation's capital. In the early
1880s, Cassius left Washington, D.C., and relocated his family to Indiana,
finding work in the coal mines. More importantly, he experienced a religious conversion. In 1927 he reflected on his movement into the fellowship
of Churches of Christ: "But as I stand on the threshold of eternity, I am
forced to turn my head, and look back over a life full of mistakes and
short-coming, and I see myself as I was 43 years ago, in a little brick on a
side street in Brazil, Ind. After hearing a sermon on 'Faith,' from the lips
of the first Christian preacher I had ever listened to, when he gave the
invitation, though I was the only colored man in the house, I went forward
and made the good confession, and with a white man I was carried to a
pool of water and I was buried by baptism into death from whence I was
raised to a new life."[1] Cassius's testimony places his alliance with the Disciples of Christ in 1883 or 1884.

Shortly after joining the Stone-Campbell Movement, Cassius began his
preaching career. Hiram Woods and W. R. Jewell, white leaders in Illinois,
first encouraged him in a career of ministry. "Elder Hiram Woods and
Elder Jewell gave me my first letter of commendation," Cassius testified in
1927. "They have gone to their reward. But I am still trying to carry their
opinion of my ability to preach the Word." Three years later Cassius remi-
nisced about the men who shaped his religious development. "Sitting here
today, at the dawn of the new year, my mind runs back to the spring of
forty-five years ago, when I laid aside a kit of mining tools and took a letter
from the hands of Brother Hiram Woods, one of the elders of the church

at Danville, Ill., and started out in the world to teach my people the plain, simple way of the Lord."[2]

Significantly, Cassius received instruction, baptism, and inspiration from white Christians in the post-Reconstruction era when white parishioners often barred African Americans from their congregations. Cassius himself recalled being rejected by a white seeker at the altar call: "When I was quite young and had no better sense, I let a white preacher persuade me to go to the 'mourner's bench.' On that same night, a white man went to the 'mourner's bench,' and it made him so mad to think that a 'nigger' was mourning at the same bench with him that he quit mourning and 'wouldn't get religion,' and I went around two or three days hoping to catch him out and fight him, because he did not want to mourn with me."[3] Cassius's positive encounters with teacher Frances W. Perkins and several presidents in his formative years had tempered such negative racial and religious experiences and did not lead Cassius to distrust all white people.

Indeed, in the years following his baptism, the life and work of Alexander Campbell (1788–1866) fundamentally influenced Cassius, who embraced Campbell as a hero whom God used to fight against sin, sectarianism, and Catholicism in the United States. When attempting to establish his Tohee Industrial School in Oklahoma in 1898, Cassius, seeking to thwart the progress of Catholicism in the Tohee community, alluded to the 1837 debate between Campbell and John Purcell, the Catholic bishop of Cincinnati. The Campbell-Purcell polemic, in Cassius's view, raised Campbell to heroic status in Protestantism.[4]

It will also be remembered that the religion of the white people as it grew in this country, partook more and more of Catholicism, until it became evident that the American white people would have to be evangelized or their religion would drift them back into Catholicism. It was then came Alexander Campbell, that great man of God—for if there has ever been a man in America sent of God, he was one; sent not to start a new religion, but to show men that they were going slowly but surely away from God and heaven, and drifting surely into Catholicism and hell; and you all know that the influence of that man's voice in the wilderness of sin and sectarianism was so loud and far-reaching that it arrested the attention of every denomination, and brought them back to the Bible and God. As a result, Catholicism received a blow from which it has not yet recovered (but if you folk do not stop stealing Catholic days and worship, you will soon be where Alexander Campbell first found you—that is, if you are not there now).[5]

Cassius inherited from Campbell and other white leaders in the Restoration Movement a vigorous anti-Catholicism which he retained throughout his life, and Cassius's opposition to the Catholic Church in Oklahoma mirrored Campbell's battle against Catholicism. With Campbell, and perhaps because of Campbell's teaching, Cassius shared a deep aversion to Catholicism. Perhaps Cassius viewed himself as a black Alexander Campbell whom God raised up to steer Churches of Christ away from those Catholic practices that were not founded on biblical teaching and to stamp out Catholic influence in the state of Oklahoma.

Cassius heaped more praise on Campbell in 1901 after digesting the Campbell-Rice Debate. "I received the Campbell and Rice debate on the Holy Spirit, while I read it as it ran through the columns of the *Christian Leader,* and was pleased with it. I find it still more interesting in book form. Every Christian should have a copy of it, so that their children could see how earnestly our old founder of the restoration movement contended for the faith."[6] From the Campbell-Rice discussion, which took place in 1843, Cassius learned the polemical arguments for the role of baptism and the Holy Spirit in conversion. As a debater himself, Cassius found in Campbell's arguments practical tools to expose what he perceived as doctrinal error. Beyond Campbell's skills as a debater, in Cassius's mind Alexander Campbell was the "founder" of the Restoration Movement. While Cassius acknowledged the good work and contributions of Barton W. Stone and John F. Rowe, he gave primacy to Alexander Campbell.[7]

Conversely, Cassius reserved his most severe condemnation for those who, in his evaluation, followed religion as a path to profits. In 1902, while visiting Churches of Christ in California, Cassius denounced preachers who used "their calling as a business profession for the sake of the compensation that is in it," criticized professional male singers who reminded him of "a wounded bear growling to keep off its assailants," and castigated trained female singers who reminded him of a "cat smiling in the dead hours of the night out on some back fence." Cassius yearned to "hear God's children pour forth their souls in song" but lamented the "lifeless, soul-

less and meaningless organ [that] jars upon your ear drums like a bray-
ing mule in a fodder stack. But it is here, and here to stay until another
Alexander Campbell is raised up to call the churches back to Christ and
his Word."[8] Together with so many members of the Stone-Campbell Movement, Cassius advocated a cappella singing in worship, disagreeing heartily
with his religious cohorts who introduced musical instruments into worship services.

No stranger to intrachurch disputations, Cassius served two years as
president of the Oklahoma Board of Colored Missions. To those who
deemed this body unordained by Scripture, he justified his controversial
position by pointing out that Alexander Campbell held the first presidency
of the American Christian Missionary Society. "A Christian preacher accused me of being 'digressive,' because I allowed myself to be made president of a mission board, yet that same preacher believes that A. Campbell
was the greatest character in the Church of Christ, and Campbell was the
first president of the American Christian Missionary Society."[9]

In 1916, Cassius linked Campbell's religious work in nineteenth-century
America with his own evangelistic activity in the twentieth century. "Campbell saw America going further and further away from God and his word,
and he saw that the only way to save them was to stop them and direct
them into the right way. So it is with the American Negro, he was started
in the wrong direction, and no half-way methods will ever cause a radical
change in the religion of my race." Just as Campbell pointed people back
to God and the Bible, Cassius believed that it was his obligation to persuade African Americans to abandon "their present system of religion" and
to "place them in line with God's word, and in full fellowship with our
Lord and Savior Jesus Christ."[10] Cassius viewed his work as a continuation
of the great Restoration Movement launched by Alexander Campbell, and
he sought to restore New Testament principles to a church cleansed from
what he perceived as latter-day impurities such as the use of instrumental
music.

Once, after attending a Christian church which had an impressive choir
"assisted by two small fiddles, two horns, a bass fiddle, a large pipe organ,
a piano and some other instruments," Cassius lamented, "I wonder what
Alexander Campbell would think, or say, if he could see some of the things
that are being done in the churches of Christ today under the name of
apostolic Christianity." After watching seekers march forward to accompa-

nying instrumental music, Cassius pondered whether "Christ could recognize his church in that ungodly mess."[11] The Alexander Campbell fixed in Cassius's mind was the one whom historian Richard Hughes has labeled "the Alexander Campbell of the *Christian Baptist.*" This more youthful Campbell, unlike the subsequent one of the *Millennial Harbinger,* was, in Hughes's view, "highly combative."[12] Cassius, who perceived no shift in Campbell's thinking, reveals in his comments no difference between an older, more open Campbell and a younger, more narrow persona. More importantly, Cassius reflects an iconoclastic, somewhat legalistic, and exclusivist mentality which apparently pervaded most African American Churches of Christ.

Cassius also came under the inspirational influence of a Restoration Movement missionary, Frederick A. Wagner (1836–1901), who inspired Cassius to toil tirelessly and shamelessly among fellow blacks whom whites despised. When Wagner died in the fall of 1901, Cassius prayed for his successors: "Oh, Jesus, help them to be faithful. Draw very near unto him upon whose shoulders falls the mantle of F. A. Wagner, is my prayer, for Christ's sake. Amen." Wagner's labor among the Japanese abroad paralleled Cassius's involvement among black people in America. "His work was so much like mine—among a people despised, in a field surrounded by nothing but enemies, every step must be won by hard fighting and personal sacrifice. I have been too sad even to work." But Wagner's example fired Cassius's determination to commit his life to lift wayward black Americans from moral and spiritual degradation. Cassius concluded, "Brother Wagner went out not knowing whither he went. Duty called him. He did not stop to confer with flesh and blood, but went forward, doubting nothing. Thank God, he fell where I am determined to fall—on the field of battle. Go on, Bro. Wagner; Cassius is coming. You went from the dark, sin cursed land of heathen Japan. I will go from the Black Belt of sin-cursed America."[13]

For the next three decades Cassius imitated Wagner's dedication to evangelism, devoting his life to attempting to solve the race problem in America by advancing what he believed was the pure religion of Jesus Christ. Wagner, who wrote several articles in the *Christian Leader* refuting Catholicism, also contributed to Cassius's strong anti-Catholic views.[14]

Cassius, however, credited Joseph E. Cain, a white preacher in Wichita, Kansas, and editor of the *Christian Leader,* with having the greatest impact on his spiritual development. "He found me alone, naked, as it were, and he gave me food, clothes and comfort, and it is to him, more than any other man I owe my success in spreading the Gospel." Cassius never praised more highly any man—black or white—than Cain, whom he dubbed "the whitest, broadest and most Christlike man I ever knew, and, above all, he was my friend." The Cain-Cassius relationship illustrates that in the deeply segregated Stone-Campbell Movement some blacks and whites did genuinely care for one another. Cassius explained, "The white brethren indeed had great reason to love, but I had more reason than they could ever have, he came into my life twenty-two years ago, at a time that I indeed needed a friend, and from that time to the very end he remained a friend to me; if I did well he praised me for it, if I erred he gave me the benefit of every doubt, and if he rebuked me it was in a Christian spirit."[15]

This commendation offers a glimpse into the psyche of Cassius, revealing the intimate and emotional bond he felt with Cain. Cain, a white Christian, perhaps represented in some ways the father Cassius never had but doubtlessly longed for. The praise and rebuke Cain gave Cassius became the love and discipline the latter had never received from his white biological father. Cain verbally lashed Cassius in 1909, when Cassius charged that white Christians knew many African Americans were "going to hell" but hated them "too much to head them off." Cain branded the criticism "unfortunate and entirely uncalled for." Violation of the "color line" in Oklahoma, Cain insisted, would "stir up the race question, and engender race prejudice that can work only harm to all concerned."[16]

Furthermore, while Cassius portrayed the all-white Church of Christ in Meridian, Oklahoma, as a spiritually and financially strong congregation, Cain dismissed such characterizations as "far from being true." "The brethren there are making a hard fight," Cain continued, "and are carrying (for them) a heavy load, and have had some serious setbacks, especially in the loss of members by removals." Cassius's remarks about the material status of Christians in Meridian upset them because "they had been placed in a false light before the brotherhood." Cain, who often gave his friend the benefit of the doubt, concluded, "I do not say, nor do I believe, that Bro. Cassius is guilty of any intentional misrepresentation. His mistake is in not well considering the matter before rushing into print."[17] Cain's public rebuke of Cassius did not disrupt their friendship.

Such white leaders as Cain influenced Cassius not only through personal relationships but more so with their literary efforts. Cassius read voraciously, devouring all sorts of literary works. Cassius read with interest the *Christian Century's* 1903 article about Voltaire, the French skeptic who in the eighteenth century had predicted Christianity's decline. The article repudiated Voltaire's claim and cited numerous examples of Christianity's progression in the world, in particular upholding the Disciples of Christ as an example of a flourishing religious body. Cassius, however, disputed the author's findings and agreed with Voltaire, arguing, "In my judgment, Voltaire spoke truth." The religion of Jesus Christ, Cassius maintained, "has almost disappeared from the world, and in its place has sprung up a religion beside which heathenism is highly exalted." Cassius maintained that God did not recognize such religious groups as the Baptists, Methodists, Presbyterians, and others because these "different denominations" had nothing to do "with Christ or his church." Like the political muckrakers common in his era, he further dismissed the boast that various religious groups spent 36 million dollars yearly to spread the Gospel throughout the world, inquiring, "What is that small sum to so many? J. P. Morgan cleared more than that amount last year for the steel trust alone."[18]

As an impoverished preacher, Cassius often looked askance at wealth and frequently linked material prosperity with irreligion. In this respect, Cassius echoed Barton W. Stone and David Lipscomb who viewed poverty as a Christian virtue.[19] "The very fact that the denominations are growing in wealth," Cassius complained, "is an evidence that they are not following the meek and lowly Jesus." Continuing his argument that Christianity was indeed decaying, he pleaded, "If in my ignorance I am narrow minded and near-sighted, I beseech you, dear brethren, to open mine eyes, enlarge my mind and strengthen my faith by showing me the truth of the statement that pure religion, undefiled before God and man, is on increase."[20] Fundamentally, Cassius measured the growth of the Stone-Campbell Movement not by the increase of white converts but by the number of blacks who submitted to the Gospel message. So he argued that Christianity was an endangered species because Caucasian disciples were not doing enough to help him and other black preachers disseminate the Word of God among African Americans.

This spiritual thrust did not, however, lead Cassius to ignore secular literature. An avid reader of black newspapers, he kept abreast of the successes and challenges of African Americans. As logs stoke a fire, black journals fueled Cassius's rage and helped shape his angry mindset. The *Savannah Tribune,* a newspaper black Georgians published, protested that "These be terrible times through which the Afro-American is now passing, but more terrible will they be upon the future Caucasian, for they are sowing what they must evidently reap." In similar fashion, the *Washington Bee,* a journal in the nation's capital, asked, "Is there no one to come to the defense of the black man?" These two black journals, among many others, gloomily described white Southerners' attempts to disfranchise their black counterparts, prompting Cassius to lament, "The highest office that a negro holds to-day, and I may say the only one open to him, is that of a preacher—and race hatred has gone so far that the great mass of white church members do not recognize him, either as a man or a brother."[21] The invisibility of black men and the indifference of white Christians troubled Cassius profoundly.

Cassius's perusal of black newspapers, which often presented dark portraits of the status of African Americans, stirred him to lash out at white Christians as caring more about "horses, dogs and cats" than about black people like himself. "The church wept, prayed and preached about cruelty to animals until it had laws passed in every State preventing brutal people from being unmerciful to them. Are we not as good as dumb brutes?" Knowing that many religious groups opposed improper treatment of animals in Progressive Era America, Cassius challenged whites in Churches of Christ to arise and denounce the inhumane treatment of black Americans in various parts of the nation. Thus, he asked, "Is it any wonder that we should wonder if the church will arise and denounce the cruel things done to us until lynchings, hangings, burnings and disfranchisements become so obnoxious that the nation will not stand them? Has the Church of Christ the courage of her convictions? If so, may I not hope that she will labor as earnestly to give the negro humane treatment as to correct other evils existing in the world? Have we a white Christian minister who will dare speak out against the evils that are being done my race? If there is one, God grant that he may speak with no uncertain sound."[22]

The *Literary Digest,* a weekly magazine published in New York, also frequently provided Cassius with information about the plight of his fellow black Americans. In 1901 William Ellis Abernethy, president of Rutherford College in North Carolina, advised in a speech which that journal published that blacks should be expelled from the South. This was the "one solution" to the race problem in America. "Go he must. Better for black man," declared Abernethy, "better for white man. We who have girl babies will rest more easily in our graves hereafter, if we die in the proud consciousness that this problem has not been left by cowardly policy to posterity." When Cassius read these words, he cringed and railed, "Again, I say the African did not come to America, and he is not going to leave America. Disfranchise us if you choose, kill us if you desire, but that will not settle the problem. We are here, and here we must and will stay." Unlike Henry M. Turner and Marcus Garvey, black leaders who advocated migration to Africa as the solution to America's race problem, Cassius opposed both mandatory and voluntary migration outside the United States. In Cassius's assessment, the race issue in America was a "question that only the Church can settle."[23]

Cassius also read papers published by black Oklahomans. In 1904, the *Oklahoma Guide,* a popular newspaper which African Americans controlled, reproduced an incendiary speech by the virulent racist James K. Vardaman. A politically progressive governor of Mississippi, Vardaman depicted freedmen as decadent criminals unfit to be educated. Cassius denounced the governor's inauguration remarks as an "insult to every great mind on earth, and blasphemy against God." The white man, Cassius charged, was responsible for any ignorance and moral decadence on the part of the black man.

> [James K. Vardaman] says as a race we are retrograding every day; that time has demonstrated that we are more criminal as freeman than as slaves. Now let us look at this matter honestly, and see if this is true. Prior to the Civil War the negro was held in bondage amid the most degrading circumstances. He was taught no moral precepts, no sense of virtue, and no regard for the marriage ties. They were compelled to live in such a compact mass that secrecy was impossible. They were compelled to witness criminal outrages on mothers, wives and sisters, until every sense of decency was crushed out of their hearts, leaving nothing behind but a brutal desire to do the same thing. Such was the condition of the masses of the slaves in at least five States, namely, South Carolina, Georgia, Alabama, Mississippi, and Louisiana; and it was from these hotbeds of moral de-

pravity and prostitution that nine-tenths of the most revolting crimes come.[24]

Cassius's denunciation of Vardaman's racist cant underscored his interest in politics. Political decrees, Cassius understood, often bore racial and social consequences, and his personal interaction with the nation's presidents, especially Abraham Lincoln, taught him that the decisions of federal officials profoundly affected the status of blacks in America, even as the Emancipation Proclamation and Thirteenth Amendment forever changed his own life. Cassius's repudiation of the Mississippi governor's tirade further revealed the continuing detrimental effects of black bondage in the Old South. Perhaps indirectly referring to his own experiences as a slave in Virginia, Cassius insisted that the institution of slavery invariably promoted immorality and indecency, and the phrase "criminal outrages on mothers" mirrored the sexual violation of his own mother. Yet Cassius hailed spiritual enlightenment as the African American's greatest need, pleading, "Oh, that the church of Christ would rise as one man and throw a flood of Gospel light in the midst of my people. Is there not a man or woman that will give a thousand dollars to start out three colored evangelists among my people?"[25]

J. S. De Jarnette, an occasional reader of the *Christian Leader* and a white Christian from Aline, Oklahoma Territory, protested Cassius's criticism of Vardaman's speech. Cassius's "attempted criticism of the statements of the governor of Mississippi contains no proof, nothing but the allegations, the ipse dixit of Mr. Cassius." De Jarnette claimed that "many people in the 'North' were so ignorant of the true state of affairs in the 'South'" that they accepted Cassius's comments "as fact." De Jarnette then concluded, "I seriously object to discussion of political questions in religious journals, and, I believe, in this nine-tenths of your subscribers will agree with me."[26] This sort of appropriation of a religious paper to address racial and political concerns marks Cassius as a unique evangelist in the Stone-Campbell Movement. The grievous circumstances of blacks in Progressive Era America demanded that Cassius use all means to uplift his people, and most whites in Churches of Christ such as De Jarnette failed to grasp this fact.

Cassius, however, reached beyond politics for succor, resorting often to poetry. He frequently incorporated William Cowper's poem "The Negro Complaint" in his writings to justify his positions on racial issues. Cowper (1731–1800), the noted English poet and hymn writer, first published the poem in 1788 as part of a campaign against the slave trade. His verses attacked the slave traders' excuse that Africans stood innately inferior to Europeans.

Forced from home and all its pleasures
Afric's coast I left forlorn,
To increase a stranger's treasures
O'er the raging billows borne.
Men from England bought and sold me,
Paid my price in paltry gold;
But, though theirs they have enrolled me,
Minds are never to be sold.

Still in thought as free as ever,
What are England's rights I ask,
Me from my delights to sever—
Me to torture, me to task?
Fleecy locks and black complexion
Can not forfeit nature's claim;
Skin may differ, but affection
Dwells in black and white the same . . . [27]

The poem's carefully paced meter vividly depicts the horrors of slavery and the slave trade which permanently severed black family ties. The poem alludes further to slavery's economic and commercial aspects, whereby whites in Europe and the Americas profited handsomely from "the man-degrading mart." This poem profoundly impressed Cassius, who argued that "My Bible teaches me that God never made but one man and I believe it, and I firmly believe that though skins may differ, that affections dwell in blacks and whites the same."[28] Cassius often appropriated this poem to argue for blacks' inclusion in society generally and in the church particularly.

In his literary sweep, Cassius read black poetry as well. He included the works of African American Charles D. Clem (1875–1934) in some of his

Christian Leader articles. In 1902, Cassius cited two stanzas of a poem that Clem wrote in "Negro" dialect.

> Did you ebber stop ter think erbout de
> preachers of today?
> Dey ain't jes lak de ones I knowed when
> I was young and gay,
> Dey preach ebout dey 'ology, but, chillen,
> sho's you bo'n.
> Dat 'ology am gwine ter drap when Gabriel
> blows de ho'n.
>
> Dey goes off to de 'cademies and fixes up
> der mine
> Till dey kin read ole David's Psalm er
> comin' or er gwine.
>
> Dey don't sing ole time melodies, but
> hafer-lutin' songs,
> But, bless de Lord, dat's gwine ter drap
> when Gabriel blows his ho'n.[29]

Cassius clearly identified with this poem, replete as it is with references to biblical characters such as David, Jonah, Daniel, and the angel Gabriel. Most importantly, the poem reflects the criticism Cassius received as a learned preacher, whom some Christians accused of idleness. Cassius referenced this poem in response to accusations of "why I have not written more about my work; they say the brethren will think I am doing nothing. That may all be true." In defense of his perceived silence, he explained, "I get tired of repeating the same old story." Thus, he concluded, "Keep this one thing in your mind: as long as I live I will try to lead men to Christ."[30]

Cassius absorbed poetry that provided moral direction and racial uplift and in equal measure detested poems that negatively portrayed African Americans. He chided white leaders of the Southern Christian Institute, which Disciples of Christ operated in Edwards, Mississippi, where a female black student read a poem, "Chiggers," that subjected black Americans to ridicule.

Way down yonder in de contry,
Whar de watermillions grow,
Whar de cotton am a-bloomin',
An de niggers use de hoe.

On de banks ob de ribber,
Am a little shady spot,
Whar dis nigger goes a-swimmin'
When de weather it am hot.

Ah don't lack to hoe de cotton,
But I sho do lack to swim,
So I hang my yaller breeches
On de nea'-by Cyprus limb.

Dar is chiggers on my person,
And dar's chiggers in my shirt;
Ah grease dem wid de bacon rhine,
An I mop dem tel it hurts.

But de chiggers keep a-bitin',
And de seem to nebber stop;
De boss at home am a-callin',
Nigger come to dis patch.

But I ain't got no time to lissen
'Bout no cotton patch;
I sure is got a job at home,
And its scratch, scratch, scratch.[31]

Cassius scorned this poem as inappropriate for black students who attended the Southern Christian Institute to train as missionaries. "Every year when the school term closes, enthusiastic men and women go to Edwards to hear students say funny things, and they call it preparing the negro boys and girls to win the world for Christ." The poem's title, "Chiggers," rhymed with "Niggers," a term he hated deeply. Therefore, it reflected the racism of many whites in the Stone-Campbell Movement who allowed and encouraged black students to read poems that perpetuated negative stereotypes about African Americans. Such caricatures, Cassius insisted, did "my race and the cause of Primitive Christianity more harm than good."[32] Such comments reveal Cassius as more than an evangelist; he was also a sensitive race man who not only sought to save the souls of black folk but also committed to protecting the reputation and image of his race.

If Cassius hated "Chiggers," he delighted in an anonymous poem entitled "The Old Preacher," which he often cited, especially in his declining years. The poem mirrors Cassius's own life as a poverty-stricken evangelist and an underappreciated racial reformer. Referring to excerpts from the poem, he identified with many "poor old preachers" who were "turned out in this cold, cheerless world, unsung and unmoaned by those they have tried to help," as well as with the sentiments in the poem's last stanza:

> . . . I'll try to believe that what happens will
> Alwus come out for the best;
> They tell my labor is ended; 'tis time
> I wus takin' a rest.
> I've leetle o' comfort or riches but I'm
> Sure my conscience is clear,
> An' when in the church-yard I'm sleepin',
> Perhaps they may wish I was here.[33]

Spiritual songs also shaped the mind of Cassius. He especially appreciated M. E. Abbey's "Life's Railway to Heaven," which contains the following caution:

> You will often find obstructions;
> Look for storms of wind and rain,
> On a fill, or curve, or trestle,
> They will almost ditch your train.
> Put your trust alone in Jesus,
> Never falter, never fail;
> Keep your hand upon the throttle,
> And your eyes upon the rail.[34]

Charles D. Tillman, a white songwriter, set Abbey's poem to music, and the song "Life's Railway to Heaven" has perhaps been sung more among African American worshipers than their white counterparts. The hymn spoke to the double consciousness of Cassius and other oppressed black Americans. In one respect, faith in Jesus required that Christians anticipate and endure "storms of wind and rain," but at the same time followers of Christ had to keep their focus on the life beyond the grave. Cassius tellingly assessed the poem: "The above is the kind of poems that suit me; they seem alive, exciting, and full of vim."[35]

Cassius kept another song, "We'll Understand It Better By and By," in his heart. Written in 1905 by Charles Albert Tindley, a renowned songwriter in the history of the black church in America, the song describes the world as a place of "dark" trials. In 1922, Cassius referred to a verse of this song: "When I try to do my best, I wonder why the test. But I will understand it better by and by." Expressing both doubt and gratitude as he relocated from Oklahoma to Ohio, he continued: "I don't know why I came east at my time of life, but somehow it just got to the point where I could not help coming to this destitute field. And as I sit here today, I thank God that I answered the call of the Spirit." Tindley's hymn gave Cassius and countless destitute African Americans hope for a better life "by and by."[36]

Since destitution and difficulty characterized the life of Cassius, it seems clear why his favorite hymn in later years was "My Heavenly Home," written by William Hunter and set to music by William Miller. Also known as "I'm Going Home," this song empowered Cassius to look past opposition and criticism and to see beyond the grave to a better world. Feeling overlooked and rejected in his old age, Cassius lamented: "But what hurts me most is: I see among that concourse of worn-out Fords, tramp preachers, a good many who think that I ought not to stand with them, even on the brink of destination—death. But there appears to me the spirits of J. E. C. [Joseph E. Cain], J. F. R. [John F. Rowe], and W. H. M., who say, 'Don't notice their frowns, Bro. Cassius, you will soon be over here with us,' and I forget the crowd around and find myself alone with Jesus, and I begin to sing, 'I am going Home, to die no more, / To die no more, to die [no] more, / I am going Home to die no more.'"[37]

Still another song, "Lord, I Done Done," inspired Cassius to fulfill his mission as a globe-trotter. In 1929, Cassius remembered the hymn as "an old song my people used to sing":

Lord, I done done.
Lord, I done done.
Lord, I done done.
I done done
What you tole me to do.[38]

This Negro spiritual prompted Cassius to "tell the world of God's love, and of his gift," convinced that "when I have done that, I done done what Jesus tole me to do."[39]

Apart from such musical interests, Cassius also studied African American history. Before fire destroyed his library, he evidently had a copy of William J. Simmons's *Men of Mark,* which extolled African American leaders in an anti-black society.[40] Cassius relied on Simmons's book and in his own pamphlet *The Letter and Spirit of Giving and the Race Problem,* upheld Frederick Douglass, Blanche K. Bruce, Robert Elliott, and Richard Allen as examples of black men who rose from slavery to prominence. Cassius concluded that "Any of these men that I have mentioned could have been President of this Nation if it had not been for the prejudice that the pulpit cultivated against them."[41] In an era in which controlling whites degraded the character and deeds of American blacks, Cassius was one of many autodidacts whose life embellished the accomplishments of his race.

In spite of his broad interests and accomplishments, Cassius clearly understood that he was not a self-made man. He attributed his religious and intellectual development to a literate slave mother, a caring white instructor, white presidents, empathetic black politicians, and devoted white church leaders. The life and work of Alexander Campbell inspired Cassius to champion the "restoration" of New Testament Christianity; the sacrifices of Frederick A. Wagner as a missionary to Japan encouraged Cassius to endure his own personal trials as an evangelist among African Americans; and the fatherly counsel of Joseph E. Cain provided Cassius the spiritual tutelage he needed. He also devoured a mixture of secular and religious literature as well as music and poetry. Among the many literary sources in his library that molded the mind of Cassius, however, none was as decisive as his Bible.

II

The "Race Problem" in the Stone-Campbell Movement

4
"Do You Believe the Bible?"
Samuel Robert Cassius's Use of Scripture

Thy word is a lamp unto my feet, and a light unto my path.

—Psalms 119:105

"Brethren, I am no scholar," Cassius acknowledged in 1912, "but I believe that the Bible is the revealed will of God and that God requires unconditional surrender to his will and an uncompromising obedience to his laws. I believe that the law of the Lord is perfect."[1] Cassius loved the Bible above all books, and it was probably the first book he learned to read. He held Holy Scripture in high regard, citing the Bible frequently and creatively to oppose what he viewed as religious error and to challenge what he perceived as improper racial practices. But beyond this, the Word of God gave him comfort amid his trials. Cassius firmly believed that the Bible, when properly understood and diligently followed, would engender religious and racial unity in America. With most members of the Stone-Campbell Movement, Cassius held up the New Testament as the authoritative guide for all Christians. Yet Cassius was a New Testament Christian who grounded much of his racial thought in Old Testament narratives. Biblical passages thoroughly saturated the mind of Cassius, providing an answer for every race question and a solution for every race problem. "I was blessed or cursed with an average education," confessed Cassius in 1920, "and my besetting sin has been a love of books, especially the Bible."[2]

Adherents of the Stone-Campbell Movement read the Bible through the lenses of Baconianism and Scottish Common Sense philosophy. Alexander Campbell and his followers believed that by stripping away prejudices and preconceptions, which manifested themselves in Christian creeds, and by reading Scripture inductively and scientifically, all believers in Jesus could unite. An inductive study of the Bible meant a rational and logical approach to biblical texts; the Scripture, in short, was a scientific textbook that could be understood by all. More specifically, Churches of Christ embraced what one historian has called "the Canon within the Canon." That is, they built their theology and ecclesiology on the New Testament books of Acts through Revelation. "But by placing such heavy emphasis on that portion of the New Testament beginning with the second chapter of Acts," Alexander Campbell and his followers "effectively downplayed those biblical materials that spoke most directly to questions of social justice—the Old Testament prophets, for example, and the Gospels, which contain the pointed teachings of Jesus regarding compassion and social concern."[3]

While Cassius did indeed imbibe "Campbellian rationalism" and while he did share an exclusivist attitude toward other religious groups, he possessed a unique canon.[4] Unlike most devotees of the Stone-Campbell Movement, Cassius broadened his canon to include the entire Old Testament as well as the four Gospels. His transition from a piece of property as a slave to a free citizen in the United States doubtlessly influenced his reading of Scripture, caused him to identify intimately with Old Testament characters and narratives, and made him more sensitive to the ethical teachings of Jesus in the four Gospels. Hence, Cassius's appropriation of Scripture was complex and perhaps contradictory. On the one hand, he used the Bible to denounce other religious traditions; on the other hand, he handled biblical texts to champion the cause of social justice and racial equality, and to argue for the dignity and humanity of black people. Yet the very people whom he yearned to elevate socially, he sometimes bludgeoned with the scriptural texts.

Cassius's creative uses of the Bible can be seen in a passage penned while he traveled for the first time to California by train in 1902. When en route to the Pacific coast, Cassius, with biblical passages, biblical events, and biblical characters in mind, wrote:

> "Shut down the windows!" is the next command, and then our train plunged in the mountain. All was heat, smoke and darkness. I said, "Surely this is the valley of the shadow of death," but while I thought on these things a small ray of light caught my eye; then suddenly I burst forth into the full sunlight of God's day, and I felt that I was alive again from the dead. Then came a chain of mountains, monuments of God's power. I thought of Noah resting in the ark upon the mount, and of Abraham alone with God upon the mount, with living

sacrifice in his hand. I thought of Jacob and his dream upon Mount Moriah, of his wrestling with the angel. I thought of Moses fleeing into the desert, and of the burning bush. I thought of his trip up Mount Sinai to meet God, and at last of his going up in the mount to die before the Lord. I thought of Christ, his temptation, his going upon the mount to pray, his ascension on the mount, and his ascension from the mount.[5]

The foregoing excerpt, replete with references to biblical figures and scriptural events, attests to how firmly Cassius's mind grasped Scripture and how thoroughly the Word of God shaped his intellect. He intimately identified with biblical figures such as Noah, Abraham, Jacob, and Jesus, who, often in solitude and isolation, struggled to serve God. "Then I longed for the privilege to forget the past," Cassius continued, "losing sight of our pretended civilization, and going away into the high and lofty mountains away from this busy, deceitful world, so full of its heartaches, tears, sorrows and death, and then be alone with God."[6] Cassius's canon clearly included the entire Bible.

The following year, Cassius scheduled a debate with a Primitive Baptist on what he described as the following premise: "Resolved, that the Church of Christ, of which I am member, is apostolic in faith, doctrine and practice. I affirm." Disappointed that the debate failed to materialize because the Baptist preacher reneged, Cassius boasted, "I carried two large solid rocks—one in each hand. In my right hand I had the four Gospels, in my left the Acts of the Apostles, and belted about my waist I had all of the pistols of Paul, James and Peter, and between my teeth I carried the sword of the Spirit."[7] Based on this creative paraphrase of Ephesians 6:10–18, Cassius obviously viewed the Bible as an instrument to attack what he understood to be false religion, confirming that his use and understanding of the biblical canon was complex, as it was simultaneously broad and inclusive as well as narrow and legalistic.

In addition to being a tool to combat irreligion, the Bible was, for Cassius, essentially a sacred document to address and correct racial wrongs. When white racism barred Cassius from Northern pulpits in Churches of Christ, he asserted that "Men may preach about the goodness of God, and pray about loving one another, and being one in Christ, but as long as they scorn me on account of my race or color, and tell me that their people will not tolerate me as an equal, I am compelled to say to all such, 'Thou hypocrite!' Do you believe the Bible, when it says that God is no respecter of persons, or that God made of one blood all men, for to dwell upon the face of the earth?"[8] Fusing Matthew 7:5, Acts 17:26, and Colossians 3:25, Cassius found validation for his manhood and personhood.

More significantly, even though Cassius was a New Testament Christian, he often based his racial thinking and racial theology on the Old Testament. He appealed, for instance, to the Book of Ruth to oppose the repatriation of black Americans to Africa. Ruth, a Moabite pagan, formed intimate bonds with Naomi, a devout Jew, by marrying her son Mahlon. After the latter's death, Ruth refused to sever ties with Naomi because, according to Cassius, she "found consolation and a husband's love in the Jewish race; she had learned to believe in her husband's religion, and to worship and to love her husband's God. In other words, her husband found her dead; he gave her his life, his religion and his God."[9] Ruth offered a tender response to Naomi that resonated with Cassius as it has with countless others: "Entreat me not to leave thee, or to return from following after thee, for whither thou goest, there will I go, and where thou lodgest, there will I lodge" (Ruth 1:16). Considering black inclusion into American society, Cassius affirmed, "Therefore, the very thought of separation was hateful to her."[10]

Allegorically, the African American people were like Ruth. Having been informed and transformed by American Christianity, the American black shuddered at the thought of separation from the United States of America and relocation to Africa. "So it is with the American Negro. It matters not what the causes were that brought him in contact with the Anglo-Saxon race, the contact has been made, and the wild 'African,' with his barbarous life, heathen religion, and wooden god, has been transformed into an Afro-American, with a civilized life, the religion of Jesus Christ, and trust in the living God." Elaborating on this allegory, Cassius declared:

> So it is with the American negro. Though his parents were forcibly brought here against their will, nearly three centuries have caused their descendants to become entirely dead to the life, character and habits of their foreparents, and even where this has not completed the severance, amalgamation has completed the work. The white people may in all candor say, "Return to your own race," and the negro can

with equal candor ask, "Who is my race, and where shall I go to find them? Has not two hundred and seventy-years of separation from the land of my fathers, with the blood of every nation under heaven flowing in my veins, blotted out my originality, and made of me a distinct race of purely Afro-Americans?" Indeed, the American negro can say as no other people (except Indians), "I am at home." I am to manor born, "Then entreat me not to leave thee, or to return from following after thee, for whither thou goest, there will I go."[11]

Cassius's interpretation of the Book of Ruth offered an implicit attack on both white and black advocates of repatriation.

Cassius additionally intimated that white American culture and Christianity were superior to African culture and African religion. This idea that white culture in America was higher than the black culture in Africa reveals the complexity of Cassius's racial views. He rejected the alleged superiority of white Americans, yet he objected to returning black people to the supposedly backward homeland of Africa. He found repulsive the notion of black repatriation to Africa and the idea of black retrogression to barbarianism. "Now, to say to him, 'Go back to your own people,' is to say to him, 'Throw off at once over three hundred years of the highest civilization of the world, and leap back at a single bound into the barbarous life of heathenism.' You may argue that if colored people of this country would go to Africa and carry their superior knowledge they would civilize Africa." Yet civilizing uncouth Africans would, in Cassius's view, be like "turning Lake Michigan into a body of salt water. The salt would be lost, without any visible effect upon the lake."[12]

To illustrate his argument against expatriating American blacks to Africa, Cassius cited an example from Charles Henry James Taylor (1856–99), a black ambassador during the first administration of President Grover Cleveland. According to Cassius, as minister to Liberia and recorder of deeds Taylor recalled that unlearned Africans rejected his "superior wisdom." After Taylor made "one of the most profound talks," a native of Liberia "patted him on the head, and said: 'Poor fellow, the white people over in America have beat him over the head so much that he's got no sense.'" Hence from Cassius's perspective, sending blacks in the United States to Africa would prove both ineffective and impractical: ineffective because instead of "winning the respect and educating the heathen, we would simply gain their pity, or receive their contempt, and in a few years instead of transforming them to our ways, we would ourselves be compelled to conform to their ways"; impractical because the prevalence of racial and sexual mixing made it virtually impossible to distinguish all black and white Americans. Implicitly recognizing his own interracial heritage, Cassius asked:

> Looking at the race problem from this point of view, we are compelled to say that we must look for its solving in some other direction aside from separation, and should the separation idea finally prevail, where will you begin? How will you draw a line? What will you do with the Mulatto, and the Octoroon and the brown man? They are bone of your bones, and blood of your blood! Nor are the colored people to blame for the mixture, either. So, then, if you say separation must come, I ask you in the name of all that's fair and honest, what will you do with your own sons and daughters? For myself I answer that, "Where thou lodgest, there will I lodge."[13]

Here, Cassius's appropriation and application of the story of Ruth to race relations in America seem to be innovative and unique without and within the context of the Stone-Campbell Movement. Contributors to Cain Hope Felder's insightful work *Stony the Road We Trod: African American Biblical Interpretation* correctly note that black exegetes, because of political, economic, and social forces, confronted the biblical text "creatively," but they cite no examples of black preachers interpreting the Book of Ruth in the way Cassius did. Cassius's use of the Ruth-Naomi narrative to argue for black inclusion in American society appears innovative for his time. Furthermore, white leaders in Churches of Christ for the most part failed to extract racial applications from the Book of Ruth. They tended to view the story of Ruth and Naomi only as a love story replete with moral lessons.[14] Nevertheless, Cassius's use of the Book of Ruth offers a vivid example of his fusion of race and religion and his wedding of biblical narratives with the race problem in America.

For Cassius, however, the most important book in the Bible was the Book of Genesis. In it he found godly counsel to inspire fellow Christians to share their monetary resources, to combat racist theories, and to advocate racial separation. First, seeking to motivate followers of Christ to give generously to struggling evangelists such as himself, Cassius appropriated the story of Cain and Abel to illustrate proper and improper methods of benevolence. "A good gift can be ruined by not giving it in the right way, at the right time and in the right place." Giving cannot replace worship; and worship cannot replace giving. "Some people believe their worship will answer in the place of their giving, and some think that their giving will answer in place of their worship." Because Abel gave and worshiped according to God's "pattern," the Lord accepted his offering. But because Cain worshiped according to his own "idea," namely his own carnal whim, by offering fruits and vegetables that were very hard to burn, God rejected his sacrifice. Cassius, continuing his analysis, observed:

> Right here we learn a lesson. Neither giving, zeal, nor devotion or self-denial makes a gift acceptable. You might inclose [*sic*] a rattle-snake in a basketful of gold and diamonds and give it to your friend, and though he should much like to have the gold and diamonds, the snake would make the gift contemptible. So it was with Cain and his offering. He had made his altar and prepared his gift, but in his presumption he neglected to consider the kind of gift he ought to give. Being carnal-minded, he looked at worship with carnal eyes. He saw more beauty in fruit than in anything else, thinking, perhaps, that just so a man was in earnest that was all God desired.[15]

With these words, Cassius sought to inspire Disciples of Christ to worship like Abel by giving liberally to fledgling churches and destitute preachers, not like Cain who offered a perfunctory sacrifice. Certainly Cassius wanted financial support for himself so that he could evangelize African Americans, since this work, in his opinion, would solve America's racial problems. White benevolence and black evangelism thereby went hand in hand.

Cassius presented the patriarch Abraham as an example of notable generosity. In Genesis 22, God instructed Abraham to offer his only son, Isaac. Cassius explained that Abraham, who "separated himself from the world in order that he might be alone with God," showed great faith in and supreme loyalty to God by "giving up all he had that was dear to him, but what was that to him? He wanted to please God." Cassius contrasted sacrificial giving and non-sacrificial giving, citing Abraham as exemplary of the former with Andrew Carnegie and John Rockefeller as illustrations of the latter. "Mr. Andrew Carnegie last year gave away over $3,000,000 without sacrificing a cent," explained Cassius, "because his income during the same year was over $21,000,000. Or, do you think that Mr. Rockefeller, the Standard Oil King, made any sacrifice by endowing the great Baptist College in Chicago, or that General Drake made a sacrifice by making Drake University what it is to-day?" Cassius answered his own questions: "I tell you Nay." These men gave, he pointed out, "because they choose to give." But they did not give sacrificially. Cassius's remarks about Francis M. Drake, a former governor of Iowa and a Disciple of Christ, angered D. L. Ammons, a white preacher in Seymour, Iowa. Ammons replied, "I am both grieved and disgusted at [Cassius's] reckless statements. It seems that a man professing Christianity should not render such harsh judgment against such men as General Drake, charging him with being without love or respect for God."[16] There is no known response by Cassius to Ammons's rebuke.

Irrespective of such charges, Cassius further addressed the concepts of generosity inherent in the social Darwinism then popular among some religionists of his era. Cassius appealed to the Book of Genesis to refute the racial theories emanating from Charles Darwin's concept of biological evolution. Cassius's skeptical view of Darwinism was "that man evolved from an atom to a flea, and from a flea to a cricket, and from a cricket to a tadpole, and from a tadpole to a frog, and from a frog to a monkey, and from a monkey to an ape, and from an ape to a gorilla, and from a gorilla, to a negro, and from a negro to a white man: and then God gave the wheel another mighty turn and it broke down, so that a white man became God's greatest work of art. You don't believe a word of this, neither do I."[17] Rather, Cassius took seriously the biblical account of God's creating the world and making man and woman in his own image. According to Genesis 1:27, which says that "God created man in his own image; in the image of God created he him: male and female created he them," African Americans were not beasts, as contemporary racial theorists alleged, but human beings fashioned by an Almighty Creator. To Cassius, any discounting of the Genesis story of man's origin would entail a denial of his own humanity.

The Genesis 11 account of the Tower of Babel, which describes how God scattered abroad people who endeavored to build a structure up to Heaven, played a constant part in Cassius's argument for racial separation. On the one hand, according to Cassius's reading of this biblical narrative, God sanctioned the separation of different races. "God saw that in order that the earth should be peopled and subdued, that the children of men must be separated, not simply by putting them in different places, but that he must put a difference between them; he must make it so they could not understand each other, and thus force them to build up nations to fit the language that God had given them." Cassius referred to the Tower of Babel story to show that God opposed the biological mixing of races. "And if this is not enough to you that it is not the will of God that one kind of people should mix with another kind of people, turn to the eleventh chapter of Genesis and read the first eleven verses." The Lord, according to Cassius, destroyed Noah's contemporaries because "the wicked and the good amalgamated," and he will pour out his "wrath" on individuals and nations who "mix or merge" with different races. "And woe," Cassius warned, "be unto the man or nation that find themselves fighting against God."[18]

Black racial thinkers contemporary with Cassius viewed "separation" positively and "segregation" negatively. The former dignified African Americans and meant separate and equal; the latter dehumanized black people and meant separate and unequal.[19] Cassius was a proponent of the former view. Cassius used the Book of Ruth to argue for black inclusion into American society, but he appropriated the Genesis narrative to endorse black separation in the United States. Ironically, white supremacist groups in the civil rights era of the 1950s and 1960s used the Tower of Babel narrative to argue for segregation.[20]

While relying heavily on Old Testament writings, Cassius of course moved also into the New Testament to seek scriptural foundation for his views. As he considered Jesus's teaching on marriage and divorce in Matthew 19:6, "What therefore God hath joined together, let not man put asunder," Cassius applied this to race relations in America, concluding, "That which God has put asunder, let not man attempt to put together."[21] But while Cassius appropriated other biblical passages to support his opposition to miscegenation, he always returned to the Book of Genesis as his lodestar.

Throughout his life Cassius extensively used Scripture, which he viewed as God's inerrant word. When seeking support for his evangelistic endeavors, he cited Jesus's words in Acts 20:35, "It is more blessed to give than to receive," and Ecclesiastes 11:1, "Cast thy bread upon the waters." When

Mississippi governor James K. Vardaman berated black freedmen whom he claimed retrograded toward barbarism and indecency, Cassius cited Galatians 6:7: "It is the fulfilling of God's word, 'Whatsoever a man soweth, that also shall he reap,' let it be good or bad. The white man for two hundred years sowed vileness in a whirlwind."[22] Cassius, thoroughly immersed in the reaping and sowing principle, often interpreted natural disasters and national tragedies as expressions of divine judgment on white Americans for their wrongs against their black counterparts. He construed the 1900 hurricane's destruction of Galveston, Texas, as God's retribution for white racism and oppression. "God intends that the American negro shall remain here, and he is fighting the negro's battle . . . God demanded ten thousand lives in Galveston. If space would permit, I could show that hundreds of white people have met violent deaths for every negro that has been burned at the stake, but it seems that hate has blinded the eyes of the American white man." Continuing, Cassius used Galatians 6:7 to insist that the Almighty Creator was "taking notice of the great fight that is being made against the negro of America." In the context of contemporary black racial thought, Cassius seemed ordinary, but in the milieu of the Stone-Campbell Movement, he stood unique.[23]

Cassius further tended to find parallels between himself and his circumstances and the lives of various characters in the Bible. When Christians throughout the nation came to his rescue with monetary aid in 1901, Cassius compared himself to downtrodden Israelites who found themselves oppressed by Egyptians and cried out to God for deliverance in Exodus 2:23 and 3:7. In Cassius's words, "Then I cried unto God and he heard me, and has put it into the hearts of his children to deliver me. Brethren, my heart is full of gratitude to God and you." His release from financial servitude convinced Cassius that "God is directing every move of my life."[24] Two years later, Cassius both identified with the children of Israel and compared himself to Moses. When the Israelites battled the Amalekites as told in Exodus 17, the former prevailed as long as Moses held up his hands, but they failed when he lowered them. Cassius noted that his success as an evangelist depended on the generosity of Christians. "When the children of Israel fought against Amalek, they could only prevail, when Moses had his arms stretched out. So in order that they might prevail, Aaron and Hur built two pillars under Moses' arms, so that they could keep them up. If I succeed, it may be that my arms will have to be held up once more."[25]

Cassius also likened himself to Elijah, who, after being threatened with his life by Jezebel, felt alone and abandoned. Elijah lamented, "I, even I only, am left; and they seek my life, to take it away" (1 Kings 19:10). Citing the words of the prophet, Cassius expressed disappointment that he received insufficient support to evangelize unsaved blacks, complaining, "No, I am not winning souls. How can I, when I don't go where they are, to win them?" Preaching to believers, in Cassius's view, was like "shooting decoy ducks, always hitting, but never killing." Convinced in 1907 that fellow Christians had forsaken and forgotten him and other "pioneer gospel preachers," Cassius grumbled, "A brother had the supreme gall to ask me, not long ago, why I did not preach in his town. I came very near asking him why he did not make it possible for me to do so."[26]

A decade later, during the Thanksgiving season, Cassius compared his own destitute life in Oklahoma to the trials of Abraham, Jesus, and the early disciples. "I am poor and needy; I am almost out of doors; so are many that will read this. But what of it?" He further asked, "Was not Abraham a stranger in a strange land? Was not Jesus without a place to lay his head? Did not the early Christians have to wander clothed in skins of beasts and sleep in caves and tombs and dens of the earth? If they, amid all of these disheartening things, could give thanks unto the Lord, how much more should we, who have food, raiment and freedom of speech and action, give thanks unto the Lord for giving food and shelter?"[27]

During his own hardships, Cassius found a source of strength and encouragement in the struggles of Old Testament patriarchs and New Testament saints as he personalized biblical stories and figures, applying them to his own life and struggles. In 1921, when Oklahoma governor James B. A. Robertson "stood in Representative Hall of the state capitol and declared lynching the most brutal crime known to the world and lynchers the most depraved and brutal beings that ever cursed the earth," Cassius identified with ancient David as he quoted from Psalms 136:1: "I am more blessed than David was, for I have seen and heard what he did not dream could come to pass. O give thanks unto the Lord: for he is good: for his mercy endureth forever."[28] The Book of Psalms seemed to Cassius more than a mere collection of praise anthems to God, as he linked the goodness of

God with Governor Robertson's denunciation of lynching, again fusing race concerns and biblical references.

In challenging racial practices in Churches of Christ, Cassius often appealed to New Testament texts as well. In 1897 Cassius contributed an article, "Negro Evangelization," to J. J. Limerick's book *The Gospel in Chart and Sermon*. Expounding on Matthew 23:26, "Thou blind Pharisee, cleanse first that which is within the cup and platter," Cassius applied the verse to white leaders in the Stone-Campbell Movement who "poured money" into foreign missions but virtually neglected African Americans. Cassius reminded readers that "the Bible teaches that God is no respecter of persons, and that all men must be saved on the terms of the gospel." He maintained that contemporary Churches of Christ were "a net of deception" and that most contemporary preachers were "a set of hypocritical shams." To support these charges of hypocrisy, Cassius referred to his own personal experiences:

> There are churches that would not allow me to enter their pulpits, on no other ground than that I am a negro. There are church-members that would not eat at the table with me, nor take me in their houses. I know Christian elders that have paid my lodging at a common hotel, where cursings and swearings and vulgarity was all that I heard. All this I have had to endure, not because I could not interpret the word of God, or was not as well recommended, or did not wear as good clothes as white men, but simply because I was a negro, and either himself, wife, daughter or son would not endure my presence for a single day or night. I say again, there is not a populated mile of ground on the earth that is not in need of evangelization. Then, why talk of negro evangelization more than any other?[29]

No mere jeremiad, Cassius's article laid out a plan for how white and black Christians could collaborate in spreading God's Word among African Americans. He concluded that "the way to evangelize the negro is to begin where, and, as the apostles did, among the poor and needy, regardless of race or color, teaching the simple truths of the gospel. But, let the man be white or black, he must forget who he is, and what the nationality of the people is to whom he is preaching." The black or white evangelist, Cassius continued, "must feel at home everywhere, and must show the same spirit at all times, and, above all, he must possess so much of the spirit of Christ that every class of people will be impressed with the fact that he is not only in earnest, but that he is personally interested in their spiritual welfare. Such men will win souls for Christ, and such men have always won souls for Christ."[30]

Cassius's exposition of "Negro evangelization" and Matthew 23:26, a vivid example of his merging of race and Scripture, pleased those who read his article. D. M. Oliser, a white Christian, responded by commenting, "I think S. R. Cassius on 'Negro Evangelization' is just splendid. I can say it is the best book of the kind ever published by any of our brethren." P. W. Adams, another white Disciple, added, "Bro. Cassius' sermon on negro evangelization is well worth the price of the book. It is one of the grandest books ever published by one of our brethren."[31] Significantly, Cassius's treatment of Matthew 23:26 mirrored Frederick Douglass's antebellum assessment of that same chapter. Douglass had distinguished the "Christianity of Christ" from the "Christianity of the land"; the former was pure, good, and loving, but the latter was impure, corrupt, and detestable.[32]

In 1901, an unidentified Christian from Kansas complimented Cassius's tracts on biblical issues as the "best I have seen on the subjects you treat." Expanding his commendation of Cassius's pamphlets on scriptural matters, the Kansan added, "They are grand, and I will send you $1, and hope it will do you good. I read everything I see from your pen, and hope and pray you may not weary in well-doing."[33] After he published his self-described "little book" *The Letter and Spirit of Giving and the Race Problem,* Cassius described the "words of praise" he received from friends and foes alike. Indeed, many Christians peppered Cassius with so much encouragement that he requested that more copies be printed. "So much am I encouraged that I will have 2,000 more of 'The Letter and Spirit of Giving' printed." Cassius wrote enthusiastically, "I want every member of the Christian Leader family to have it."[34]

Several years later Frederick L. Rowe, editor of the *Christian Leader,* invited Cassius to contribute an article on "Unity" in *Our Savior's Prayer for Unity: A Symposium on the Seventeenth Chapter of John.* Cassius submitted an analysis of John 17:9: "I pray for them: I pray not for the world, but for them thou hast given me; for they are mine," essentially treating the subject of prayer. Christians, he argued, had no obligation to pray for the world "because it is not consistent with the gospel plan of salvation. At no time and in no place in God's word has any part of the world ever been granted eternal life because someone prayed for it." An explicit attack on religious groups who advocated salvation by the "Sinner's Prayer," Cassius's remarks held that a person received salvation "upon hearing, believing and obeying what was taught to them by the preacher or teacher."[35] By "the gospel plan of salvation," Cassius clearly meant that human beings must act on God's Word. Cassius's emphasis, shared by other leaders in Churches of Christ, was not God's acting on humans' behalf, but instead humans' complying with God's "plan of salvation." This plan involved the "five finger exercise," a teaching device of Cassius's fellowship common in the nineteenth century, wherein a hand's five fingers represented five essential steps toward salvation: hearing, believing, repenting, confessing, and being baptized.[36]

Cassius's pamphlet "Faith, Repentance, Confession and Baptism" underscores his appropriation of the "five finger exercise." In this booklet, Cassius's statement "Water is a substance or liquid that God did not create" ignited controversy.[37] A respondent from California replied, "I would not dare say that God did not create water out of which to make [the seas]. [The seas] were made by causes." Cassius argued for the priority of water, for the Spirit and water worked in unison "in the beginning, and we see them acting in union in every move of God with the children of Israel." In essence, Cassius argued for the essentiality of baptism wherein God and human united. Citing numerous New Testament passages (Matthew 3:16, John 3:1–7, 1 John 5:8, Revelation 22:1), Cassius continued his argument: "God and water are inseparable; through it God comes to us, and through it we must pass to get to God." Cassius's handling of such passages of Scripture suggests the legalistic and combative tendencies of his religious thought. Cassius in fact delighted in controversy, advising others, "Brethren, don't fear to oppose me; it's the strength of my life."[38]

Taking him at his word, in 1912 some Christians accused Cassius of "being unsafe, unsound and disloyal." Cassius insisted that the charges surfaced for three reasons. First, he preached "to people that do not follow the teaching of the Scripture as they are taught in the New Testament." Second, some believers indicted Cassius for going "unto people of any denomination and preach[ing] to them." Third, Cassius appealed to a brother for assistance, who said that "one of the best friends that I had in the Church of Christ told him that I was not 'loyal.' " Distraught over these allegations, Cassius asked J. H. D. Tomson, a reputable white leader in Churches of Christ, to intervene in his behalf. Cassius pleaded, "Now, Bro. Tomson, you have been a great help to me in the answers you have given others. I now beg of you to be a help to others by the answers you give to me." Tomson defended Cassius's interaction. "I see nothing wrong in your going to those Sabbatarians," Tomson insisted, "with the open Bible and trying to show them that Sabbath days, weeks and years were shadows." Tomson further denounced "a few blind zealots who think that everybody is dis-loyal, except those who ride behind them on their hobby-horse. Let all of Christ's loyal ministers prove their loyalty to him by faithfully obeying him in all he commands them to do."[39]

More specifically, accusations of Cassius's disloyalty stemmed from his insistence that the "seventh-day was still in force." Francis M. Turner, who argued that the Old Testament command to observe the Sabbath day did not apply to twentieth-century Christians, came under Cassius's censure: "It surely is strange that our very best and strongest men will continue to defend the keeping of the first day, by trying to repudiate the seventh day. . . . It strikes me that Bro. Turner gets on mighty thin ice, when he tries to reason the seventh day out of the way, without, at the same time, doing away with the other nine commandments." Unlike most members of the Stone-Campbell Movement who believed with Turner that the death and resurrection of Jesus obliterated the Ten Commandments, Cassius held that the Decalogue still applied to contemporary Christians. "The facts are that Christ did keep the Sabbath," Cassius replied, "and taught the Jews the real meaning of the Sabbath." Continuing his assertion that Jesus and "all of the apostles kept the seventh day," Cassius maintained, "I think the greatest trouble is, we are afraid that we will be called Advents if we admit that the seventh day is yet a law, when the fact is *all Christians are Advents.* But Advents are not Christians."[40]

The Cassius-Turner exchange reflects the ambivalence of the former's religious thought. On the one hand, it demonstrates the breadth of Cas-sius's canon, which he refused to confine to Acts through Revelation. He had no misgivings about viewing the Old Testament as equally authorita-tive with the New Testament, but such a view clashed with the prevailing perspectives of Stone-Campbell followers. On the other hand, despite the expansiveness of Cassius's canon, he maintained an exclusive and combative mindset. A broad canon failed to translate into more openness, acceptance, and tolerance of other denominations.

Cassius later sparked more controversy in the Stone-Campbell fellowship with his article "No Room in the Inn." In this discourse, Cassius extolled children as the foundation of home and family life, expressing that without children "Home is only a place to rest, eat and sleep. There is no merry laughter, no romping children; not even the glad bark of a dog is heard, for dogs will not stay where there are no boys." The absence of children engendered "discontent, discord, strife, envy, malice, and, above all, the abolition of affection, because it is the underlying instinct of mankind to reproduce his kind, and the chief ambition of every real red-blooded woman, to feel the warm breath of her child at her breast. Robbed of this happiness, she will lose interest in hope, for, after all, '*What is home without a baby?*'" Cassius further indicted Americans for what he perceived as their prevailing anti-children sentiment; and he blamed Catholicism for the rise of sterility in American homes. "Catholicism has for years sown the propaganda of sterility among Protestants, and fertility in the homes of all Catholic families, and it can only mean that the 'Pope' is capturing America by shutting up and cutting off the source of production, and with the loss of children in the home come all those things that destroy a nation."[41]

To corroborate his stance concerning the rise of anti-children feeling in the United States, Cassius referred to Luke 2:7: "Because there was no room for them in the inn." Cassius interpreted the verse to mean that Bethlehem innkeepers rejected Joseph and Mary as customers because the former did not want an annoying baby interfering with "worldly pleasures." He explained:

> I do not believe that it was because of the lack of room in the inn that Mary and her husband could not find lodging. It was because Mary was about to become "*a mother*" and it would have spoiled the pleasure of the guest to be annoyed with the plaintive cry of a *babe,* therefore the Son of God found no place to lay his head except among the dumb brutes of the earth. You may ask what was the matter with the Jews at that time, that they hated children. The answer is "*Sin.*" The women had learned from the other nations the secrets

of sterility. They could enjoy all of the worldly pleasures without being bothered with "*little crying brats.*"[42]

In Cassius's mind, the hatred of children, as manifested in the Christmas story, caused the Jews to lose "their country, their religion, and their God." Consequently, the rejection of children by Americans prompted Cassius to inquire, "*Are we not tending downward, too?*"[43]

Theo Delong, a Christian in Bens Run, West Virginia, disputed Cassius's interpretation of Luke 2:7 and accused him of denying the validity of Scripture. Delong inquired, "Is it possible that Luke could have been mistaken in regard to this matter, and some poor preacher, away down here, almost two thousand years, can stand up and say he does not believe it?" Startled by Cassius's remarks, Delong continued, "I am surprised that an intelligent man would make such a statement before intelligent people. I can not understand just what he means, unless denying this Scripture gives him a channel through which to go to say a lot of other things that no preacher of the Gospel ought to say." Delong also challenged Cassius's statement that "a home where there are no children is a pit of hell and the woman a she devil," by referring to Sarah and Elizabeth as biblical examples of "barren" women whom the Lord used in significant ways. Delong insisted, "We could give many more Scriptures, but it is not necessary; for any one with good eyes can see how bad he is off." He refuted Cassius's idea that dogs will not live in a home without children, concluding, "[Cassius] says that a dog will not stay where there are no boys. Wrong again. I know this is not true. We have had three dogs, and never had a dog to leave us, yet one lived to be so old he went blind with age. Still, he wanted to stay, and we had no boys, either. I know of at least four homes in this community that have no children, but each has a dog, and there is not one of these homes a pit of hell, and not one of the women a she devil."[44]

The editor of the *Christian Leader,* Frederick L. Rowe, intervened in the dispute to appease his readership. Rowe admitted that Cassius's "language is a little strong, and perhaps a little unguarded, giving grounds for criticism." Yet Rowe, attempting to assure his audience of Cassius's good intention, stated that Cassius was "too reasonable and sensible to make his charge against homes where Nature has interpreted and made it impossible to carry out the universal decree of God in Gen. 1:28." He also reminded readers of Cassius's sense of humor, noting, "But we must remember that

Bro. Cassius is somewhat of a humorist. I will leave him to fix up his contradiction of Luke's statement in 2:7."[45]

In reply, Cassius explained the real motive behind his article as well as his controversial rendering of Luke 2:7. In 1922, when Cassius and his second wife, Selina, relocated from Guthrie, Oklahoma, to Cambridge, Ohio, they and their twin grandchildren received cordial treatment until they reached Columbus, Ohio. There, they "found lots of places, and there was no objection to us, until the question was asked, 'Have you any small children?' and when we admitted that we had two little grandchildren, the answer would be, 'We are very sorry, but we can not have children about the house; they are such a nuisance, you know,' and, Bam! The door would be shut in our face." Discrimination against children, especially his two grandchildren, enraged Cassius and inspired him to write the article "No Room in the Inn." He gave a more elaborate example of the rejection he, his wife, and his grandchildren experienced when they faced one landlady, explaining:

> When we told what we wanted she was all smiles. We liked the rooms, and I liked the landlady. Then she asked, "How many children have you, and how old are they?" Wife answered: "We have a boy and a girl and two little grandchildren," and just as soon as we told how small they were, the lady went right straight up in the air. Even the "bull pup" she was raising showed its teeth. No, she didn't want no little "brats" in the house. I got mad then, and told her that I saw a fine litter of hound pups over in Missouri, and I was sorry I had not traded the twins off for the pups, so that my pups could be company for that bull pup of hers. Bam! went the door, and we and our twins were together again, among a whole city full, but home we had none. This was my reason for writing "No Room in the Inn."[46]

Cassius doubtlessly reacted also to the sexual teachings of Margaret Sanger, the "woman rebel,"[47] who coined the term "birth control" in 1914. Born and reared in an Irish-Catholic family, Sanger advised that premature and multiple childbearing experiences of women trapped them in "endless travail and enslavement," while smaller families meant happier marriages.[48] Cassius, however, objected to the idea of limiting a family's size because he viewed solemnly the instruction of Genesis 1:28, "Be fruitful and multiply," and he himself fathered twenty-three children. Cassius's exegesis reflected his entrenched anti-Catholic views, for he detested the celibacy of Catholic priests and nuns.

More significantly, however, Cassius's experiences with white racism affected his view of the Luke 2:7 Scripture. He linked the rejection of his two black grandchildren by the white female landlady in Columbus, Ohio, to the exclusion of Joseph, Mary, and baby Jesus from a Bethlehem hotel. In a personal letter to Homer H. Adamson, a preacher and writer for the *Christian Leader,* Cassius explained, "What made me write what I did, was because we have two little fatherless grandchildren that we are trying to raise. But because of them, I could find no place to stay, and I had to leave the city of Columbus, O., as no one would rent us rooms because of those two babes." Adamson in reply chided fellow whites for their racial discrimination. "Now, white folks, how does a letter like that make you feel? . . . 'No room in the inn' for Jesus; no, and no room for black folks; no, and sadly no, no room for babies and blessed little children."[49] Cassius obviously read his personal experiences into Luke 2:7.

Moreover, his views on procreation emphasized Cassius's hermeneutics which placed equal value on both the Old and New Testaments. "Brethren," he firmly declared, "I believe in every word of God." Not only did he embrace all of God's Word, but it was also his conviction that no group of people in the United States held the Bible in higher regard than African Americans, because they had virtually no exposure to man-made tenets. Cassius, when urging white Christians to help him preach the Gospel to black Texans, explained: "Because, as a race, the colored people, believe more fully in the Bible than do any other race of people in the United States, for the very simple reason that they have always been taught the Bible was the word of God, and have not had access to the doctrines of men, to materially change that belief."[50]

Cassius himself loved the Bible intensely and valued it most highly. Nine months before his death, Cassius again asked readers of the *Christian Leader,* "Do you believe the Bible? If so read, Gen. 11:1–10, then if you believe the Bible, stop trying to deny what it says, but rather, Go into all the world and preach the Gospel to every creature telling them that he that believeth and is baptized shall be saved, and he that believeth not shall be damned, Mark 16:15, 16."[51] The fusion of these Old Testament and New Testament verses succinctly summarizes Cassius's handling of the Bible. He made Genesis 11:1–10 a pivotal part of his argument for racial separation, even as he appropriated Mark 16:15–16 for the basis of his evangelistic activity. Hence, when Cassius asked the question, "Do you believe the Bible?" he was not merely raising a theological issue; he was also asking a social and racial question. Cassius, like Henry M. Turner and countless other blacks in post–Civil War America, essentially demanded, "Am I not a man, because I happen to be of a darker hue than honorable gentlemen around me? . . . Am I a man? Have I a soul to save, as you have?"[52] For Cassius, then, the Bible was certainly a scientific textbook for the guidance and union of all Christians, but it was much more. He extended his canon beyond Acts–Revelation to include Genesis–Malachi as well as the four Gospels. But while personalizing biblical texts and applying them to the race problem in America, Cassius could never extricate himself from the legalism and exclusivism he had inherited from white comrades in the Stone-Campbell Movement.

5

"The Whole Thing Is a Pious Fraud"

Samuel Robert Cassius and the Missionary Society Controversy

> Even so ye also outwardly appear righteous unto men, but within ye are full of hypocrisy and iniquity.
>
> —Matthew 23:28

Shortly after joining the Stone-Campbell Movement around 1883, Cassius began protesting against what he deemed the unbiblical racial views of some white Christians. Oscillating between natural optimism and a pessimism fueled by the realities of his times, Cassius never resolved the inner tensions of American racism. His optimism compelled him to look to Churches of Christ to solve America's race problem, and in 1901 Cassius expressed his confidence in white Christians' ability to solve the race issue, affirming that "it is a question that only the Church can settle." Yet later that same year, he lamented pessimistically that "even our religion is a great trap of ostracism into which we have run, to shut up like rats in a trap."[1] Cassius lived a life of recurrent frustration as a black evangelist in the Restoration Movement, since many of the same people he relied on to relieve the race problem only aggravated it by viewing African Americans with both suspicion and disdain.

Historian Joel Williamson has identified three racial mentalities in the postbellum South. These included what he called racial "liberals," "conservatives," and "radicals." Liberals such as Atticus G. Haygood, a Methodist bishop in Atlanta, Georgia, expressed optimism about the future of ex-slaves in the nation. Liberals believed that with proper supervision from white Southerners in integrated churches and schools, black Americans could experience spiritual and intellectual elevation. Racial conservatives in the New South, holding to the idea of the biological inferiority of black people, assigned them to a perpetual place of subservience. Racial radicals such as Virginia author Philip A. Bruce and North Carolina novelist Thomas Dixon, Jr., envisioned the emergence of the "New Negro" who reverted to beastly behavior.[2] Whites in the Stone-Campbell Movement imbibed these liberal, conservative, and radical racial mentalities, which did not go unchallenged by Cassius.

David Lipscomb, a prominent white preacher in Churches of Christ and editor of the *Gospel Advocate,* typifies racial liberals in that fellowship. Like most New South paternalists, Lipscomb lamented the demise of slavery because black freedmen were "turned loose in our midst without protectors and advisers." The abolition of black bondage, in Lipscomb's mind, meant that ex-slaves would abandon true religion for false religion, white evangelical Christianity for heathenism and fanaticism. "These sad truths bring impressively to bear upon our minds the thought that a weighty responsibility rests upon us to try, if possible, to deliver the negroes from the fearful superstition and degrading barbarism from which they were, to some extent, delivered, but into which they now seem rapidly relapsing. The duty rests upon us . . . to elevate, educate, and Christianize them."[3]

William K. Pendleton, another prominent post–Civil War minister in Churches of Christ and editor of the *Millennial Harbinger,* shared Lipscomb's sentiments. "The disruption of slavery has broken up also the family ties, which furnished and fostered the religious culture of the negro. The new relation of freedom has put a distance between the races, and isolated the one from the instruction and sympathy of the other."[4] White Southern paternalists in the Stone-Campbell Movement believed that slavery had blessed blacks, but freedom now cursed them.

Notwithstanding Lipscomb's view of black retrogression, his friendship for African Americans continued beyond the 1860s. In 1878, when white Christians in McKinney, Texas, rejected a black man who "presented himself for membership," Lipscomb denounced the action of white believers, contending, "We believe it sinful to have two congregations in the same community for persons of separate and distinct races now. The race prejudice would cause trouble in the churches we know." After all, he inquired, since God saves both black and white, "can one claiming to be a child of God say no?"[5]

Lipscomb's liberal outlook derived from his upbringing by and among African Americans. "I was raised among negroes," Lipscomb wrote. "My mother died so early I do not remember her." He justified the existence of integrated churches in the New South by recalling his daily interaction with, and his constant dependence on, slaves in the Old South. "I was cared for, for some years, greatly by a negro woman. Negro children were my playmates. I have always had the kindliest feelings for them." Lipscomb's intimate ties to both "Aunt Milly" and other blacks remained unsevered throughout his life. Lipscomb's biographer Robert E. Hooper has observed that the editor's relationship with blacks, although paternalistic, moved him "well beyond most Southerners of his era."[6]

In 1907 Lipscomb unsurprisingly defended his white friend and colleague Edwin Alexander Elam and his wife for caring for a black girl and bringing her to the worship services of a white congregation in Bellwood, Tennessee. S. E. Harris, representing members of the Bellwood Church of Christ, wrote to Elam, grumbling that "There is a great deal of complaint in the church at this place in regard to the colored girl that lives at your house." Elam responded that "God is no respecter of persons, but he who objects to worshiping where this negro girl does is a respecter of persons." Continuing his defense of the black girl's presence in a predominantly white church, Elam insisted, "She is an innocent and honest Christian girl, and all the church at Bellwood know that she cannot be sent away from my family to the negro church without exposing her to the temptation of such weakness and sins [that] are common to her race."[7]

Lipscomb intervened in the Harris-Elam dispute, arguing, "No one as a Christian or in the service of God has the right to say to another 'Thou shalt not,' because he is of a different family, race, social or political station. While these distinctions exist here, God favors or condemns none on account of them." Recalling with fondness his own relations with blacks in the pre–Civil War South, Lipscomb stated, "I have never attended a church that negroes did not attend. While they were slaves, we in the country were glad for them to attend and become members of the churches." Indeed, Lipscomb often partook of the Lord's Supper at two separate congregations on Sunday, one "with the white brethren" and another "with the blacks to show as Christians we are one." Lipscomb repudiated separate churches for whites and blacks because segregated assemblies prevented so-called superior whites from instructing and interacting with supposedly inferior blacks.[8]

For Lipscomb, white paternalism meant black elevation; to Cassius, however, white supervision meant black degradation. In the fall of 1889, after attending a national convention of the Disciples of Christ in Louisville, Kentucky, Cassius wrote his first known extant letter in the *Christian*

Evangelist objecting to the appointment of J. W. Jenkins, a white "superintendent of colored missions." Denouncing what he viewed as paternalistic attitudes of white leaders in the Stone-Campbell Movement, Cassius defended his race: "I hope you will again allow me to speak through your valuable paper, in order that I may defend my race because according to Bro. Moffett's report concerning colored missions, as it appears in last week's supplement; one could be inclined to think that the 'NEGRO' was so inferior from an intellectual point of view, and so weak from a spiritual stand-point, that it was a matter of impossibility to a colored man with enough common sense to do evangelistic work among his own people." Cassius insisted that black men were as well qualified as white men to hold leadership roles. "Now I say," Cassius maintained, "and I think I speak the sentiment of every intelligent colored man in the Christian church, that we have colored ministers that are every way as well fitted for the work of an evangelist as any minister in the Christian church that could be secured for the position that Bro. M. mentions, and if a colored man can not do the work, it will be utterly impossible for a white man to do it."[9] Cassius clearly interpreted this appointment of a white superintendent as blatant paternalism which threatened black elevation and black independence. From Cassius's perspective, the board's decision to appoint a white supervisor over black missionary activity revealed white leaders' fundamental unwillingness to grant African Americans economic control.

In response, James H. Garrison, editor of the *Christian Evangelist,* took issue with Cassius's remarks and defended Robert Moffett's report and the board's action of placing a white evangelist over black missions. Garrison explained that the "let-alone policy" of Northern politicians was not beneficial to black Southerners, and postbellum African Americans needed both monetary and spiritual supervision. "They need and deserve outside help," Garrison stressed, "help not only in money but chiefly in wise counsel and leadership and sympathetic oversight; not because they are colored, but because the mass of them are ignorant, of necessity, and need education and religious training." To refuse financial assistance and spiritual guidance from white Christians, Garrison concluded, would deprive blacks of a "higher religious life" and "superior advantages." Garrison concluded that most black ministers in Churches of Christ did not share Cassius's independent views.[10]

Garrison's response to Cassius's protest plainly reveals the racial ambivalence pervasive in the Stone-Campbell Movement of post–Civil War America. Even though there was genuine concern to assist and elevate black Americans morally, spiritually, and financially, white paternalism and white racism often accompanied this beneficence, as whites viewed themselves as superiors reaching down to uplift supposedly inferior, childlike blacks. Herein Cassius found his most difficult challenge. The very institution that Cassius looked to for freedom of thought, movement, and expression ironically suppressed his efforts to liberate himself and his people from white domination.

Like Garrison, Clayton C. Smith, corresponding secretary of the Board of Negro Education and Evangelization, claimed in 1893 that American blacks needed Christian education for at least five reasons: protection, domestic life, religion, citizenship, and labor. "All know," Smith elaborated, "that by somebody, the ignorant, inexperienced, improvident, childish negro has been wronged out of much of his hard-earned wages, and that will continue so long as he is unable to take care of himself, which will be so long as he remains in ignorance." Furthermore, Smith added, biblical teachings obligated white Christians to educate the black man "to give him a home," "to give [him] a religion," and "to make him a citizen." "It was not the negro's fault," Smith continued, "if he never discovered any relation between his religion and his morals," for the religious practices of American blacks essentially blended emotionalism, heathenism, and American Christianity. "The only religion possible to him has been the religion of emotion, and ofttimes it is but little better than superstition and idolatry, even though it was named after Christ." Smith vehemently rejected granting voting rights to what he deemed as unlearned, untrained, and undisciplined blacks. Smith rationalized that the chief issue was not race, but what he called "fitness." "We have learned to our sorrow that an act of Congress cannot make a citizen. We also know that there is nothing so dangerous to the peace and prosperity of a country as an ignorant ballot. I had rather be ruled by a King than by ignorance. We talk about making men free; the truth only can make men free. It is not, it must not be a question of color; only a question of fitness. No nation can stand long as a republic unless intelligence is vastly in the majority. Not only education, but compulsory education for all our citizens, if need be."[11]

In Smith's view, only education for blacks could help them develop the resources of the South. "One of the great hinderances to growth to the

South has been and is ignorant labor." Black "skilled laborers," Smith predicted, "at the bench, at the forge, at the lathe, in her mines and quarries, in the fields and groves, building her temples and fashioning her granite and marble into things of beauty," would enable the South to "appear in her true loveliness and strength." Smith also regarded black household servants as morally superior to black field laborers. The former, "brought into intimate relations with the best whites," experienced the "realization of an Eutopian [sic] dream." The latter, "meeting seldom with the whites," were "as wild as when lassoed in the jungles of Africa."[12]

Smith's pompous and self-serving racist portrayal of African Americans enraged Cassius. He excoriated Smith for his contention that the "negroes in the South are so ignorant that they don't know beans with the sack open, and that they live in such close quarters that secrecy is impossible, and virtue is an unknown quality, and that negro women have not sense of chastity, nor any regard for the marriage tie. This is the gist of Bro. C. C. Smith's set speech that he has made for five years."[13] Cassius fiercely resented the corresponding secretary's smug assertion of white superiority and black inferiority. Hence his antipathy for missionary boards and societies developed, not merely from what he viewed as doctrinal error, but also from the anti-black racism expressed and practiced by some white leaders in the Stone-Campbell Movement.

If Lipscomb, Pendleton, Garrison, and Smith represented racial liberals in the Restoration Movement, John M. McCaleb, a talented evangelist, hymnist, and missionary to Japan, typified racial conservatives among them. In 1907 McCaleb, convinced that the black man needed "proper training" because "his language is something awful, and his thought crude and disconnected," devised a plan to provide spiritual uplift for black Southerners. His plan included training for the "colored preacher." McCaleb argued, "We accept the Turk, the Armenian, the Greek, the Japanese, the Korean, or Chinese, but not the American African." He proposed that Christian schools, owned and operated by white members of Churches of Christ, partner with colleges such as Fisk University and Tuskegee Institute to teach Bible classes. McCaleb cautioned, however, that the collaboration be carried out "'professionally,' but not socially," for blacks must always be kept in their "proper place."[14]

"Place," consequently, stood foremost in the mind of McCaleb and like-minded conservatives who held that blacks must be treated as human beings but certainly not as social equals. "The white people should remember that the black man, though black, is a man, a member of the great human family, and that he has rights which should be duly respected. He should be dealt with and in every way treated as a man." Black Americans, McCaleb stressed, "should also clearly understand that while the white people are their friends, they insist on their remaining in their proper place and as to what this place is there is a pretty general consensus of opinion."[15] The black man's "proper place" was one of submission and subservience, a "place" of clear inferiority.

McCaleb further emphasized that black Americans should be "true to themselves and fair to others" and realize the "vast difference between them and us." Claiming that blacks despised their own physical appearance and wanted to be white, McCaleb stated, "The black skin, the flattened nose, and kinky hair are hated by the blacks themselves, and every one of them would change to white people if they could. I do not blame them for this, but let us remember that this difference in race is the work of God and not of man. Since God has made the difference, let us not fight against him nor deceive ourselves about it. What I mean is that the colored people would greatly smooth their own path, and would remove the barriers that keep the white people from doing more for them if they would cease their silly and unseemly efforts of trying to be the same as white people."[16]

To illustrate his argument about "place," McCaleb recalled a young undisciplined black coachman who called a daughter of a white Christian man "'Bessie' in the familiar style of her own white brother." "I believe," McCaleb protested, "I voice the sentiment of the brotherhood generally when I say that boy was out of his place. That upstartish disposition, especially among younger negroes in which they vainly try to be white people, has done much harm." By "younger negroes," McCaleb meant "New Negroes" who, because they were untrained by the institution of slavery, frequently violated the social order of the New South. Historian Leon Litwack has noted that "the New Negro violated white expectations of black people, confounded their feelings of superiority, and violated stereotypes long assimilated into the white people."[17] This was especially true of racial conservatives in white Churches of Christ such as McCaleb.

McCaleb strongly admonished the young black student to "remember his place and race, ask necessary questions, and speak courteously when he is spoken to, but carefully avoid intruding on the feelings of others. Let him seek familiar companionship with his own race." Black "intrusions" into the space and "place" of whites, McCaleb stated, would lead to racial and sexual mixing, an idea that gave rise to a neurotic fear pervasive among white Southerners. "Give him the privilege of attending our schools," McCaleb articulated, expressing a deep and common concern of Southern whites, "and next he will be making love to our daughters and will seek a place in the social circle."[18] Fundamental to white Southerners' insistence on "place" was the issue of interracial sex.

Clearly, some whites in Churches of Christ absorbed what journalist Wilbur J. Cash has called the "Southern rape complex." Cash explained that "What Southerners felt, therefore, was that any assertion of any kind on the part of the Negro constituted in a perfectly real manner an attack on the Southern woman." To whites this Southern rape complex "justified violence toward the Negro as demanded in defense of woman." This neurotic disposition derived from any imagined black assertion and black aggression. The abolition of slavery brought about a degree of political advancement, social elevation, and educational opportunities for African Americans during the Reconstruction era. Such unwanted advances, white Southerners commonly feared, entitled blacks to the "ever crucial right of marriage." The intermarrying of blacks (the so-called inferior race) with whites (the alleged superior race) vitiated the perpetuation of white supremacy and white superiority, "the great heritage of white men."[19]

Cassius understood that many whites in the Stone-Campbell Movement harbored a visceral fear of black males interacting with white females, and he argued that "the fear of social equality" prevented Churches of Christ from becoming the most dominant religion in the United States. White evangelists, according to Cassius, refused to reach out to black Americans because they shuddered at the thought that such outreach would lead to racial and sexual mixing. "It was then like Banco's Ghost that 'Social Equality' raised its hideous head and 'Howled that if the American negro is converted to Christ he will want to fill your churches and homes and drawing rooms and court your daughters, and in every way be your social equal.'" But Cassius insisted that white Christians' fear was unfounded. "The whole life of the Afro-American has proven that every one of the above allegations are false and absurd. The American Negro as a whole does not want to mix with any other people under heaven." Expressing his sense of black pride, Cassius asserted, "We believe we are just as good morally, and socially as any other people on earth."[20]

In addition to racial liberals and racial conservatives, racial radicals were also part of the Stone-Campbell Movement. For example, in April 1899, a crowd of white Georgians brutally murdered and tortured Sam Hose, a black worker in rural Georgia who allegedly killed a Mr. Cranford and raped his wife. After burning Hose, the bloodthirsty mob removed his heart and liver, cut them into several pieces, and crushed his bones into small particles. A month after the atrocity, an unidentified member of Churches of Christ sent Cassius ten cents for a tract titled "Religious Expansion" and asked, "But what do you think of that 'fiend,' Sam Hose, whom the good people of Georgia burned?" Cassius angrily replied, "My brother, you had better ask what I think of the 'fiends' who did the 'burning.'" Admitting that Hose may have committed murder, Cassius insisted that Hose did not rape Mrs. Cranford. In a tone of rage, disgust, and frustration, Cassius affirmed, "Just think of burning a man and then cutting up his body in small pieces to send to their friends! Ouh! They even sent the Governor of the State a slice of his heart. And this brother asks me what I think! If you had signed your name I would have sent your ten cents back, because I don't want a cent of money in my work that comes from a man who believes in mob violence."[21] This exchange reveals more than Cassius's rage; it demonstrates as well that racial radicals were members of the Restoration Movement. The remarks addressed to Cassius further suggest that some whites in the Stone-Campbell Movement viewed black men as predatory beasts who desired to assault white women and that some approved of mob violence against black males who ventured to attack white womanhood.

The attitudes of racial radicalism in Churches of Christ are further illustrated in a nameless woman's correspondence to David Lipscomb in 1901, when she wrote the editor of the *Gospel Advocate* that "negroes are a separate creation and beasts." Swayed by the contentions of Charles B. Carroll's *The Negro a Beast,* the correspondent continued, "Because of their attacking Southern women, the two-footed black beasts are being killed— saturated with oil and burned to death—every week somewhere in the South; indeed, one often reads in the paper accounts of as many as three or four such horrible crimes. What but a beast could do such a thing?"[22] This woman, like other white Southern racial radicals, viewed black men as predatory beasts who yearned to rape white females.

Lipscomb, however, refused to regard black people as beasts. He declared that the "negro is a human, not a brute," and he fiercely opposed lynching because it made a "hero and martyr of [the rapist] in the eyes of himself and his race" while making "cowards and demons of his tormentors." Lipscomb advocated castration instead of lynching since it would strip the culprit of his martyr complex and make him an "object of scorn and ridicule among his people, that none would desire to emulate."[23]

Cassius, sensing that many white Christians held similar anti-black views, took issue with both Lipscomb and his nameless female correspondent. "Now if 'A Woman' who wrote this article really believes what she says, the question is, how many more hold the same view?" Espousing such erroneous notions that blacks were beasts, Cassius maintained, would infect and inflame the minds of countless white racial radicals in America. "A little spark sometimes kindleth a great fire. How long then would it take the idea that the Negro is a beast to fix itself firmly in the minds of a great number of people, and once fixed there, especially from a Bible standpoint, what a work of extermination would be carried on in the name of God." The woman's citation of the Bible to support her contention especially alarmed Cassius. He concluded that if white Americans could find biblical sanction for black bestiality and race hatred, their black counterparts would soon vanish, victims of racial genocide.[24]

From Cassius's perspective, however, anti-black sentiment in Churches of Christ moved beyond the South. When he traveled and raised funds in the North for his Tohee Industrial School, white leaders in Churches of Christ refused him an audience in "their congregations because I was a negro." "Never, since I have been a Christian," Cassius complained, "have I seen so much real race prejudice in the Church as exists at the present time."[25]

D. L. Ammons, a white preacher of the Stone-Campbell Movement in Seymour, Iowa, disputed Cassius's claims of mistreatment by Northern Christians and expressed disgust over Cassius's remarks. Ammons, responding to Cassius's claims in his *The Letter and Spirit of Giving and the Race Problem,* stated that Cassius "came to Seymour about six years ago an entire stranger, and told me he was out of money." Continuing his refutation of Cassius's statement about his unpleasant experience with Christians in the North, Ammons retorted, "I was in the midst of a protracted meeting. I took him in, let him preach at night, took up a collection for him, furnished him bed and board in my own house, and when he left he promised to write as soon as he reached home, but he never did." In Ammons's judgment, Cassius overstated the case about Northern racism in Churches of Christ. Ammons concluded, "I think much of what he said had better have been unsaid—better for him, better for the colored people, and better for the cause of Christ in general."[26] There is no record of Cassius's response to Ammons's charges and criticisms, but there is ample documentation of racist sentiment in both Northern and Southern congregations.[27]

Cassius's assessment of his experiences among Northern Christians, correct or not, affected his view of the missionary societies then expanding in churches of the Restoration Movement. In 1895, for example, Cassius assessed the Board of Negro Education and Evangelization's annual financial statement and criticized its unjust compensation practices. Adoniram J. Thompson, a white instructor at the Louisville Bible School in Kentucky, whom Cassius labeled a "failure as a teacher of white students" in Illinois, received $1,500, while Octavius Singleton, a black instructor in the same institution, earned $255. Singleton "is a negro," Cassius observed, "and teaches in the same school that is presided over by A. J. Thompson. Yet notice the difference in the pay the white man gets—$1,245 more than the negro—and I honestly believe the negro is the smarter of the two." Cassius further noted that African American evangelists M. Powell of Missouri, J. G. Keys of Mississippi, and J. H. Rodgers of Florida received one hundred dollars, fifty dollars, and thirty-five dollars respectively. "It's a wonder," Cassius jested, "that these men don't let prosperity kill them." Such conspicuous inequity by white board members prompted Cassius to conclude of missionary societies, "The truth of the whole matter is, the whole thing is a pious fraud. There never was anything in it, either for the negro or the cause of Christ."[28]

In the spring of 1896, Cassius acknowledged that he received help from the Board of Ministerial Relief, a benevolent auxiliary designed to assist impoverished preachers among Disciples of Christ. Brother Atkinson, the corresponding secretary of the board, sent Cassius twenty-five dollars. "At the time I received it I was very much in need," commented Cassius. "Everything seemed dark before me, and I cried unto the Lord, and, bless his name, he answered me through the *Board of Ministerial Relief.* Brethren, if God uses it to answer the cries of his suffering children, let us be very careful how we fight it; let us rather help it, and fight these Boards that have great, high-salaried heads, who sit as popes over the Church of Christ." Although Cassius had a positive experience with the Board of Ministerial Relief, he continued to indict leaders of missionary societies who "fear a mule [mulatto] and hate a negro."[29]

In a reply to an article in the *Christian Leader* which criticized African Americans for their "incorrect idea of personal rights and obligations," Cassius affirmed his indictment of missionary societies by blaming the white man for the black man's deficiencies. "It must be remembered," Cassius responded, "that the American negro is morally and physically the American white man's duplicate. In intellect, both worldly and religious; in habits, both private and public; in affairs, both domestic and general, he is the white man's understudy." Cassius thus chided white missionary societies for their failure to elevate the black man. "The fault is the societies, and not the negro's, because these great benevolent and religious institutions have always tried to make their work 'a fad,' with no real purpose but to gain the applause of men." Cassius then challenged board leaders to treat the African American with courtesy and respect. "If the American negro is in need of one thing more than another, it is that he be given more brotherly kindness on account of his nearness, and less heathen methods of evangelization, as though he was in Africa. Treat him like you would like to be treated, remembering that he worships your God, believes in your Savior, and reads your Bible, and hopes to reach the same rest that you are working for."[30]

In 1897, Cassius compared the missionary activity of first-century Christians and late-nineteenth-century Christians and saw profound differences. The former, under the influence of the Holy Spirit, "believed that at all times and in all places it was their duty to do whatsoever the Lord commanded." The latter, under the guidance of "the Board," operated with the "most selfish motives." Cassius asked, "Did you ever take a careful look at one of the great, big, take-the-world-for-Christ advocates? If you have not, you do so the very next time you see one, and you will see a conceited, well-dressed, must have-a-singer, twenty-five-dollar-a-week preacher that will not go beyond the limit prescribed by the 'Board.' "[31] Flamboyancy and self-centeredness, in Cassius's assessment, characterized contemporary missionary society leaders in contrast to the altruism and sacrificial qualities of the first Christians. Beyond this, Cassius's distrust of white board leaders stemmed from his refusal to be controlled by the white paternalists who supervised black missions. The desire for black independence inspired Cassius to establish his own journal, the *Industrial Christian,* the "first colored paper ever published by colored disciples, free from 'Board' influence."[32] Like that of other black leaders in Oklahoma who started their own newspapers, the creation of the *Industrial Christian* clearly reflected Cassius's attempt to provide a spiritual uplift for African Americans free from white dominance.

The same year, at a mass meeting in Panama, Nebraska, some white leaders questioned Cassius's loyalty to Scripture because of his affiliation with the *Christian Leader,* a religious paper that some in Churches of Christ deemed "progressive." Paraphrasing Jesus's denunciation of the Pharisees in Matthew 23, Cassius lamented, "I am sorry to say that some of our dear, good brethren were too everlasting particular about 'gnats' and too careless about some of the camels they were freely swallowing." He further deplored that some white Christians "based their ideas of loyalty on 'papers' rather than Christ." Conservatives in the Stone-Campbell Movement expressed doubt at Cassius's commitment to biblical teachings because he frequently contributed to the *Christian Leader.* "My loyalty was called into question because I wrote for the C. L., and I was told that I would not be assisted by the loyal brethren unless I took a stand against the C. L., and condemned it as a 'prog' paper, and that I must set forth my position immediately or I would be considered a 'prog.'" Delineating his views on issues such as missionary societies and instrumental music then threatening to unravel the Restoration Movement, Cassius set forth his affirmation:

I condemn every attempt to substitute human forms, plans and ideas for the plain written word of God contained in the Bible, believing that God has given us a complete revelation of his will, and that he will not accept any addition to or subtraction from his word. I believe that it is a sin to place an organ in a congregation to use in "worship," and that all societies are ungodly. I also believe that the *Primitive*

Christian, Echo and Review are very good religious papers, but do not believe that they are so good that loyalty to them should be made a test of fellowship.

Now, to those who say that I must denounce the C. L. as "disloyal" and Bro. John F. Rowe as a "prog," I have this to say: I believe that the C. L. is still the most "loyal" paper published by our brotherhood, and that John F. Rowe is the most able editor and safest Christian I have ever read after, and I will further say to those parties that demand my written statement on this matter, you now have it, and if I must sacrifice my love for the C. L. and my love and respect for Bro. Rowe in order to get their support, I do not want it.[33]

These passionate paragraphs reveal three significant aspects of Cassius's views and the friction between "loyals" and "progressives." First, the passages attest to Cassius's unwavering commitment to Scripture. He took seriously the Bible as the "complete revelation" of God. Second, the two issues that created the rift between Disciples of Christ and Churches of Christ were missionary societies and instrumental music in worship. Third, and most significantly, Cassius's refusal to allow white conservatives to dictate which paper he wrote for and which editors he supported marks his quest for intellectual freedom as he vehemently spurned the white believers' attempt to restrict his thinking and his writing.

Homer E. Moore, an attendee of the Disciples convention in Panama, Nebraska, and a reputable leader among the "loyals," replied to Cassius's accusations and branded them as "untrue from first to last." Explaining his perception of the affair in Panama, Moore said, "We were not calling in question his loyalty; but simply stating to us that he wrote for the *Christian Leader* was no guarantee to us that he was loyal." "Simply because," Moore stressed, "when we pick up the *Christian Leader* we find loyal brethren, digressives and even Presbyterians represented there." Moore, representing those who allegedly questioned Cassius's fidelity, continued, "What we wanted to know was whether he was loyal, in favor of the 'little organ,' a digressive or a Presbyterian. He soon satisfied our minds, however, that he himself was loyal." Moore further recalled that when Cassius arrived by train in Panama, he and other white Christians treated him as "kindly as we knew how to treat him" and gave him the "same care and privileges as the other brethren." On Sunday afternoon, Cassius, according to Moore, "preached us an excellent sermon, after which he made an appeal in behalf of his work in Oklahoma." At the close of the meeting, Moore said, "The brethren flocked around Brother C., and, as rapidly as he could write, some fourteen or fifteen names were put down as subscribers of his paper" [the *Industrial Christian*]. Some Christians gave personal donations, while the congregation in Panama "gave him the last dollar they had in their treasury." Moore concluded, "Actions speak louder than words, and now, dear reader, you have our actions before you, and we leave you to judge for yourself as to whether Brother C.'s accusations are true or false."[34]

Cassius, however, insisted that some preachers who attended the Panama meeting did indeed question his loyalty. Cassius boasted, "I preached the deepest, strongest, *shortest,* and most thoughtful sermon of the whole meeting. Brethren, you know I did." Following his sermon, according to Cassius, Brother Gray of Edenville, Kansas, sought to "kill the influence of my sermon and turn the brethren against me by rebuking me for being so unsound as to support a 'prog' paper as the *Christian Leader.* Brethren, you know he did that very thing, but when he found that I was not as green as I was black, he dropped me like a hot potato." Certain that men in Panama doubted his devotion to the Word of God, Cassius felt engulfed in a "vail [*sic*] of suspicion." "They came to hear me preach, and Brother Gray tried to treat them to a black burying picnic; but I guess he thought I was a pretty lively corpse." Even though Moore and other white leaders said "nice things" about Cassius, the latter indicated that "it is general custom to say good things about a dead man, especially at his funeral." Acknowledging that Christians in Panama did indeed give the "last dollar," Cassius offered clarification: "Yes, the brethren at Panama did give me the last dollar (not the last they had) because they saved out that last dollar to give me; and it was the only dollar they gave me, too, although they knew that I was 500 miles from home, and that I had to pay full fare, notwithstanding they had given Brother Bohlen to understand that they would help pay my fare back home." Sensing that the leaders treated white evangelists better than himself, Cassius noted that "all they cared for was to get me out of sight, while every white preacher that wanted was provided some point to preach at, besides getting all 'but that last dollar' of the money that was in sight."[35]

The Moore-Cassius conflict attests to the role journals played in creating division in the Stone-Campbell Movement. Papers that preachers wrote for and journals that members subscribed to became a measuring stick for one's loyalty or disloyalty to the Bible. "We judge a man," Cassius remarked sarcastically, "by the company he keeps." The verbal skirmish between Moore and Cassius also contained racial overtones, since Cassius refused to bow before white paternalists who, he felt, sought to treat fellow white Christians to a "black burying picnic."

Cassius continued to intertwine the race problem with issues centering on missionary societies. He consistently and creatively linked racism and paternalism with "progressivism." In the fall of 1902, after noticing the program for the Disciples of Christ convention in Omaha, Nebraska, Cassius complained that the "American Negro has entirely been left out." Suspecting that board leaders used black people as tokens "to pull a few dollars out of Christian pockets that could not be got any other way, with no intention of making any effort to give him a pure Gospel," Cassius concluded, "I am now convinced that that was the sole intention of the Board from start to finish. Are Indians, Japanese and Chinese better than Negroes? If so, why, how and when did they get better?" After attending the convention, Cassius lamented that white leaders of missionary societies devised "plans to spread the Gospel in the world, while not a word is said for nor a plan suggested to reach 12,000,000 [black] people in their own midst, I am forced to ask, 'What right has such a body of people to call themselves Christians? Can a Christian use race discrimination and do the will of God and of Christ?"[36] The display of both indifference and impatience by white "society men" toward black Americans frustrated Cassius. "I have seen for ten years that it was the purpose of organized societies in the Christian Church to drop the negro as a religious failure." White leaders of the Board of Negro Education and Evangelization deemed outreach to African Americans a failure, Cassius explained, "because there has never been a real, pure effort made by the societies of the Christian Church to carry the Gospel to the colored people of America."[37]

Together with a lack of diligence on the part of white board members, Cassius listed several other reasons why organized societies failed to reach black Americans. From Cassius's perspective, white Christians at times engaged in mission work among blacks to "get rid of" their "few negro members." A missionary endeavor among American blacks, guided by ulterior motives, necessitated the separation between "loyals" and "progressives" in the Restoration Movement. White leaders and members of the Stone-

Campbell Movement also frequently enlisted spiritually and intellectually unfit black missionaries and black evangelists. "The man selected to organize the congregations is seldom, if ever, chosen because of his spiritual and intellectual fitness, nor because he is desired by the people he is expected to build up. But he is the 'fad' or 'whim' of some member of the white congregation, who thinks they see in him a great future." Additionally, white Christians who regularly contributed to missionary societies to aid in the evangelization of black people became "tired of being taxed [pressured] for [monetary] support" by the board. Seeing insufficient money contributed, the board reduces its support, "and the work dies without accomplishing anything except ridding the white congregation of its objectionable negro members. This is the kind of work the Boards have been doing among the colored people all these years."[38]

Most importantly, white leaders of missionary boards excluded competent black preachers from participation in decision-making roles and refused to give black and white evangelists equal treatment. "An able colored preacher is not tolerated among the great leaders in the mission work of the Christian Church. They say that able colored preachers expect too much simply because they ask the same treatment given to white missionaries."[39] In the mind of Cassius, the racism and paternalism of white "society men" fundamentally hampered efforts to evangelize blacks in America.

The apathy and anti-black sentiment espoused by some white board members disillusioned Cassius and stimulated him to organize the Missionary Executive Board of the Colored Disciples of Oklahoma in 1909. While the organization primarily sought to "insure more and better missionary work," as the organization's president, Cassius insisted that racial hatred drove a wedge between white and black Christians in Oklahoma, asserting that "the time has come for colored Christians to form themselves in a class by themselves, because the white Christians have plainly shown that he is not wanted among them. For this reason I think it is far better for us both that we separate." For Cassius, the separation fundamentally concerned the issue of race with theological issues involved as well. "In this way," Cassius maintained, "we will be saved from the sad spectacle of making believe that we love one another."[40]

Dissension over the missionary society in the Stone-Campbell Movement occurred in the late nineteenth century. The fracture between Disciples of Christ and Churches of Christ was not formalized, however, until

1906. A decade after the split, Cassius continued to connect the problems of race with missionary societies, and he attributed the Board of Negro Education and Evangelization's lack of success to white leaders who regarded themselves as morally superior to black people. Efforts failed "not because we did not need the help our white brethren were trying to give us, but because they underestimated our intelligence and overestimated their ability to give us what we needed then and still—a pure gospel." The rupture between the "loyals" and "progressives," according to Cassius, derived not from doctrinal differences alone, but from racial tension as well, which remained a fundamental contributing factor. "They tried to start a system of evangelization among my people and at the same time ignore the colored Christian preachers that were building up a strong work without the aid of any human organization." The neglect of black evangelists by white leaders of the Board of Negro Education and Evangelization not only resulted in "a failure," but "division, which is doing us much harm."[41]

Cassius reiterated this point in the fall of 1916. "Twenty-five years ago a great movement was made to educate and evangelize the Negro. But instead of choosing Negroes to carry the gospel to Negroes and intrusting the work into the hands of Negroes, white men and white women were chosen to carry on the work, implying by action that the Negroes were not to be trusted to evangelize their own race." Here Cassius revealed the impetus behind his aversion for missionary societies. Cassius felt that white board leaders refused to place black evangelists in leadership roles because of the blacks' perceived incompetence. Cassius explained why he believed the white "society men" used the wrong plan and why his own plan was better:

I fully believe that the promoters of the plan were strictly honest, and were zealous toward my people as I am this day, but their zeal was not according to knowledge. They forgot that four hundred years of slavery had bred a prejudice that even zeal for the cause of Christ could not overcome, and that in the mind of every white man lurked the thought [that] the Negro was, in some way, inferior and that Negro himself had been taught to suspect and fear the white man. If, as I then suggested, that the work had been placed in the hands of colored men, and our white brethren had simply encouraged and financed the work, I feel safe in saying that where we now have a few hundred colored disciples we would have had tens of thousands.[42]

Cassius added that while the "great society movement may be all right for the white race who have grown strong and wise, and can perhaps carry out their plans, and still keep in that strait and narrow path, but for the Negro race, who have been only a half century out of slavery, it's all wrong."[43] In the mind of Cassius, black people longed to hear the Gospel from evangelists of their own race.

Cassius correctly observed that white board leaders underestimated the lingering effects of slavery. Former slaves such as Cassius distrusted white leaders who offered and extended financial assistance to black preachers. But black bondage also influenced the way white clerics viewed ex-slaves, even though some such as Cassius had become self-taught, committed evangelists in the Stone-Campbell fellowship. Cassius deplored that white believers "attempted to make [the black man] a spiritual equal and a social outcast. Brethren, it cannot be done." Ed Harrell notes, "Most Disciples had discarded biblical theories of racial inferiority, but few had abandoned the idea that blacks were inferior. The characterization of blacks as 'indolent,' 'ignorant,' 'chicken thieves,' all too frequently found its way into the church papers."[44] Cassius linked such caricatures with the white-dominated missionary organizations affiliated with the Stone-Campbell Movement.

But Cassius failed to recall the monetary assistance he received from the Board of Ministerial Relief in 1896, and the contributions the Board made toward the evangelistic and educational efforts of Preston Taylor, Rufus Conrad, H. S. Howell, J. G. Keys, and other black ministers. He sometimes forgot the kind white saints in the North and the South who befriended him, and Cassius at times incorrectly stereotyped all white leaders and members of the Restoration Movement associated with missionary societies as anti-black. Harrell has claimed that the motives of many white leaders were "above reproach." Indeed, Cassius himself admitted in 1917 that David Lipscomb "regarded the negro as a man, and a negro Christian as a brother." Cassius lamented, "In his [Lipscomb's] death the colored disciples have lost one of their best friends."[45] Cassius did not, however, view all white leaders in the Stone-Campbell Movement as comrades.

Cassius, in short, became ensnared in the vortex of doctrinal divisions between "loyals" and "progressives" in the Stone-Campbell Movement. Conservative leaders in Churches of Christ labeled him both a "digressive" and a "progressive" because he wrote for the *Christian Leader.* Liberal ministers among Disciples of Christ dubbed him an "anti" because he adamantly opposed missionary societies and mechanical music in worship. One group sought to restrict his freedom of mind as an independent thinker, while the other worked to curtail his freedom of movement as an evangelist among black people. Behind all these attempts at control, Cassius detected racist assumptions of black inferiority and white superiority. His preoccupation with race influenced how he viewed such theological issues as missionary societies, for in Cassius's perspective racial liberals, racial conservatives, and racial radicals, whom he encountered in the broader American society, also enjoyed membership and leadership roles in the missionary societies of the Stone-Campbell fellowship, and they brought their anti-black attitudes with them. This troubled Cassius deeply and contributed to his profound antipathy for and aversion to the missionary-society program. There were no mitigating circumstances in Cassius's view: "The whole thing is a pious fraud."

III
From Heaven to Hell:
The Oklahoma Experience

6

"No Race Suicide on This Ranch"

Race, Family, and Finances

> Lo, children are an heritage of the Lord: and the fruit of the womb is
> his reward.
>
> —Psalms 127:3

Samuel Robert Cassius was more than a Bible expositor and race man; he
was also a family man, an ardent believer in Holy Scripture, and an earnest
believer in large families. In 1909, Cassius proudly confessed, "I have a large
family—no race suicide on this ranch. I am only the father of nineteen
children." With such statements, he sought to demonstrate that American
blacks were strong and fertile while many whites, by limiting the number
of offspring they had, were weak and sterile. Cassius thus observed thirteen years earlier, "We may be short on money, but as a race we are long
on children."[1] The responsibilities of church planting while meeting his
family's needs, however, constantly frustrated Cassius, as parental demands
often hampered his evangelistic efforts. "I visited ten places during the
year," Cassius wrote, dejectedly recounting his limited accomplishments
for the previous year, "and only baptized one person. My traveling expenses
have been $108.50, and I received from all sources $94." The imbalance of
expenses and income combined with failing crops to leave Cassius despon-
dent at times. "It's part of my life to go from place to place and preach the
gospel. I work hard when I am at home, but somehow I don't seem to get
along." While Cassius had a strong passion to carry the Good News to
African Americans, he frequently struggled to do what he loved most because of the burdens of financial and family matters. "I am not complaining," Cassius concluded, "but just simply telling the truth."[2]

Careful scrutiny of his correspondence in the *Christian Leader* reveals
Cassius as a man who cared deeply for the spiritual and material necessities
of his family. Although little detail is known of his family, according to his
obituary Cassius fathered twenty-three children, eleven with his first wife,

Effie Festus-Basil, and twelve with his second wife, Selina Daisy Flenoid.[3] His first wife, a native of Ohio, died in 1895 in Oklahoma, and three years later he married his second wife, a Texan by birth and twenty-five years his junior.

The United States Census of Oklahoma for 1900 reveals that the Cassius household consisted of his second wife; a daughter Julian, born in 1875 in Washington, D.C.; a son Isaiah, born in 1886 in Indiana; a daughter "Allice" (probably Alice), born in 1888 in Iowa; a son "Amus" (probably Amos), born in 1889, also in Iowa. The census showed that a son, William, was born in 1898 and another son, Franklin, was born the following year. In 1901 Cassius told the *Christian Leader* that he had the "sad misfortune to lose my little boy on July 22," but he did not divulge the son's name. The 1910 census reported that the Cassius family included six more children: Mary Juanita (age eight), Jennie B. (seven), Benjamin C. (five), Anthony B. (three), Effie F. (two), and Ferris C. (one and a half). A decade later, the census registered the names John F. Rowe Cassius (age twenty) and A. Brudis Cassius (thirteen), whose names were left off the 1910 census.[4]

Cassius gave three of his sons biblical names: Isaiah and Amos in honor of God's prophets and Benjamin in honor of the patriarchs Abraham, Isaac, and Jacob. Cassius viewed himself as a prophet whom the Lord used to proclaim the pure Gospel. After relocating from Oklahoma to Ohio, Cassius wrote, "I would not be in this state if I had not been sent by those who could not go themselves, and I said to them here I am, send me," with the ending phrase alluding to the prophet Isaiah's declaration in Isaiah 6:8.[5] Cassius probably expected his sons to become evangelists. To honor the life of John F. Rowe (1827–97), founder of the *Christian Leader,* Cassius named one of his sons John F. Rowe Cassius.

Besides the names of some of Cassius's children, we know very little about them. Cassius published an invitation in the *Western Age* about the forthcoming wedding of his daughter Alice to Mr. Ed Persio on May 17, 1908. The paper, after acknowledging receipt of the invitation, extended well wishes to the couple. The same newspaper announced that Cassius "spent Sunday in Langston administering to the spiritual want of the christian denomination. Mrs. Cassius and children were with him."[6] The announcement suggested that Cassius and his family were known in Logan County.

In 1914, the father happily reported in the *Christian Leader* that two of his children, "by confession and baptism," became Christians. "This makes seven of my own children that I have lived to see enter the church of Christ. Truly, I can say, of those thou hast given me I have lost none; ten children are dead, seven are converted, and six remain to be saved." In the same report, Cassius informed his audience that his son Amos contemplated entering the ministry: "My son, 'Amos,' wrote me not long ago that he was studying hard that he might be able to keep the name of Cassius alive as a gospel preacher." Two years later, Cassius shared more good news when his daughter Jennie B. and his second wife, Selina, confessed Christ and received baptism. "At Meridian, Sunday, Nov. 5th, my daughter, Jennie B., age thirteen, made the good confession, and was baptized; and my own wife, who has long known the truth, but because she was afraid of offending her people, who were Baptists, has hesitated to come out from among them, she, too, on last Lord's day, threw off the yoke of bondage, and accepted the truth." Cassius continued his testimony about his family: "This has long been a great source of sadness to me, and has somewhat hindered my work, but now I feel that I can go forward to more and better work. I lived to see both of my wives stand firmly on the Rock, Christ Jesus, and have heard the good confession come from the lips of eight of my children, and praise the Lord I have not coaxed one of them into the church. I have simply taught them the truth by precept and example. I may lose my home, but I want to be able to say to the Father, 'Of those that thou gave me I have lost none.'"[7]

This foregoing testimony allows a deeper glimpse into the Cassius family. Not only was Cassius serious about providing spiritual direction for African Americans in general, but he was also concerned about leading his own children in the way of the Lord in particular. Before his wife's conversion there was religious division in Cassius's house, as he was a staunch member of the Stone-Campbell Movement while Selina was a Baptist. Cassius felt relieved when his wife made the "good confession." In John 17:12, Jesus, referring to his relationship with the twelve apostles, stated, "Those that thou gavest me I have kept, and none of them is lost." Cassius applied the verse to his own family; he viewed himself as a custodian of his wife and offspring.

In 1918, Cassius told his supporters that the federal government stationed two of his sons in foreign lands to fight in World War I. Noting the impact the war draft had on his congregation in Guthrie, Oklahoma, Cassius observed, "The war is proving to be a very serious factor in church work. All our young men are being drafted into the army, and I fear that our work will be very much injured." Cassius, pointing out that the war touched his own family, continued, "One of my boys, John F. Rowe Cassius, is in France, and William M. Cassius is in the Philippines, and three more of my married sons and two sons-in-law will have to go if they make another call." Cassius expected the United States government to aid soldiers' "parents and other dependents, but I don't know of any colored families that are being helped. We have not received a cent." Notwithstanding his disappointment, Cassius used the context of World War I to argue that the "negro is no slacker!" Cassius optimistically believed that "When this cruel war is over and the boys (my boys and your boys) come marching home, they will find a new country." Blacks' participation in the war meant that race relations would be better. "A whole lot of things that now exist will have been washed away in a tide of human blood," Cassius asserted. "[I]t will be then that the Church will have a chance to make the religion of Jesus Christ stand out as the saving power of God for all mankind."[8]

Amos Lincoln Cassius is the best known of the Cassius children. William T. Milligan, preacher for the Avalon Church of Christ in Los Angeles, California, and a close friend of Amos, compiled Amos Cassius's obituary. According to Milligan, Amos enrolled in Tuskegee Institute in Alabama in 1906. While a student at Tuskegee, he worked in president Booker T. Washington's house and studied under renowned agricultural scientist George Washington Carver (1864–1943). At Tuskegee, Amos Cassius acquired skills as a chef. Student records at Tuskegee Institute, however, reveal that Amos attended the institution for only two terms, from 1909 to 1910. As a student, young Cassius studied in an experiment station during his first year and in a dairy barn in his second year.[9] Thus, Amos Cassius would have worked alongside Professor Carver, who depended on "student labor" to "cultivate experimental fields" for livestock and assorted vegetables.[10]

In 1910, Amos returned from Alabama to Oklahoma and was baptized. He developed cooking skills while working in large hotels in Chicago, Illinois, as well as Houston and Dallas, Texas. Near the end of World War I, Amos served as a cook in the Nurses' Corp of the United States Army in Douglas, Arizona. With the coming of peace, Amos and his wife, Beulah, relocated to California, operated a restaurant, and co-established the first African American Church of Christ in southern California in 1922. Amos, with assistance from his father, Samuel, founded other churches in the Los Angeles area. The younger Cassius, like his father, helped raise funds to erect church buildings in Statesville, North Carolina; Delray Beach, Florida; Riverside, California; Hobbs, New Mexico; and Nassau in the Bahamas. Milligan, when eulogizing Amos, wrote, "He was an eagle willing to flock with us sparrows. He was eloquent. His eloquence was ever present but seldom used in order that we might understand him. He was greatness clothed with humility. He was maturity clothed for our sake with a touch of childhood."[11] Amos Lincoln Cassius devoted his life to the spiritual uplift of black Americans, as he perpetuated the evangelistic legacy of his father.

Samuel Robert Cassius frequently exulted in his large family, happily acknowledging his clan of twenty-three children. In 1918 he rejoiced, "I have spent thirty-five years of my life in the ministry, and I am yet strong and active; and, with God's help, these remaining years shall be spent trying to overcome some of the mistakes I made while caring for a family of twenty-three children. Ten are dead; two are somewhere at the front fighting for the freedom of the world, and three more will have to go in the next call; and, best of all, all of my boys have made that good confession." A dozen years later, Cassius continued to express delight over his large family, writing, "I have raised a large family of very intelligent children. I have given them fair education. I have seen 12 of them baptized into the one Body. We have buried 10 children, and there are thirteen living now. For nearly 45 years it has been a race with us to keep in sight of the breadwagon, but as David said, I have never been forsaken, neither have my children had to beg bread. All my children are poor, but praise the Lord, none of them are criminals."[12]

Although Cassius burned with a fervent evangelistic urge, the difficulty of caring for a large family clashed with his passion for preaching. In 1897, Cassius reported sadly that his children had been shoeless for eight months. "Think of it; it is the 25th day of November, and my children have not had on a shoe since last March. Some will ask me why I don't stop preaching until times get better." Basing his response on Luke 9:62, Cassius replied, "I am my brother's keeper; so are you. We may evade our duty, but we can not evade the consequence of not doing our duty."[13] And he held his primary duty to be the spreading of the Gospel. Five years later Cassius illuminatingly portrayed his family life, as he struggled to meet the physical needs of his own children and the spiritual needs of God's children. "I have a wife and six healthy children to feed, and three congregations to break the bread of life to, and at least one-third of my time. Then, again, I live in the worst old log cabin of any of my members, and the centipedes and tarantulas are getting so bad under it that I am compelled to build some kind of a shack this winter, so you see these poor old hands of mine must keep busy. I am not begging," he insisted, "I am simply telling some things that hinder me." Refuting any speculation of idleness, Cassius continued, "Maybe you think I am not busy, but if you had to do as much work to feed your wife and children as I do, and then do as much free preaching as I do, you would wonder how I get even time to think. Oh, yes, I am getting awful rich."[14]

That which gave Cassius the greatest pleasure, however, sometimes created the most acute tension in his life, as he juggled preaching assignments and family concerns. In 1903 Cassius enunciated his burden to preach: "My course is laid out. I can not go back. God has committed to me the glorious privilege of preaching the Gospel to the colored people of Wagoner, I. T. [Indian Territory]." So determined was Cassius to devote his life to full-time evangelism that, in 1904, he offered to sell his farm. "I have a good farm," announced Cassius, "worth $2,500, and if I can sell it I will settle my family in some town, and once more throw my whole life into the work of the ministry. I can not serve two masters." Two years later, he held firm to his intent to "devote as much of my time as possible to preaching the Gospel out on the firing line of our civilization. My determination is to preach Christ where others will not, or dare not, go." In 1907, Cassius disclosed a plan to wipe out his monetary debts so that he could "devote all my time to the ministry" the following year. "This is my earnest desire. Not that I am not willing to work, but because I love to preach." Giving his most articulate expression about his passion for preaching, he continued, "I had rather preach the gospel for what I can eat, than to live in plenty at anything else. God has raised me up for this very work, and I am not happy or contented at anything else."[15]

Cassius reiterated his frustration over the clash of his two duties in 1907, explaining that "eleven people put their feet under the table at my house three times a day. Six of them are under nine years, with twenty-year-old appetites; so you see I have not much time to give to new work." In 1910, when a friend from Kansas offered Cassius a monthly salary of twenty dollars to preach the Gospel full time, Cassius answered "no" and explained, "I am convinced that no man living can now enter the field and support his family and devote his entire time to the ministry of the Word unless he had an assurance of not less than $10 a week and what he could gather in his work." Cassius realized that with nine children "in size giants' appetites" and a "great, big, able-bodied, always-hungry" wife, he needed more than twenty dollars a month to survive as a full-time evangelist. Cassius, now at age fifty-seven, knew the value of having sufficient financial support in order to commit himself solely to evangelism. He concluded, "Let me say that if you will give me food to eat and clothes to wear, I will devote my whole time to the preaching of the Word, and never by word, look or act will I even associate with hard work." Later in the same year, Cassius admitted that he made "some money" and that he did "work hard," but he lamented that "with crop failures, and a large family, it keeps me always at home."[16]

In addition to toiling to provide food and clothing for his wife and children, Cassius often struggled to keep them healthy. During the winter of 1904, Cassius reported that he did limited evangelism work because of sickness in his family. "I have only preached three or four sermons during this time. I have been sick all winter, and for eight weeks I have had from two to five sick at once." A variety of illnesses afflicted Cassius's children. "At this writing my wife and four of my children are sick. The children have the measles, and the worst coughs I ever heard. It is the worst case of measles I ever saw, and those afflicted with it go as near death as it is possible to go without dying." Cassius, too, informed his supporters that it cost $5.50 to have a doctor visit, "and even now I am more than $25 behind for medicine." The following year, Cassius reported that one of his daughters "was creeping back from the grave with a live body and a dead mind—for, be it known unto you, her mind is dead—a brother in the West sent me $11." Although it is unclear whether Cassius's little girl was mentally ill, he called the gift from the West "a miracle of God." In 1913, Cassius acknowledged that sickness again infiltrated his home, noting, "I have been sick and several of the children are now sick, but, thank God, I still live and have bread enough and to spare." Half a decade later, Cassius related to his *Christian Leader* audience that "yellow jaundice and several other diseases" permeated the state of Oklahoma and debilitated "four of my children." Thus, the following month, when Christians from Missouri sent him a "box of meat," disciples from Kansas assisted him with a "box of clothing," and believers from Iowa gave him ten dollars, Cassius exulted, "For all of these blessings I most fervently thank God."[17]

Cassius and his family, consequently, lived off of the generosity of mostly white congregations. Disinterested in wealth and affluence, Cassius preached the Gospel without monetary compensation. Therefore, the Globe-trotter relied on the charity of white Christians, whom he believed possessed more resources to aid black evangelists. "The white brethren have this advantage over us," Cassius explained in 1916, "they have the means to support preachers and buy tents, while if we get these things, the whites will have to give them to us." Five years later, when Cassius announced his plan to leave Oklahoma and take up residence in the Ohio Valley, he explicitly stated that his transition would be impossible without the benevolence of whites in Churches of Christ. "I hope the brethren along the Valley," wrote Cassius, "will remember that I am depending on them to get away from here [Guthrie, Oklahoma] at the appointed time." W. W. Thornberry, a white preacher in Jerusalem, Ohio, urged readers of the *Christian Leader* to support Cassius financially. Thornberry pleaded, "Let us give Bro. Cassius a chance among his people in the Ohio Valley by holding up his hands. What say you?" The next year, when Cassius and his wife relocated, he indicated that they were homeless, acknowledging, "I have no home now. Wife and I are doing our best to make good." Explaining that he rented his house in Guthrie, Oklahoma, Cassius confessed, "We don't want to make money. We only want to live."[18]

After eventually settling in Cambridge, Ohio, Cassius encouraged his supporters to fulfill their promise of financial assistance to him. Reminding his backers that monetary gain was not the impetus behind his move to the Ohio Valley, Cassius reaffirmed, "I don't want to make money, but I do want to be God's free man to do the work that you can not do."[19] Cassius understood that help from white churches made it possible for him to evangelize African Americans.

While Cassius left behind his family for several months to preach the Word, his wife and children lived off the kindness of white supporters. After preaching for several weeks in West Virginia, Cassius requested in 1920 "Please remember my wife and children until I get home again."[20]

Two years later, when a windstorm demolished his house in Guthrie, Oklahoma, Cassius reported, "I have no money today to send my wife, but somewhere, the sun is shining and God will take care of me and mine. I will thank God for any kindness shown my wife in her need while I am away."[21] After completing a four-month preaching and fund-raising tour for his ministerial work in Ohio, he commented, "I am sure no one will object to me going home after a four months' trip of hard work. Remember a kindness shown my family is a kindness shown me."[22]

A devoted and considerate husband, Cassius left home to preach the pure Gospel to African Americans in the fall of 1922 with five dollars and returned from an evangelistic campaign with but seventy-five cents. "I was feeling sad," Cassius admitted, "but when I entered the wife was all smiles." While Cassius was absent, a Brother Moore of Sisterville, Ohio, sent four dollars to Selina Cassius just before her husband returned. She spent some of it on "the best dinner (it seemed to me) that I ever ate. I guess it was because I saw in it the loving hand of my heavenly Father." The providence of God perhaps expressed through the beneficence of white followers of Jesus made Selina a happy woman and her husband a grateful man. Cassius, however, explained why he returned home *broke as usual.* When returning to his wife and family in Cambridge, Ohio, Cassius visited a Church of Christ, a pro-instrumental and pro-missionary society congregation. The preacher arranged for Cassius to preach a Thanksgiving sermon. When church officers discovered that the visiting minister was Cassius, a fierce opponent of instrumental music in worship and missionary societies, they "raised Cain." After the church leaders refused to allow him to preach, Cassius explained that he "had too much regard for my brother's kindness to even want to speak. That's why I got home *broke as usual.*"[23]

Cassius's love and concern for his wife, Selina, became evident when she developed three tumors on one of her arms in 1923. The condition of his wife's arm consumed his mind. When preaching in Fairmont, West Virginia, Cassius received forty dollars. After taking care of his expenses of twelve dollars, Cassius gave his wife twenty-five dollars "to have her arm treated. She has, so the doctors say, a tumor on her arm, which is giving her much trouble." Cassius, continuing to express concern for his wife's predicament, wrote, "I only hope I will be able to get her cured, so that she can be the help to me that she left the comforts of home for." Selina's infirmity made it virtually impossible for her to sew and sell quilts to help earn money for the family. A week later, while in a worship service in Fairview, West Virginia, Cassius said, "I thought of my poor wife at home, 'winged' with a tumor on her arm." Cassius, after noting that he recently celebrated his birthday on May 8, pleaded with the *Christian Leader* readership: "I ask the brethren to help me do two things, preach the Gospel and have my wife's arm operated on."[24] Not surprisingly, Cassius placed his preaching tasks above his wife's health.

The next week, Cassius informed his readers that the operation on his wife's arm would "cost me $100." With a blend of humor and gravity, he continued, "After [the doctor] operates on her arm he will operate on my poor old pocket; and, say, he ain't giving me a thing for my nerves! I sure do wish I had his nerve." Seven days later, Cassius acknowledged receiving ten dollars from a Church of Christ in Hundred, West Virginia, "to help me have my wife's arm operated on." Cassius needed financial assistance from white Christians to bring relief to a suffering spouse. In June, Selina Cassius had a near-death experience, when an "old wornout gas range" exploded and "burned her pretty bad, but not enough to disfigure her." The explosion, according to Cassius, "singed her hair and burned her eyebrows off, and scorched her afflicted arm pretty bad." Pentecostal groups interpreted Selina's misfortune as an act of God, who was "punishing her because she won't join the Holy Rollers." Cassius dismissed so-called Christians who held "God responsible for all their meanness." Selina, however, did not receive her successful operation until 1927, after she and her husband took up residence in Colorado Springs, Colorado. Her husband thanked God and all Christians, confessing, "It was only through the mercy of God and the kindness of our white brethren that she is a living woman today."[25]

Cassius himself was not exempt from physical maladies. In 1916, he admitted that he was unable to do evangelistic work because he had been "sick for six months." To make matters worse, Cassius was "too poor to buy medicine that I need, so I just sit and wonder." A year later, "la grippe" (or influenza) forced Cassius to abandon a preaching tour and "to stay close around home the rest of the winter." Knowing that he was "getting too old for the rough life of a pioneer" and sensing that "automobiles, moving pictures, the European war and about a hundred other kinds of ungodliness" made the "Gospel plan of salvation" less appealing to sinners, Cassius confessed, "I have given all I had for the sake of a pure Gospel. I came into this world naked and hungry, and it looks like I am due to go out the same way, except somebody sends me a box pretty soon."[26]

In the fall of 1924, while traveling from Winfield, Kansas, to Oakland, California, Cassius suffered a back and hip injury on a train. He considered the accident as providential, as it ultimately allowed him to reach his destination, California. He wrote:

> A peculiar thing happened to me on this trip that shows me just what strange means God uses to answer a Christian's prayer. I was on the Union Pacific railroad train, coming from Denver to Ogden, Utah. I lacked twelve dollars of having money enough to carry me from Ogden to Sacramento, Cal. I was asking the Lord to open the way for me to continue my journey, when the train stalled on an up-grade, and in order to start it again it made a sudden lunge forward while I was standing and threw me in such a manner that my back was strained so that I could not walk without great pain. The railroad doctor examined me and as I was only temporarily hurt, they agreed to give me $20 to relieve the railroad from further responsibility.
>
> You may say it was too little, but I saw in it God's answer to my prayer, and I took it. By accident I had a twenty-four hour insurance in my pocket, and I hope to get something out of that.[27]

Cassius's hip injury hindered him from assisting D. C. Allen, a black preacher for Churches of Christ in Oakland. A frustrated Cassius lamented, "There has been no additions since I came, but perhaps that is partly due to the fact that my hip hindered me from getting around among the people."[28]

Cassius and his family clearly lived a life of hardships and disappointments. Financial problems and family concerns consumed Cassius's energies as much as did evangelism and the race problem in America. Indeed, the web of race and economics ensnared the household of Cassius, who certainly understood that his preaching the Word to African Americans depended on the support he garnered from white believers. In 1922 he acknowledged, "I have not gone to the white churches because I liked to preach to white folks. I went to them to get aid that I might go to my own race. There was nowhere else to go." Cassius preferred not to "face a white audience," but he interacted with white disciples because they had "my bait in their pockets" and because "I had a work to do." "Many of them," he confessed, "have received me as a man of God in spite of my race and color, while some have received me as they would a case of small pox." Five years later, Cassius boldly declared, "I will leave home tonight, hunting for some place where I can say or do something that will cause a sinner to repent, as you brethren know I am dependent on the Churches of Christ (white) to enable me to go." Anticipating that critics would say that he ought to wait until sent for, Cassius responded, "But the word of our Lord was that his preachers should go, and if it is my lot to die somewhere among strangers, I intend to go and preach the Gospel." Cassius then left a sickly wife in the "hands of God" and to the "care of his saints" in order to go and do what he loved most.[29]

Having to divide his interests between evangelizing and caring for his enormous family frustrated Cassius. Insufficient monetary support from white disciples also disappointed him. When a tornado destroyed part of his house in Guthrie, Oklahoma, Cassius commended the liberality of white Christians, who contributed toward repairs for his "humble home." Simultaneously, Cassius explained that the donations enabled him to shelter his family but did not help him to spread the Word of God among black Americans, his primary passion. "Don't you see that the money they are giving me don't help the work I want to do? It only helps me to keep my family under shelter." "I thank God," expressed Cassius with a mixture of praise and criticism, "for such kind friends in my hour of need. But it does not help me to build up the Cause of Christ in this barren field." After reporting that he had received sixty-five dollars from generous Christians, Cassius divulged that he sent forty dollars to his wife and kept the balance for personal expenses. He also confessed his embarrassment over reporting money he received from fellow believers, stating, "Somehow I don't like the idea of parading the monies I receive in the papers, there is something about it that is not right." That Cassius regularly disclosed the amount of donations and how he used them was a testament to his integrity. And while he was always faithful in monetary matters, the lack of funds forced Cassius into an itinerant lifestyle.[30]

Cassius moved to Ohio in 1922 but then departed the state in 1924. He then went on a three-state odyssey from Rockford, Illinois, to Minneapolis,

Minnesota, to Los Angeles, California, before settling in Colorado Springs, Colorado, where he died in 1931. Notwithstanding his evangelistic trek throughout the United States, Cassius explained why he left the Ohio Valley, which he once deemed a most promising field for black evangelization. "I left Ohio because only four congregations made any attempt to support me, and forced me to drift around half of my time, edifying congregations to get money to live on." Lack of ample financial support crushed Cassius's dreams of reaching black people in America with the Gospel of Jesus Christ.[31]

Consequently, race, economics, evangelism, and family were inseparable issues in the mind and experience of Cassius. On the one hand, his large family impeded his efforts to get "out on the firing line." In 1907, for example, Cassius lamented, "Brethren, I could put in every day and night, if I was able to afford it, but I have a wife and eight children at home to feed and clothe, therefore, I shut my eyes and ears, and will neither see nor hear the cries of these people except when I find myself with a few dollars to spare. Then I go among them, and do all I can." His immense family, the source of his pride and joy, became in many ways a massive burden. On the other hand, Cassius, who relied on the benevolence of white Christians, frequently chided them for diverting monetary resources to foreign lands. In 1910, Cassius lamented, "I am getting old now, and am still doing all I can to carry the gospel to those that need it. For that reason I sincerely need all that is given me. Now, brethren," Cassius complained, "if you sling your tears plumb across the ocean at those heathen over there, and your contempt at the negroes and the heathens over here, there's nothing to it." A dozen years later, after returning home from a preaching engagement *"broke as usual,"* Cassius asked whites in Churches of Christ, "Is the Negro a man? And did Christ die to save him as well as other sinners? And above all, can a man have the love of God in his heart and hatred toward other races at the same time?" In Cassius's view, the racial antipathy of some white Christians toward the souls of black folk caused his meager financial aid, which led to his family's destitution. In 1930, Cassius, reflecting on his ministerial career, lamented, "I have tried for the past 45 years to go, but instead of preaching all the time to my people, as you make it possible for others to do, it takes most of my time trying to raise a little to feed my family, pay R. R. fare and keep up an appearance." Cassius further deplored that there were "only a few loyal colored Christian preachers" who were "willing to go out into the world and try to convert sinners" because the "white brethren will not hold up their hands."[32]

More specifically, Cassius and many other evangelists in Churches of Christ lived in poverty because the congregations they served were poor. In 1920, the *Christian Leader* reported that the Disciples of Christ had 1,226,280 members who gave $8,797,820, "an average of $7.10 per member," while Churches of Christ had 317,937 members who contributed $679,000, "an average of $2.10 per member." The editorial sarcastically concluded, "I'm not saying a word, are you?" The statistics speak loud and clear, however. Earl I. West notes that after the 1906 split, the noninstrumental group was "stronger numerically" only in Texas and Tennessee, but in the North, it was a "different picture" as the pro-instrumental group swept up Northern congregations and grew considerably. Thus, by 1920, Churches of Christ generally were neither financially nor numerically strong. Consequently, many preachers, white and black alike, struggled to provide for their families while building and guiding fledgling churches. Struggling congregations translated into impoverished evangelists, who often overextended themselves and sacrificed their families to teach people the Gospel message.[33]

Hence, Cassius lived in poverty, partially because he relied on white churches that were weak monetarily, partly because some white parishioners divided their resources between foreign and domestic missions, but mainly because he put the spiritual needs of his race above the physical needs of his large family.

7
"The Booker T. Washington of Oklahoma"
Samuel Robert Cassius and the Tohee Industrial School

And thou shalt teach them diligently unto thy children, and shalt talk
of them when thou sittest in thine house, and when thou walkest by
the way, and when thou liest down, and when thou risest up.

—Deuteronomy 6:7

From 1895 to 1915, Booker T. Washington was unquestionably the most
influential black man in the United States. His influence spilled over into
the Stone-Campbell Movement. In 1897 Washington addressed a Disciples
of Christ convention in Indianapolis, Indiana, where the *Christian Evangelist* called Washington's talk "one of the most remarkable speeches, in its
point, power and pathos, to which we have ever listened." Whites in the
Restoration Movement learned Washington's story, and they admired his
meteoric rise from poverty to prominence. "In simple manner," the paper
continued, "he recited his early history of poverty and want, his thirst for
knowledge, his efforts in getting to the school in Hampton, Va., and the
work which he undertook [after his course of study at Hampton] at Tuskegee, Ala., in the midst of the 'black belt,' and has carried forward with
such remarkable success. Mr. Washington seems to be a philosopher, an
orator, a teacher, a prophet, and a practical philanthropist, all in one."[1]

Caucasian members of Churches of Christ venerated Washington partly
because he rose from a slave in Virginia to a reputable educator in Alabama, but mainly because he refused to insist on social equality. Historian
Joel Williamson has aptly assessed the reason for Washington's widespread
appeal to whites in America. "[B]y giving up demands for integration in
public places and universal male suffrage, he seemed also to surrender any
claim to the 'social equality' that so thoroughly frightened whites." The
Christian Evangelist lauded Washington for urging fellow blacks to commit
themselves to "industrial and agricultural education" and for demanding
that fellow blacks stay out of politics because of its "demoralizing influ-

ence."[2] In the minds of most whites in the Stone-Campbell Movement, Washington represented a progressive yet nonthreatening "Negro."

African American leaders in Churches of Christ, too, admired Booker T. Washington. Marshall Keeble, the highly acclaimed twentieth-century evangelist, said that he read Washington's *Up from Slavery* "from lid to lid." Working primarily out of admiration for Washington's efforts in academia, Annie C. Tuggle, a female educator in Churches of Christ, vigorously championed educating black hands and minds. "I was deeply impressed with what he did during his lifetime to make the world a better place in which to live." G. P. Bowser's educational pursuits in Tennessee, Arkansas, and Texas were in large part attempts to duplicate the work of Booker T. Washington.[3]

But none of the above persons experienced life as a slave in Virginia, as did Booker T. Washington and Samuel Robert Cassius. Thus, Cassius's identification with the Tuskegee president was more real and more significant. Washington instilled in Cassius a sense of black pride and inspired him to imitate the former's racial posture and educational philosophy. Cassius himself noted striking similarities between the two. "We were both born [Washington in 1856, Cassius in 1853] in the same State, both of slave mothers, and both were the sons of white men." Both men came to advocate industrial education. As a consequence, both relied on the generosity of white philanthropists for their success, and both embraced the racial creed of separate but equal.[4] In the 1890s, Cassius emerged as a Booker T. Washington–like figure in the Stone-Campbell Movement and won the hearts of many white believers.

Cassius, a lover of poetry, reproduced in one of his own books "Know No Color," a poem by M. A. Majors who wrote the verse to celebrate Washington's receiving an honorary master's degree from Harvard University. The second stanza of the poem goes:

Our Booker Washington now stands
With leading men of letters,
Of North and South, yea, foreign lands,
He ranks among the better.
His reaching high lifts all the race
To heights where mankind measures
The worth, where all may take his place,
The place where souls are treasures.[5]

Not only does Cassius's choice of this poem clearly reflect his interest in poetry, but it also reveals his appreciation for Washington as well as his preoccupation with race. The achievement of one black man "lifts all the race."

The year 1895 was pivotal for African Americans, as the death of their premier statesman, Frederick Douglass, created a void of leadership in the black community. When Douglass died in February, Ida B. Wells, an antilynching advocate, temporarily assumed the leadership mantle until Booker T. Washington's September Atlanta Exposition address catapulted him into national and international fame. Later known as the Atlanta Compromise, Washington's speech urged blacks to stay and labor in the agricultural South. The Tuskegee educator argued that Southern states offered black people the best opportunity for economic advancement. "And in this connection it is well to bear in mind that whatever other sins the South may be called to bear, when it comes to business, pure and simple, it is in the South that the Negro is given a man's chance in the commercial world, and in nothing is this Exposition more eloquent than in emphasizing this chance."[6]

Washington's speech advised both blacks and whites in his audience. To black Southerners, he stressed that they pour "brains and skills into the common occupation of life" and that they start at the "bottom of life" rather than the "top." At the same time, he denounced African Americans who pushed for social equality. "The wisest among my race understand that the agitation of questions of social equality is the extremest folly, and that progress in the enjoyment of all the privileges that will come to us must be the result of severe and constant struggle rather than of artificial forcing." In Washington's view, advancing economically bore more importance than stirring up the issue of social and political equality. Washington also encouraged white Southerners to employ faithful ex-slaves who had proved past fidelity by "nursing your children, watching by the sick-bed of your mothers and fathers, and often following them with tear-dimmed eyes to their graves, so in the future, in our humble way, we shall stand by you with a devotion that no foreigner can approach, ready to lay down our lives, if need be, in defence of yours, interlacing our industrial, commercial, civil, and religious life with yours in a way that shall make the interests of both races one." The Tuskegee Wizard additionally urged white employers in the South to rely on black laborers, not immigrants of "foreign birth and strange tongue and habits for the prosperity of the South." More significantly, Washington's address sanctioned racial separation by declaring, "In all things that are purely social we can be as separate as the fingers, yet one as the hand in all things essential to mutual progress." Not only did the Atlanta Compromise exalt Washington as "the leader of his race," but it also made him, in the view of historian C. Vann Woodward, "a leader of white opinion with a national following, and he propounded not merely an educational theory but a social philosophy."[7]

Washington's racial views profoundly impacted Cassius's life. A month after Washington's November 14, 1915, death, Cassius wrote a eulogistic article in the former's honor, observing, "Not during the past half century has a man of any race achieved a greater distinction than that Booker T. Washington achieved as a leader, educator, and originator. This was not because he was born great." In Cassius's opinion, Washington's success as president of Tuskegee Institute derived not from his birth and education but from his own ambition and white philanthropy. "His parentage was so obscure that he neither knew who his father was nor the day or year of his birth. Neither was it because he was endowed with a great education." Cassius, continuing his assessment of Washington's achievement as a business and educational leader, explained, "Being a natural orator, a deep thinker, and a convincing speaker, [Booker T. Washington] soon found that some of the great religious, financial, and political leaders of this nation were willing to help in the uplift of the negro race. He was not long in winning them over to the support of his work. The tide once turned in that direction, it did not recede until he had the greatest school of its kind in the United States. All the honors that were showered upon him were not only merited, but acted as a stimulus to higher and greater things."[8]

The foregoing passage suggests that Cassius obtained his knowledge of Washington's life most likely from two sources. First, Cassius's praise of Washington's successful development of the Tuskegee Institute implies that Cassius had read *Up from Slavery*. Second, the *Christian Leader* at times published speeches and talks Washington gave while on tour and upheld him as a model citizen. A frequent contributor to and an avid reader of the *Christian Leader,* Cassius doubtlessly paid close attention to the impression the Tuskegee educator, a black man of humble origins, made on the mindset of American whites. Moreover, when the president of the Tuskegee Institute toured two Oklahoma towns, Guthrie in 1905 and Boley in 1906, Cassius was probably in attendance and met the renowned educator personally.[9]

Regardless of how Cassius acquired his knowledge of Washington's life, the two men unmistakably shared similar racial beliefs. When the Tuskegee Wizard asserted that the "agitation of questions of social equality is the extremest folly," Cassius agreed, attesting, "But amid it all, Booker T. Washington did not forget the fact that he was a negro, and showed his great common sense by staying in the race, as far as social equality was concerned. It meant nothing to him. He made for himself a place in the whole nation, based upon manly achievement, and not upon social or racial distinction. In other words, Booker T. Washington was in a class by himself. His race did not make him great, but he reflected greatness on the race."[10] The key terminology, in Cassius's thinking, was "social equality," which meant racial and sexual mixing. Throughout his life, Cassius opposed interracial marriage, stating emphatically in 1903, "It has long been demonstrated that, as a rule, negroes are as much opposed to mixing with whites as whites are to mixing with negroes."[11] Cassius believed God himself opposed social equality because he "made the line of race distinction too broad and deep to be bridged by man's inclination without causing a serious rupture in the human family." Yet divine power—namely, the Spirit of God—enabled different races to "believe the same thing, hope the same thing, and do the same thing, to the glory and honor of God."[12]

Cassius opposed social equality on biblical grounds. Years later, referring to Acts 10:34 which reads in part "God shows no partiality," Cassius believed that African Americans were "just as good morally, and socially as any other on earth." From observation of the animal kingdom, however, he learned that beasts and fowls "mingle, but do not mix"; consequently, the Lord required the same for humans. This was the proper understanding of social equality. "If then the created thing guided only by the natural instincts of life can live together, enjoy life, liberty and the pursuit of happiness and still remain true to their kind, why cannot man, who was made in the likeness and image of God, governed by the wisdom and knowledge of God, live the same temporal, spiritual life, enjoy the same blessings and hope for the same reward that is promised to all mankind regardless of race, color, or previous condition of servitude?" In short, human beings, like animals, were capable of living together harmoniously without mixing sexually.[13]

Yet Cassius believed that social equality, improperly understood, was the work of Satan. The devil's distortion of the meaning of social equality created hostility and division between blacks and whites in America. "The devil never invented a better plan," Cassius insisted, "than when he invented the idea that the righteous, honest dealing of one race with another meant social equality and social intercourse."[14] The issue of racial and sexual mixing was not only a potent and divisive tool of Satan, but it was also the greatest obstacle preventing Churches of Christ from reaching African Americans, Asians, Mexicans, and Native Americans with the Gospel. Many white evangelists, according to Cassius, viewed social equality as a threat to white supremacy because they interpreted that the opening of their church doors to black people also meant granting blacks access to their bedrooms.[15]

Cassius not only adopted a similar racial posture to Washington, but he also imitated the Wizard's educational philosophy. In 1895, Cassius announced plans to establish an industrial school for African American children in Tohee, Oklahoma Territory. "Here in this new country," wrote Cassius, "God has given us the means of solving the social, religious and political problems of this age; for this is indeed an age of reason and development, and the negro, as well as other races, is trying to rise higher in the scale of the world's civilization, and will hail with joy any effort that can or will be made to help him on to progress and recognition. At this present time the Industrial School is the great need of my race." Cassius believed that a practical education should complement a theoretical education. Admitting that some industrial schools had already been established, he regretted that "it is not true that the Disciples of Christ are doing anything in this direction." Cassius essentially sought to duplicate in Oklahoma what Washington had accomplished in Alabama, exclaiming, "Think of it! Fifteen years ago it was Booker T. Washington alone. Now, look at what a change has been wrought!" Comparing the humble beginnings of his own educational project to the modest origins of Tuskegee, Cassius found hope for his Tohee Industrial School. "Booker T. Washington began his school in a house beside which this building would seem a palace, yet in a few years it has become one of the greatest centers for the education of the colored children in America." Cassius, knowing that Washington enlarged his college from such an insignificant start, concluded, "WHY SHOULD I NOT DO LIKEWISE?"[16]

Like Washington, Cassius envisioned a school "to educate both minds and hands," an institution which would produce not only readers and writers but also cooks, washers, barbers, preachers, waiters, and waitresses.

"Education," in Cassius's reasoning, involves "develop[ing] both mind and matter—it means the strengthening of both the physical and intellectual part of man." By training black students to use both their hands and their intellect, Cassius argued, "you produce a happy, independent people, who will be a credit to the nation and a safeguard to the republic. Industrial schools are the only means of bringing about this result. And as the Disciples of Christ have no such school for the lifting up [of] the colored race, I take pleasure in offering a plan that will surely do more to lift up my race than anything that has yet been inaugurated by any of the great church organizations."[17]

Indeed, when Booker T. Washington addressed a crowd of ten thousand in the Oklahoma Territory of Guthrie on November 18, 1905, he urged black Oklahomans to become property owners. And he reminded them of the dignity of labor by stressing, "We must continually train our children, setting the example ourselves, that there is no disgrace in any kind of labor, but that there is a disgrace in all idleness. There is as much dignity attached to working on the farm, in the kitchen, in the factory or on a brick wall, as it is to teach in the school room or to preach the gospel." Cassius probably heard these words, and two decades later he similarly emphasized that "industrial education" must "go hand in hand with an intellectual education." Witnessing ex-slaves learning to read and write thrilled Cassius, "but how much more wonderful," he continued, "it would have been to have seen their hands taught to execute the things that their minds planned."[18]

Unlike Washington's Tuskegee Institute, however, Cassius's Tohee Industrial School involved an important religious component. Cassius planned to use his school as an evangelistic instrument to rescue black Americans from sectarianism and Catholicism, and he constantly pleaded with readers of the *Christian Leader* to help him purchase a building for his educational enterprise. In the summer of 1896 Cassius wrote, "Now, brethren, I have stayed here and eaten too much dirt to suffer a 2x4 little Catholic priest to come here and take these children away from me. I have an average attendance of children in this Sunday-school of thirty every Lord's-day." Cassius viewed himself as a bulwark against the "spread of Catholicism" in Oklahoma, asserting, "It will be a race for the next ninety days between the Catholics and me, and it is for you to say who shall succeed."[19] He sought to prod his supporters into action with the observation that a woman from the East gave three hundred dollars to start a Catholic church.

The Tohee educator, fearing Catholic encroachment in black Oklahoma, expressed his dismay the following year: "I do not believe all the money sent into Oklahoma by the disciples of Christ during the past year would, as a sum total, amount to as much as the Catholics are spending each thirty days right around me here in Logan County. They are certainly showing their faith by their works." The presence of Catholic priests and the proliferation of Catholic students both impressed and alarmed Cassius. "We have seven hundred colored children in the city of Guthrie alone that are of school age. Of this number there are 150 in the Catholic school, or one in every five of the colored children of Guthrie are under Catholic influence."[20]

Moreover, Cassius cited other illuminating sources in highlighting the success of Catholics in the Oklahoma Territory and contrasting the prestige of Catholic priests and the poverty of preachers among the Disciples of Christ:

[Catholics in Oklahoma] already own the best church within ten miles of here. Their missionary priest owns a fine team and buggy, and has a hired boy to drive him; while our poor preachers have not where to lay their head. Now let us look at the Governor's report of 1896, under the head of the Catholic Church of Oklahoma (proper): Churches, 24; chapels, 4; stations visited, 73; missionaries, 15; membership, 10,000; academies, 4; college for boys, 1; schools for boys and girls, 2; convents, 4; monasteries, 1; value of church and school property, 60,000. All other denominations have church property to the amount of $96,315. Thus you will see that the Catholic Church owns over one-third of all church property of this Territory.[21]

The numerical, material, financial, spiritual, and educational advancement of Catholics in the 1890s in the Oklahoma Territory prompted Cassius to challenge leaders in Churches of Christ to focus less on foreign missions and more on domestic missions. "Brethren, the foreign field is, indeed, worthy of all, and far more than all, you are doing, but is not there a greater need at home? The foreign work you ought to do, but this you can not afford not to do." The "greater need," Cassius declared, was his Tohee Industrial School in the Oklahoma Territory, which would "prove a blessing to our country and a safeguard to the religion of our Lord and Savior."[22]

Contemporary black Oklahoma newspapers mirrored Cassius's understanding of the vigor of the Catholic advance. The *Western Age,* a paper Cassius read and wrote for, consistently praised Catholics who worked diligently to uplift African Americans morally and intellectually. The editor of the same paper applauded black nuns in New Orleans, Louisiana, who displayed "much intelligence and marked administrative ability."[23] He insisted that most whites in Presbyterian, Methodist, and Baptist churches were "opposed to the Negro" and he touted the Catholic Church as being less prejudiced toward "the Negro than any other denomination in the world. It is also true that most all other denominations have adopted rules and passed resolutions to bar out the Negro." The popular black newspaper further linked the demagoguery of racist politicians with the three major religious bodies, which "declare that the Negro is not good enough for him to serve God with them." "Tillman, Vardaman, Williams and their associates," the *Western Age* editor continued, "belong to the Southern Methodist denomination, and so long as they continue to be members of that denomination, there is no hope for the Negro Baptist, Presbyterian and Methodist." Since Catholics were more "favorably disposed" to African Americans, the paper concluded that "there is nothing for the Negro to do but to join the Catholic Church."[24] In short, from the perspective of many black Oklahomans, Catholic parishioners treated their black counterparts like "human beings and not as cattle." The only criticism some blacks leveled against the Catholic Church was its prohibition against shouting. "The only objection the colored [C]hristian may have to the Catholic Church is a restriction that the church may place upon his shouting proclivities. The colored Protestant Christian like[s] to shout."[25]

Notwithstanding the appeal the Catholic Church had for African Americans, even in educating their children, Cassius worked diligently to establish a school for black children in the territory of Tohee. To generate financial support for his project, Cassius grew and sold various vegetable seeds such as potatoes, onions, beans, peas, cabbage, and tomatoes. Sixty percent of each dollar, the horticulturalist-educator announced, "goes into the school." He also published a newspaper, the *Industrial Christian,* to market his school and to solicit funds. "I will send the *Industrial Christian* one year to every one that contributes either to the school, paper or evangelistic work of my race, and I will report at least once a month in the *Industrial Christian* and the LEADER just what is being done."[26] Cassius also sold books in support of his school, stating in 1897, "If I could only sell those 100 books that I received from Bro. J. J. Limerick, 'The Gospel in Chart and Sermon,' I could finish my school." He earnestly pleaded with members of the Restoration Movement, "Brethren, please don't forget me and my motherless children and my Industrial School."[27]

To answer criticism from "A Disciple" asking "when you will get that school built," Cassius scheduled preaching appointments in Missouri and Ohio. He emphasized, "I make no charges. I will simply take what I can get. I want the money to finish my school."[28] His reports in the *Christian Leader* revealed that he garnered most of his support from Christians in the Northwest, Midwest, and Northeast. Canadians contributed to the project in Tohee as well. Church leaders such as Joseph E. Cain of Missouri and John F. Rowe of Ohio personally visited the Tohee site and encouraged Christians to assist Cassius's educational endeavor. White believers such as Henry and Mary Van Deusen of Omega, Illinois, also contributed generously to Cassius's work.[29] A letter from an Illinois teenager especially touched Cassius.

> Rinard, Ill., July 6, [1898]
> Dear Bro. Cassius.—Please find inclosed $1.65. It is not much, but it is the best I can do. We are only poor farmers, but we have always been blessed with plenty to eat and wear. I hope this will help you a little. I have worked and earned every cent of it myself. I am thirteen years old, and live on a farm four and one-half miles east of Rinard, Ill. I am a member of the Church of Christ at Pleasant Hill. If this money helps you any, I may send you more some time. May the Lord bless you in your good work, is my prayer. Your sister in Christ,
>
> Etta Duke[30]

This heartfelt letter suggests that most of Cassius's monetary support came from poor farmers who often gave sacrificially to the cause of Christ. Unlike Booker T. Washington who garnered generous financial gifts from wealthy white philanthropists, Cassius was a destitute farmer, preacher, and educator who received donations from struggling white farmers. Yet this fact also demonstrates the influence and charm of Cassius. While out-spoken on the race issue, Cassius seemingly possessed a winsome person-ality, one which touched young and old, black and white. Furthermore, even though Cassius graciously accepted contributions from Caucasian Christians, he never allowed white generosity to translate into white con-trol; Cassius intended his Tohee Industrial School to be a school with black students under black supervision. Cassius doubtlessly communicated his intent to his closest friend, Joseph E. Cain, who communicated Cassius's desire to remain independent of white control. "This is not a school for the colored people to be conducted and controlled by white men, but it is a school for the colored people and to be controlled and conducted by them. This is as it should be."[31]

Cassius had planned to open his school in the fall of 1897, but inclement weather, failing crops, and insufficient support forced the suspension of his paper and delayed his educational undertaking. On Thanksgiving Day, after discontinuing his paper, Cassius voiced his disappointment: "I am not thankful for having to suspend the Industrial Christian, nor am I thankful that I can not raise enough money to start it again." Yet, at the same time he confessed gratitude: "I am thankful that there are still a few Christians that believe that I am pleasing God, and I firmly believe that he will grant me the privilege of completing the work that he has put into my hands to do."[32] Two summers later Cassius wrote appreciatively of contributions from Esther Keiser, a ninety-year-old Christian widow whom he believed the Lord kept "alive for my sake, and not only her." After mentioning four other Christian women, an eighty-one-year-old Illinois widow, a fifty-five-year-old widow, and "two good sisters in Pennsylvania whom God has given me for this work," Cassius concluded that while "men may tire of me, these women never will."[33] Residents of Logan County also took in-terest in Cassius's project. Inman E. Page, president of Langston University, visited Tohee and declared that Cassius's work "was a credit to the brethren and the negro race." Showered with encouragement but burdened with debt, Cassius prayed, "O God, help me to build this school for Jesus' sake. Help! Help! Lord, help me."[34]

Cassius's dream for his school finally materialized on Monday, July 24, 1899. "It is done," Cassius sighed with relief. "The Tohee Industrial School is a fact." Although unpleasant weather shrank an opening-day ceremony gathering of seven hundred to four hundred, after the storm passed 250 wagons and buggies and "one hundred saddle horses" were hitched around Cassius's house. Joseph E. Cain, the event's featured speaker, considered leaving the ceremony until, in Cassius's words, "one hundred loaded wagons pulled in sight, bringing with them four hundred men, women and children, some of whom had come forty miles to hear Elder J. E. Cain." Cassius expressed satisfaction that he had given to the Lord and "to the brotherhood a school that has in its two rooms 20 by 42 feet of seating capacity, and I can safely say that I have done more for the cause of our blessed Master and for the upbuilding of my race, with the amount of money given me, than any other man, white or black, in our brotherhood." Cassius delighted in a poem that Roxanna T. Lydic, a white Christian from Cookport, Pennsylvania, composed in celebration of the school's opening:

"The Tohee Industrial School"
To S. R. Cassius came the happy thought
To raise his people from their lowly lot;
To patiently teach them to work with skill,
That in life their place they may nobly fill . . .

Our country still owes the poor negro a debt
Which her good people never have canceled yet;
Let us, then, put in practice the old Golden Rule,
And do what we can for the Industrial School.

Then come, my kind friends, and help our good brother,
And be blessed in the deed by helping another;
Or I am afraid our consciences will lash us,
If we don't send more money to good Brother Cassius.[35]

More congratulatory statements came to Cassius from Fred Rowe, an editor of the *Christian Leader*, who wrote, "I send you this letter of greeting and congratulation, for the untiring effort, on your part, which has enabled you to throw open to your community the Tohee Industrial School. I hope and pray your institution will prove a lasting and growing benefit, and that the next decade may see you standing out among our brethren as the Booker T. Washington of Oklahoma."[36]

The Tohee Industrial School's curriculum offered reading, writing, and preaching classes as well as courses in cooking, sewing, and washing, because Cassius believed in developing the "physical and intellectual part of man." In the first week of August 1899, Cassius added night classes to serve nine students. A. F. Ayres, with assistance from Cassius, offered reading, writing, arithmetic, grammar, geography, and history. Cassius reported that expenditures for the month comprised $25.25, while income was $20.90; he also indicated that his school needed a blacksmith, a wheelwright, a carpenter, and a seamstress. In October, Cassius requested a stove and two sewing machines. He informed his supporters that he had only "nine scholars," but "as soon as the cotton is picked, the school will fill up."[37]

Financial woes, however, quickly doomed the hopeful enterprise. In January 1900, after announcing that he "successfully conducted four months of school," Cassius reported the school's closure. "Last night I closed the school," he lamented, "until I can get out of debt. I will now keep only the Bible school going on Lord's day afternoons." Cassius noted that during the past two months, Tohee's operational costs amounted to $62, while its receipts came to $41.11. "One of the chief reasons for closing the school for the present is because it takes all I receive to keep things going, and doesn't give me a chance to catch up. Another reason is that owing to the short cotton crop, the people are so discouraged that they have lost interest in everything but their debts." The next year, Cassius admitted that he had not kept detailed records of "all that has been given me." Thus, he speculated that he probably received "from all sources" six hundred dollars, which he spent to build his school, to publish tracts and his *Industrial Christian,* to meet the needs of his family, and "to preach the gospel to these poor people, without being a burden to them."[38]

More specifically, Cassius attributed the decline of his Tohee Industrial School to the rise of the Colored Agriculture and Normal University (now Langston University) in 1897. "The erection by the government of so much better and finer buildings, made mine useless." Although blinded perhaps by both ambition and lack of foresight, Cassius boasted that his paper and his school paved the way for the college in Langston. "I could not foresee this, neither could my friends, but it was my school that aroused the interest that built Langston University." Cassius, consequently, refused to view his Tohee Industrial School as a failure. "But was my effort a failure? I answer no, because if it had not been for my beginning it is doubtful if

Langston University would have ever been a fact."[39] He reaffirmed his conviction that his paper, the *Industrial Christian,* led to the establishment of the school in Langston, acknowledging, "I made a mistake in starting 'The Industrial Christian,' but I still feel that it proved a great blessing, because it aroused a desire for an institution of higher learning for our boys and girls, and Langston City College resulted. I firmly believe that that university would never have been built but for that little paper."[40]

In 1902, avid supporters of the Tohee Industrial School attempted to revive interest in the defunct institution. Sister Soule, a white Christian from Weston, Ohio, "has again aroused the Tohee Industrial School by sending me $25." Because of past experiences, however, Cassius vowed to proceed more cautiously: "I will move slowly, but surely; therefore I will not do a thing toward reopening the school until I have enough money to carry it on one year. It will take about $2,000 to do that; therefore it will be some little time before I am ready." While Cassius's Tohee Industrial School struggled to get off the ground, its neighboring college, the state-supported Langston University, started with an initial budget of five thousand dollars and flourished under its first president, Inman E. Page, growing from 41 to 650 students from 1898 to 1915. Hence, while Langston University grew and expanded, Cassius's educational project simultaneously declined and died.[41]

Cassius, nevertheless, sought to follow the path of Booker T. Washington in racial, social, and educational endeavors. Notwithstanding these notable similarities, there were stark differences between the two men. According to historian Louis Harlan, Washington's premier biographer, there were two Booker T. Washingtons: a public, unassuming, and accommodating man who wore a mask and a private, outspoken, and vindictive man who denounced racial injustice. Washington, consequently, was not an Uncle Tom; he was a Brer Rabbit and a "secret militant." "While Washington publicly seemed to accept a separate and unequal life for black people," Harlan observes, "behind the mask of acquiescence he was busy with many schemes for black strength, self-improvement, and mutual aid."[42]

While Washington may have worn what Harlan calls a "mask of accommodation and morality," Cassius did not. He never disguised his true feelings about race. Indeed, he confessed in 1903, "I may have my faults, but hypocrisy is not one of them."[43] Beyond this, Cassius's preoccupation with spiritual matters also distinguished him from the Tuskegee Institute president. When eulogizing Washington in the *Gospel Advocate,* Cassius deplored, "There can be but one regret; and that is, his great work was for the temporal rather than the spiritual uplift of the Negro race." Cassius devoted his life to the spiritual elevation of African Americans, while Washington advocated the material and economic uplifting of his people. Thus, the former pleaded, "O, that we could arouse a like spirit in the church of Christ for the spiritual betterment of the negro race!" In the *Christian Leader,* when comparing his effort with Washington's work, Cassius was more elaborate and more emphatic, asserting:

> I think I can claim originality in the race problem. I am positive that I am the first man to publicly proclaim the negro question as a problem. Also, when I was in my twenty-third year I took the stand that industrial training was the negro's greatest need, but in both of these issues I was hampered by the early training of that Christian woman. I could only see the accomplishment of such a work through the Church, and doubting the righteousness of all sectarian churches, I advocated the idea that the future of the American negro rested with the Church of Christ. It was this stand that got me in bad with my race and has kept me there. Yet it is the naked truth. If the Church of Christ does not step in and rescue the American negro he will be hopelessly lost in the great onrush of racial ambition.
>
> On the other hand, Booker T. Washington thought he saw the negro's future along the same industrial lines that I did. Whether he gathered his idea from me or whether it was an inspiration does not now matter. The facts are he built up the greatest system of industrial education that has ever been built up in America. But you will ask why could not I, who gave birth to the idea, have done as he did, or even better? My answer is, there are several reasons, among which lack of financial support stands out the most prominent.[44]

Cassius's position of religious exclusivism limited him to raising funds for his school in Tohee only from members of the Restoration Movement. He "looked to the Church of Christ to see the need and fall in line and help me push the work." White believers, Cassius noted, "cheered me on in the work with their prayers and words of encouragement, and now and then a few dollars, perhaps just enough to keep me moving, but not enough to enable me to accomplish the work in hand, while the entire nation got behind Washington and made it impossible for him to fail." Too, Cassius had divided interests, as his desire to educate his people conflicted with his duty to care for his large family as well as his primary passion to evangelize African Americans. Thus, he asked his readers, "But did I fail? Nay, verily," Cassius answered. "I not only succeeded, but succeeded so well that to-day I can truthfully say I have done more to advance the cause of Christ among my people than any living negro in the Church of Christ."[45] He was probably not the only "Booker T. Washington of Oklahoma," as Fred Rowe purported; Cassius was more accurately one of many Booker T. Washingtons in the African American Churches of Christ.

1. Samuel Robert Cassius (1853–1931) poses before a chart that distinguishes the Old Testament from the New Testament. This photo was taken in 1896. (Courtesy of the Disciples of Christ Historical Society, Nashville, Tennessee)

2. Samuel Robert Cassius was the most vocal and most visible African American preacher in Churches of Christ during the Progressive Era, 1890–1920. A racial separatist who based his racial thought on biblical texts, Cassius insisted that whites and blacks in America could "mingle, but not mix." (Courtesy of the Disciples of Christ Historical Society, Nashville, Tennessee)

3. Selina Daisy Flenoid Cassius (1878–ca. 1935) was Samuel Robert Cassius's second wife. A native of Texas, Selina Cassius was a staunch encourager of her husband from the time of their marriage in 1898 until his death in 1931. (Courtesy of the Disciples of Christ Historical Society, Nashville, Tennessee)

4. Clayton Cheyney Smith (1845–1919), a racial liberal in the Stone-Campbell Movement, was corresponding secretary for the Board of Negro Education and Evangelization. In this position, Smith worked diligently and paternalistically to provide spiritual uplift for African Americans. (Courtesy of the Disciples of Christ Historical Society, Nashville, Tennessee)

5. David Lipscomb (1831–1917), editor of the *Gospel Advocate,* insisted that white Christians bore what he called the "weighty responsibility" of elevating and Christianizing African Americans in the South. As a racial liberal in Churches of Christ, Lipscomb championed the causes of black education and black evangelism throughout his life. (Courtesy of the Disciples of Christ Historical Society, Nashville, Tennessee)

6. John F. Rowe (1827–97) established the *Christian Leader* in 1886. Samuel Robert Cassius never forgot the kindness and warm reception he received from Rowe, who invited the black evangelist to write for the *Christian Leader* as early as 1895. Cassius honored Rowe by naming one of his sons John F. Rowe Cassius. (Courtesy of the Disciples of Christ Historical Society, Nashville, Tennessee)

7. Frederick L. Rowe (1866–1947), son of John F. Rowe, served as editor of the *Christian Leader* for many years. A friend of Samuel Robert Cassius, the younger Rowe published two editions of Cassius's *The Third Birth of a Nation* in 1920 and in 1925 respectively. (Courtesy of the Disciples of Christ Historical Society, Nashville, Tennessee)

8. Joseph E. Cain (1846–1918), an editor of the *Christian Leader* and a prominent preacher in Churches of Christ, was perhaps Samuel Robert Cassius's closest friend. Cassius called Cain "the whitest, broadest and most Christlike man I knew, and above all, he was my friend" (Cassius, "Bro. Cain Is Dead," *CL* 32 [Aug. 27, 1918]: 5). (Courtesy of the Disciples of Christ Historical Society, Nashville, Tennessee)

9. Amos Lincoln Cassius
(1889–1982) continued the
evangelistic legacy of his father,
Samuel Robert Cassius. The
son, much like his father,
traversed the United States,
preaching the pure Gospel
and planting congregations
in California, Colorado,
New Mexico, and Arizona.
(Courtesy of Greta Leverett,
great-granddaughter of Samuel
Robert Cassius)

10. Henry Atkins Van
Deusen (1818–97) and
Mary E. Van Deusen
(1818–98), two Christian
philanthropists in the
Stone-Campbell Movement
from Omega, Illinois, were
avid supporters of Samuel
Robert Cassius's evangelistic
and educational efforts.
After her husband's death,
Mary E. Van Deusen
continued to support
Cassius and often wrote,
"Brother, my husband
loved you." (Photo taken
from the *Christian Leader*,
1903)

8
"Tried in the Fire"
Life in Black Oklahoma

> That the trial of your faith, being much more precious than of gold
> that perisheth, though it be tried with fire, might be found unto praise
> and honor and glory at the appearing of Jesus Christ.
>
> —1 Peter 1:7

Cassius first entered the Oklahoma Territory in 1891, among a large company of African Americans who flocked to the "new country" in search of better social and economic opportunities. Writing a decade later, Cassius recalled, "In August 1891, I arrived in Guthrie, Oklahoma, a stranger among strangers." An avid reader of national newspapers, he had undoubtedly digested the reports concerning the Oklahoma Territory, which editors in the early 1890s portrayed as a land pulsating with boundless advantages for black Americans. The *Langston City Herald,* a black paper established by William L. Eagleson, played a major role in promoting black towns in Oklahoma. Advertisements such as "Come to a land where you can be free," "Home, Sweet Home," "Freedom!" and "A LAND OF PROMISE" tantalized American blacks who found that the iron grip of segregation had reduced them to a status of legalized inferiority just twenty-five years after emancipation.[1]

In 1890, the editor of the *New York Times* described Edward P. McCabe (1850–1920), founder of Langston City, Oklahoma, as a gubernatorial candidate of the Oklahoma Territory, who planned to "make a Negro state" out of Oklahoma where African Americans "can remove the laborers from one State to another at will, always having in view the control of enough of the black race to found a new State where they themselves will have full power."[2] The blacks' desire to control their own political and economic destiny unquestionably appealed to the mind of Cassius, whose experiences in Oklahoma amid blacks who worked as politicians, doctors, lawyers, sheriffs, educators, and entrepreneurs helped convince him that African Americans would succeed best if separated from their white cohorts. He saw, then, great opportunity in Oklahoma.

Studies on the subject of blacks in Oklahoma reveal several divergent perspectives, evidently shaped by the authors' proclivities. Advocates of utopianism perceive the influx of African Americans into Oklahoma as an example of blacks' search for a utopian society,[3] while proponents of separatism or black nationalism have attributed the movement of American blacks to the Oklahoma Territory in the 1890s to the impetus of these urges.[4] The eclectic school has credited a variety of issues such as race, politics, and economics with the influx of black immigrants into Oklahoma. Booker T. Washington, after touring the all-black town of Boley, Oklahoma, in 1907, noted that African Americans entered the territories for several reasons, concluding that "Boley is another chapter in the long struggle of the negro for moral, industrial, and political freedom."[5]

For Cassius, one of these migrants, black Oklahoma offered both religious opportunities and economic advantages. Exuding confidence about evangelistic potential the Oklahoma Territory furnished, Cassius believed that "God has opened a door for us and invited us to enter; there is no place in the United States that offers our plea such opportunities as are to be found in this territory. Every village, every town, is willing to donate ground for a church." The propagation of the Gospel was Cassius's primary motivation when he left Sigourney, Iowa, and moved to Tohee in the Oklahoma Territory. He determined to introduce African Americans to what he viewed as pure and primitive Christianity, convinced that "it was the purpose of God that the colored people should settle this country." While attempting to establish his Tohee Industrial School for black children, Cassius pleaded with his supporters, "Don't you see the open door through which the disciples of Christ can enter into a field of labor that is ripe and ready for the harvest? God offers you Oklahoma. Will you take it?"[6]

Economic possibilities also influenced Cassius's decision to relocate west. Cassius wrote, "It has long been conceded that Oklahoma was made for the colored man, and the colored man for Oklahoma. Here it is he will demonstrate to the world his fitness for an equal show with the more dominant race." Much like his hero Booker T. Washington, who maintained that "No race that has anything to contribute to the markets of the world is long in any degree ostracized," Cassius held that what he termed economic "fitness" would eventually lead to social and political equality. Continuing in a vein of optimism, Cassius maintained that "Already [the black man] has assumed the responsibility of making Oklahoma the most prosperous land in America, for without a dollar or team, hoe, plow, or in fact anything but his wife, children and dogs, he has snatched this country out of the jaws of famine and the hand of ruin by raising over three million dollars' worth of cotton."[7]

In 1898 Cassius reaffirmed his conviction that "Oklahoma is the American negro's battle field, on which he will win his right to be called the equal of any other man." Convinced that the successful economic performance of black Oklahomans would eventually command whites' respect in America, he pointed out that "Here he can learn trades, acquire an education, amass wealth, and serve God without fear." Nine years later, Cassius singled out the all-black town of Boley as a model community, one which African Americans controlled. "There is not a white person in the town," wrote Cassius, and the black residents of Boley operated a "good school, with plenty of children to fill it. (Race suicide has not reached this town.)" The presence of black depot agents, black bankers, black pharmacists, black grocers, black hotel clerks, and black educators also impressed Cassius, who called the "purely negro" town "one of the best governed and most orderly towns I ever saw. Just think, only one arrest in a year, and not a single house of ill-fame in the town." From Cassius's perspective, then, the Oklahoma and Indian territories presented black Americans with educational prospects, economic opportunities, and religious freedom, all apart from white hegemony, harassment, and interference.[8]

In black Oklahoma Cassius himself held a variety of positions. He farmed, growing an assortment of vegetables to raise funds for his prospective Tohee Industrial School. Although he raised cotton, he detested it as the "bane of the white man, and the curse of the negro. It's a relic of barbarism, a breeder of ignorance, and an enemy to the cause of Christ." The cultivation of cotton, according to Cassius, prevented black people in Oklahoma from advancing both academically and spiritually. Relying primarily on the donations of poor cotton pickers, Cassius lamented having to "preach and labor another year without a dollar from those to whom I preach, and my Industrial School, from which I hoped such great things, it seems as though I will never get enough to finish it." Cassius also wrote prolifically, publishing several tracts and a short-lived paper, the *In-*

dustrial Christian. While living in Oklahoma, he contributed regularly to the *Christian Leader,* writing beneath the banner "Among Our Colored Disciples," to keep the race issue fresh in the minds of his readers.[9]

He also served as postmaster, having received the appointment on July 13, 1897. The office of postmaster was a "position of significance because of the federal recognition it brings,"[10] and Cassius used his role to advance evangelistic and educational projects. His postmastership allowed him to send bulk letters, pamphlets, and advertisements at a cheaper rate. When asked how he was able to distribute so many personal letters and financial requests, Cassius explained, "Being postmaster, I get the proceeds from my cancellations. This I freely put in the work, asking nothing and expecting nothing from my friends." Cassius added that as postmaster he could disseminate five hundred letters for three dollars, but "'through the regular channels of the Church,' the cost of sending out 500 letters would be about $13.50; and, as the negro can not get into the regular channels of the Church (except by proxy), he ought not to be blamed for launching his boat on the river of life."[11] This situation earned Cassius a certain freedom from white domination and control, feeding his preference for black independence rather than white paternalism. By holding such prominent positions in black Oklahoma as postmaster, writer, and preacher, Cassius developed a mind-set and practice of independence, yet this same autonomy engendered friction between him and white paternalists in the Restoration Movement.

Cassius's most important role in black Oklahoma, however, was not as an educator but as a preacher and race man. When a white preacher, A. J. Hopkins, raised questions about Cassius's evangelistic work in Oklahoma, Cassius replied, "I am not hunting believers. I am seeking those that do not understand our 'plea.' I am not shooting at dead ducks. I am hunting sinners that I may bring them to Jesus." From around 1883, when he began his preaching career, until his death in 1931, Cassius evangelized among black Americans and established more than forty churches throughout the United States. Heartened by the growth of African American Churches of Christ in Oklahoma, Cassius named the territory the "'Mecca' of colored disciples."[12]

Cassius often compared his evangelistic activity to a soldier who was "out on the firing line." "They pay the man sixteen dollars a month to call men to arms," Cassius observed in 1903, "but they pay the man two hundred dollars a month to lead them on to victory; so it is in doing mission or evangelistic work in a new field, a man can and does consider himself blessed if he gets food to eat and clothes to wear while he is out forming the line of battle. He is not the general that is to fight the battle; he is simply the agitator that is to arouse the people to action, or if he is a general he can not show his ability until he gets an army."[13] Cassius viewed himself as a soldier or "agitator" fighting erroneous religious and racial practices, so he admonished his brothers, "When you are preparing to make Merry Christmas think of us poor preachers out here on the firing line, barely living and afraid to see a strange face."[14] He urged believers to support him and other struggling evangelists, explaining in 1905, "Not that I do not need more help, but I am sure that our true and faithful men out on the firing line need help also, though they have not suffered as I have."[15] In 1907 Cassius wrote to readers of the *Christian Leader* that despite his many difficulties, he had not deserted his post as preacher. "I want to say right here that I am still out on the firing line, doing, as far as in me lies the power, my whole duty, but I am trying to live without begging." Providing for his family while serving as a full-time evangelist deeply frustrated Cassius, who laid out his priorities: "I want it now to be well understood that whether I write or not, as long as I live, and have full use of my mind, I shall preach the gospel."[16]

A dozen years later, Cassius articulated exactly what he meant by the expression "out on the firing line": "For thirty-five years I have been as faithful as I possibly could be to my work as a minister. I have not turned to the right or left, neither have I sought the paying fields of labor, but away out on 'the firing line' of our work I have fought for the principles of the Gospel, living off of the chips and whetstones that have been thrown at or to me. I thought of the great army of Christians behind me, and said within myself: 'They will see me some day and come to my rescue.'"[17] For Cassius, then, "out on the firing line" involved constantly preaching, teaching, laboring, toiling, and fighting for what he believed was the truth, while living in destitution if necessary.

In addition to the burdens of evangelism and family, Cassius also shouldered the more intractable encumbrances of racism. Cassius's preoccupation with the region's racist environment led to his involvement in the Negro Protective League in Oklahoma. Organized in 1905, the League sought to unite blacks in both the Oklahoma and Indian territories and to arouse these African Americans to the "importance of safeguarding our political and civil rights." Leading a membership of two hundred thousand black residents in the Indian and Oklahoma territories, S. Douglas Russell chaired the new organization and proposed to recruit two lecturers to organize clubs in the regions that would fund and send delegates to the nation's capital. Cassius, "in the interest of the Protective League," crisscrossed the two territories as one of these lecturers, raising funds and advocating social and political rights for black Oklahomans.[18]

Apart from ordinary goals, the Negro Protective League and similar organizations such as the Blaine County Colored Protective League opposed the push for Oklahoma statehood. African Americans in Oklahoma feared that the transformation of the two territories into a single state under a new constitution would signal the end of their political and civil rights. They sensed that a new state constitution would engender Jim Crow laws, statutes sure to bring discriminatory and dehumanizing practices, and would lead Oklahoma to emulate the inequitable policies of the New South. In 1904 the *Oklahoma Guide,* a newspaper published by blacks in Guthrie, Oklahoma, predicted that "When this territory becomes a state the colored man will be deprived of equal rights as protection of law, and will be mobed [*sic*] and lynched without law, and will be treated as other colored people are in the southern states." Three years later, the *Guide* captured the essence of blacks' anxiety about statehood: "All the Negroes of Oklahoma demand is a square deal, that we'll have. He will not stand no Jim Crowing, let there be one law for all."[19]

Despite the resistance of African Americans, however, President Theodore Roosevelt formally declared Oklahoma's statehood on November 16, 1907, and the state with its Progressive constitution entered the Union as the forty-sixth member. What white newspaper editors and legislators saw as a Progressive constitution, however, blacks in Oklahoma viewed as a Jim Crow constitution, for the "first order of business" of the 112 white lawmakers was to enact separate and unequal policies.[20] Cassius himself experienced firsthand the blight of segregation when traveling by train through Oklahoma in 1908. He recalled with disgust that he had to sit in the Jim Crow section, "the most filthy place I ever saw, in even a village," "devoid of all regard for comfort," scattered with "whiskey bottles," and "used by bums and toughs of both races."[21] Oklahoma meant its segregated railcars not only for despised blacks but also for derelict whites.

While on the train Cassius mistakenly opened and entered the bath-room door reserved for white women. Cassius wrote that "The difference between it and the one for the colored women, was about the same differ-ence that we preachers place between heaven and hell." Angry that segre-gation degraded his wife and daughters in particular and black Americans in general, Cassius railed, "My God, is this the place that I must bring my family? Surely such treatment as this will only end to put murder in peace-able men's hearts." Continuing his vivid description of his experiences in Jim Crow cars in Oklahoma, Cassius noted:

> It was just half of an ordinary smoking car; in one end there was a toilet for both men and women. The Gods, think of it! Our wives, mothers and daughters compelled to take chances with men, in order to preserve their health and comfort. There were, in this car, two colored women who had to endure the smoke of two brutes, one black the other a dirty Turk, who did not have sense enough to go among the whites; the train porters pretended to believe he was a Negro. Bosh! White men will risk their positions even on the rail-roads, in order to protect their women from even low down white men, while we Negroes are powerless or too much of a coward, I don't know which, to even protect them from any body.[22]

Like other African Americans in the Progressive Era, Cassius learned that "separate but equal" really meant separate and unequal, with clean and comfortable facilities for whites and unsafe and unsanitary accommoda-tions for blacks. Frequent encounters with such stark, legalized disparity doubtlessly strengthened his views as a black separatist and profoundly shaped his racial thought. His travels in and out of Oklahoma on Jim Crow railcars convinced Cassius of segregation's degrading effects, which he detailed in *The Third Birth of a Nation*.[23]

More than dividing Oklahoma communities, segregation also perme-ated the state's churches. In the fall of 1908, Cassius pointed out that Jim Crow practices in the forty-sixth state touched every facet of life, including the Christian church. "The lines are tightening about us so fast that it's only a question of time until the poor, homeless colored man will not be tolerated among the white people of this country. Even now the mines, mills, factories, and, in fact, every line of industry is being closed up against us." Most regrettably, Cassius lamented, "Even the Church has Jim Crowed us; therefore to me there remains but one course, colonization. The time has come that we must stand on something stronger than pity, hate or fear." Cassius urged blacks in Oklahoma to relocate to southwest Kansas and eastern Colorado to "preserve our lives, manhood and freedom." Cassius himself, however, would remain in Oklahoma for at least a dozen more years, tenaciously following his commitment to evangelism.[24]

The clash between the dual burdens of evangelism and racism plainly marked Cassius's 1921 visit with members of a white Church of Christ in Oklahoma City who had recently dedicated the "best and most commodious house of worship owned by the loyal brethren in the State." Although impressed by the spacious edifice, Cassius actually went there "to see their new house of worship" as well as "to see if they were doing anything to help give my people the same pure truths they seemed to understand so well." The white Christians' references to black people as "Nigger" and "Darkey" convinced Cassius that "I could not expect them to help me get my people on the right road, if the poor negro was no more to them than was indicated in their expressions." But after an elder from the congregation gave him a five dollar donation, Cassius admitted, "I sure was glad to get it. It sort of made me forget the 'Nigger' and 'Darkey' part of the meeting."[25] Cassius clearly fused the burdens of race and religion in Oklahoma and viewed them at once as complementary and contradictory: complementary, in that blacks and whites collaborated to reach the African American people with the Gospel; contradictory, when white racism and paternalism impeded the evangelization of these same people.

Despite his struggles in shouldering the burdens of preaching the Word and solving the race problem in Jim Crow Oklahoma, Cassius remained optimistic about black people's future in the nation's newest state. In 1910 he wrote, "Oklahoma is not a white man's country. The conditions are all wrong for the white man, but they will do for the red man and the Negro. All of the legislation in the world will not change these facts. A black man feels like he is in heaven in Oklahoma, a white man feels the other way."[26] Significantly, Cassius issued this assessment just a few weeks after Oklahoma legislators passed a grandfather clause "to disfranchise practically all of its negroes." But the passage of anti-black legislation did not slake Cassius's thirst for evangelism among the state's African Americans.[27]

Notwithstanding Cassius's expression of optimism, Oklahoma was not a black man's paradise, as Cassius's experiences showed only too well. While they lived in Tohee, Oklahoma Territory, his first wife, Effie Festus-Basil, died in 1895 and left him with a house full of small children. When one of his sons died, monetary indebtedness compounded the emotional loss. "The coffin also cost us $5, for which I had to go in debt."[28] The death of livestock and the failure of crops often left him in more debt and saddled with legal woes. In 1896 Cassius reported that a hog he bought for seven dollars "died within three hours after I got her home," making "about $150 worth of good stock that has died for me in ninety days." Seven years later Cassius lamented, "There is something wrong with my stock. It seems that it is utterly impossible for me to keep horses." His livestock likely victimized by Spanish fever, then rampant in Oklahoma, Cassius noted that "I have lost three good horses since last November, and with the team of mules I have just purchased, I have bought $285 worth of stock since last November. So you see I am somewhat unfortunate with stock. This makes eight head of horses lost in seven years. Do you wonder that I am always destitute?" In the spring of 1904, Cassius rejoiced when rain ended Oklahoma's drought, but the sudden death of his mules tempered his joy. "Some people say that mules don't die," Cassius complained, "but, brethren, don't you believe a word of it. Three nights ago I had a team of mules; during the night one wandered off to a drain and fell in and killed himself."[29]

Crop failures also plagued Cassius. In the summer of 1901 he reported, "I have to keep my plow and hoe going, to try to save my crops. The dust is a foot deep in my fields, and our only hope lies in keeping the ground stirred, and then, after all that, the outlook is not promising. Corn is ruined, the earth is an oven and the heavens are brass."[30] Four years later Cassius referred to Oklahoma as a "queer country; it's either too hot or too cold, too wet or too dry. Wheat is a failure this year, and if cotton and corn is short, it will cause much suffering; but I sometimes think that a general famine would do us more good than harm." The prevalence of barren fields seemed to Cassius divine retribution, as "too much ungodly work [is] going on. Something must be done to convince men that God is not mocked."[31] In 1908, a devastating tornado ripped through Oklahoma, demolishing houses and destroying crops. Cassius called it the "worst and most general storm I have ever witnessed . . . and to-day the people are downhearted and ruined. It has been so wet for three months, and so cold, that all the cotton has either been washed out or killed, and many are homeless." The catastrophic storm tore through Cassius's own cotton field. "I had twenty acres of cotton chopped out. It's all gone."[32] Even when he successfully produced cotton, creditors waited "around like hungry wolves watching that."[33] In 1921, while on a preaching mission in Stafford, Ohio, he announced that his wife had written from Guthrie, Oklahoma, concerning medical expenses incurred from the "sickness and operations that was performed on my two children during the past spring." The "debts," which he could not then pay, were "being sued for."[34]

Among Cassius's most excruciating experiences in black Oklahoma was a fire on January 15, 1905, which rendered him and his family homeless, penniless, and without clothing. Describing his predicament to the readership of the *Christian Leader*, Cassius alluded to 1 Peter 1:7 in his theological response: "I have been tried in the fire. Nine years ago I was tried by death: my wife, child and five horses died. Then I was tried by hail and rain and wind, and lost three crops out of five. Now I am tried by fire, and if $1,500 was placed in my hand, it would not replace all I lost in forty minutes last night."[35]

Cassius then spelled out the devastating extent of the loss. "Neighbors had to bring old rags to us," he explained, "so we could cover our children from the cold, and we lost at least $150 in provisions we had stored away to make a crop on, and all of our furniture and bed clothes except six quilts. And not a cent—no credit—no food—no roof over my head." But losses reached beyond home and farm goods. An intellectual response then followed. "All of my 250 books gone. I have not even a Bible—do you understand, Bro. Rowe, I have not even a Bible! My children want clothes, my wife is naked, and I have none but the clothes I wear."[36]

A month after word of Cassius's terrible loss appeared in the *Christian Leader*, monetary gifts began pouring in from Christians throughout the United States to help him build a new house. For the month of January Cassius reported donations of seventy-nine dollars and promised to "furnish the names of the donors later on when I can write with more comfort."[37] A distraught Cassius described the terrible and destructive power of the fire that had ravaged his home:

Water leaves its soaked remnants here and there, and sometimes much can be saved with a little labor; wind does likewise. But fire— there is nothing that strikes such terror to the human heart as the cry of "Fire." Everything its fatal arm reaches out and grasps is lost; everything its horrid red tongue touches is blasted. The accumulation of a lifetime of privation vanishes into air and ashes, and it matters not whether it is caused by carelessness or accident, it is awful to be turned out of bed into a bitter cold night with nothing but your night clothes. It is hollow mockery to simply pity a family cast out of home by fire, and it's both an injury and an insult to upbraid persons who are in such a situation until after you have in some way provided for their immediate need. Even our carnal laws mix kindness with their severity in dealing with willful brutal criminals. Why should the Lord's children be less considerate?[38]

Cassius never disclosed the cause of the fire. If arsonists or White Cappers, white terrorists designed to drive prosperous blacks out of certain communities, started the fire, Cassius would have almost certainly exposed them. Some believers even hinted that Cassius deliberately set his house afire. "Since I was burned out I have received a full amount of sympathy, criticism and gentle abuse; this, too, coming from people who ought to know me too well to do any of the above things." Probably a prairie fire, not unusual in those regions, ignited the blaze that destroyed Cassius's house.[39]

Many Christians demonstrated their genuine love for Cassius and came to his rescue in these trials. "But in the midst of it all," Cassius acknowledged, "the real gold in the hearts of our brethren has been exposed and reached even unto me." J. C. Glover, an influential white preacher in Oklahoma, urged Christians to "help Bro. C. in his present distress," and H. A. Stigers, an assertive Christian woman from Kansas, prodded fellow female believers into action by challenging them to take "care of the stuff at home." She pleaded, "Now I want to put in a plea for Bro. Cassius. He is an able preacher, one who has hold of the sword of Spirit by the hands, and one who having put his hand to the plow does not turn back. He is doing a great work among his people, and his people need him, but they are poor and can not do much for him. And now this great loss has come upon him. Still he does not falter or turn back, but trusts God and fights 'manfully onward.' In fact he is just the man we need to evangelize the colored people of Oklahoma Territory. Sisters, we can help him in the field. Will we?"[40]

Stigers encouraged other Christian women to share their seeds, fruit, and meat with the Cassius family. She urged them to sell their chickens "and send [Cassius] the money." Anticipating that some believers would respond that they had nothing to spare, Stigers pointed out that "The Bible does not say anything about having any to spare, it says divide that which you have."[41] Several congregations and individual Disciples met Stigers's requests. That spring, Cassius reported receiving $291 "in round figures" from all sources. "I was burned out. You were my friends. I came to you, and told you. Your own hearts did the rest." Cassius particularly singled out Sister Stigers and sisters from Mississippi, Kansas, Missouri, and Illinois, who "helped a great deal in clothing and quilts." Overwhelmed by such generosity, Cassius asked the brotherhood to stop sending donations. "Now, dear friends, again I will say that I think it is time to call a halt. Not that I do not need more help—for I do."[42] Cassius, however, felt embarrassed that members of the Restoration Movement made him a "special object of their fellowship."[43] On May 5, 1905, Cassius and his family moved into their new house, and the next week he thanked Christians for their generosity, acknowledging, "I am now living in the house built by the saints. It is God's own gift to me."[44]

But barely two months elapsed before Cassius experienced still more trouble, when a white merchant of Logan County, Oklahoma, sued him on the grounds of "disposing of mortgaged property." Cassius admitted in court that he owed the merchant one hundred dollars for lumber and cotton, but he was unwilling to surrender his house. "I refused to do it," explained Cassius, "and he tried to sue me for selling his cotton, which, thank God, I honestly proved I did not do. But he is a white man and rich; I am a Negro and poor, and he knows that I am a man that is respected, so he thinks to force me into giving him my home to save my name. Yes, I owe him nearly $100," Cassius acknowledged, "but it would not be right for me to mortgage such a man my home." Cassius, consequently, felt obligated to explain this controversy before the *Christian Leader:* the "entire brotherhood is interested in me [so] I feel that it is right that I should make this matter clear." When Guthrie's justice of the peace declared him innocent, a relieved Cassius pointed to the white merchant's allegations as "one of the many methods that is used to rob us Negroes of our homes."[45]

Years later, yet another natural disaster victimized Cassius when a fierce tornado struck Guthrie in 1922 and demolished part of Cassius's house. The storm did one hundred dollars' worth of damage and "swept away lots of things" that Cassius and his "wife and the children needed." The wind-storm left "us in pretty bad shape. Before the storm came we were barely making out."[46]

In the face of such trials, Cassius never realized the economic independence that black promoters of Oklahoma envisioned. In 1899, Cassius had described himself as a "poor, despised negro preacher, with not a decent suit of clothes." Destitution engulfed Cassius for the next three decades. His postmastership with the Tohee Post Office was neither permanent nor prosperous; he held this post from July 13, 1897, until January 31, 1906. In 1899, Cassius earned $120.13. In 1901, he earned $71.11; in 1903, $40.90; in 1905, $29.20. The economic downturn of the Tohee community, reflected in declining postal activity and Cassius's declining wages, contributed to the community's eventual disappearance. According to Cassius, the emergence of larger, neighboring cities and communities led to the shrinking of mail delivery to smaller towns such as Tohee. Cassius explained in 1905 that "Rural free delivery has sapped the life out of all our country postoffices. Around Tohee clusters nearly all stirring scenes of the settling of this country, and for this reason it will be long remembered." Even though Cassius lamented the "passing of Tohee," he recalled the many significant religious occurrences there. While the Baptists, Methodists, and Catholics initiated their mission efforts in Tohee, more importantly, noted Cassius, "some of the greatest and most far-reaching efforts ever made in the Southwest to reach my people with the pure Gospel have been made from Tohee." He singled out his own Tohee Industrial School and the *Industrial Christian,* "the first colored paper of our faith in the Southwest," as notable achievements.[47]

Even though Cassius consistently depicted himself as a destitute evangelist, he somehow managed to accumulate several acres of land in Oklahoma in an era when land was easier to acquire than to farm profitably. Court documents from Logan County (Guthrie), Oklahoma, show that during his thirty years in the state, Cassius owned 157 acres of land. By 1923, however, he reported having lost all but twenty acres because of unpaid debts. "I had a piece of land in what is supposed to be in the next great oil belt of Oklahoma," a sorrowful Cassius explained. Because his preaching efforts often kept him away from home for extended periods of time, he admitted neglecting his financial obligations. "In the planting of twenty-one congregations, I lost sight of many things, and seven years ago

I found myself with debts that, before I could untangle myself, took all the land but these twenty acres."[48] This preoccupation with spiritual matters ruined whatever economic opportunities Cassius might have seized.

But financial woes always paled before the ubiquitous problem of racism. Newspapers published by black Oklahomans frequently described whites expelling blacks from the region. In a typical instance, the *Oklahoma Guide* reported that whites in Lexington, Oklahoma Territory, drove out their black neighbors "for no reason, but they were Negroes." The same journal announced that whites and blacks near Marshall fought and "shot each other and behaved worst than the plantation Negro did next year after the war [*sic*]." When evangelizing among the Creek Indians in Oklahoma, Cassius witnessed this racial tension firsthand. He reported that white residents of Broken Arrow denied African Americans the right to "live, buy or sell in the town." Similarly, according to Cassius, blacks in Wybark, "a purely negro town," produced a sign which read, "No white people allowed here. If you can't read just keep running."[49]

In the face of so grave a reality, Cassius struggled to maintain a disposition of optimism about black people's presence in Oklahoma. As early as the fall of 1901, Cassius indicated that de facto racial codes already restricted the movement of African Americans in Oklahoma. "White people may pull about over the country where they please, but the poor negro must be careful where he goes, or they will make a bonfire out of him. The outlook is indeed dark."[50] The following month Cassius, aware of the proliferation of back-to-Africa movements, explained why many blacks desired to leave America, asserting, "We have no rights before the law that any white man need to respect. When we lie down at night it is with the fear that before morning we will be called upon to defend our lives against lawless white men." Knowing, too, that many white Oklahomans absorbed the Southern rape myth, Cassius revealed the danger of black men interacting with white females. "It has indeed reached a point that it is not safe for a colored man to meet a white woman on the highway and speak to her, and it is almost equally as hard to pass one and not speak." Articulating disappointment of his own as well as the frustration of other black Oklahomans, Cassius confessed, "We thought that if we came here and got homes we would in a measure break down this kind of life; but it is no use; nothing but the death of the negro race will satisfy the hatred of the Southern white men."[51]

The longer Cassius lived in the Oklahoma Territory, the more his confidence in the region as a black man's paradise waned. The exodus of African Americans from the United States to Africa, in Cassius's judgment, emerged as a viable solution to the race problem in American society, partly because of the prevalence of anti-black sentiment which had led to the rapid deterioration of blacks' civil rights. Cassius's comments exude fear, an anxiety of whether a black man should or should not even greet a white woman in public. The Oklahoma Territory, the very region that black Americans had flocked to for economic independence, political freedom, and physical safety from "lawless white men," proved a bitter disappointment. When Cassius and other American blacks had rushed to the Oklahoma Territory for a better life, many of their white counterparts from the South dashed to the same region, bringing their racist views. Historian Jimmie Lewis Franklin has explained the mood of race relations in prestatehood Oklahoma: "Customs associated with the Deep South had had time to be transplanted by the region's native sons, and near the end of the nineteenth century were being institutionalized in law."[52] Hence, in due time Oklahoma's social and racial practices mirrored those of the New South.

Borne down by these difficulties, Cassius in 1903 reiterated his frustration with the intensification of white racism in Oklahoma. "The sentiment here is unusually high against the negroes, and it is for that I want the negroes to build up a church here." According to Cassius, many white people in Oklahoma viewed their black counterparts as mere beasts. "Race prejudice runs so high down this way that a negro is considered no more than a brute; he need not expect either help or encouragement from white disciples."[53] In Cassius's view, racial prejudice darkened the minds of whites in the Restoration Movement toward the African American. The racism, and at best indifference, of many white believers also pushed Cassius to espouse separatist views.

It was, ironically, the Christian church (Disciples of Christ) that drove Cassius out of Oklahoma. Convinced that white leaders of the Christian Woman's Board of Missions, whom he frequently and vehemently denounced, conspired to destroy both his image and his work as an evangelist, Cassius announced in 1921 his plans to relocate to Ohio. "I can not do any more good in this state. The C. W. B. M. is paying two colored preachers to visit the colored congregations and tells them that S. R. Cassius is an enemy to their progress, and that I am keeping them from getting the help they need." Convinced that white leaders among the Disciples of Christ plotted to turn black ministers and black members in Oklahoma against him, Cassius shrugged, "I can not do the work in the state I once did. Therefore, I am sure it is better for me to move." After raising enough funds, he announced, "I intend to leave here for the Ohio Valley."[54]

Because, then, of personal tragedies such as the loss of his first wife, a son, livestock, and house, and monetary indebtedness as well, Oklahoma never felt like the paradise Cassius had envisioned. Legal woes hounded him, while racial discrimination within and without Churches of Christ left him disillusioned and discouraged. Cassius never experienced heaven in Oklahoma; instead, he found there a hell. The religious prospects of disseminating the Restoration plea among black Americans as well as the opportunity for economic advancement lured him to the Oklahoma Territory, yet financial difficulties as well as the racial and conspiratorial practices of white religionists in the Stone-Campbell Movement drove him out.

IV

A Race Man and Globe-Trotter in Progressive America

9
Mind Poisoning
The Racial Thought of Samuel Robert Cassius

> But the Jews who refused to believe stirred up the Gentiles and poisoned their minds against the brothers.
>
> —Acts 14:2 (New International Version)

Fired in the crucible of his turbulent years as a black farmer, preacher, and reformer in Oklahoma, the racial thought of Samuel Robert Cassius reached full maturation in 1920. In this year Cassius, at age sixty-seven, published the first edition of *The Third Birth of a Nation,* a book he revised and reissued five years later. The briefer first edition included 15 chapters with 72 pages, but the second he expanded into 26 chapters of 120 pages.[1]

In the latter book Cassius added two pictures: one of his second wife, Selina, and the other one of Anthony Overton, owner of the Overton-Hygienic Manufacturing Company in Chicago, Illinois. Cassius proffered the first portrait in defense of black womanhood, castigating whites who referred to the African American female as a beast. Speaking for his wife particularly and all black women generally, Cassius insisted that his wife was not a "negress," a term he called the "most brutal assault" on black womanhood.

Cassius's second portrait touted black ability and black advancement in an effort to show that black men can succeed in business in a racist society. As his examples Cassius highlighted Anthony Overton, a black entrepreneur from Kansas who relocated his baking powder business in 1911 to Chicago, where he launched other enterprises including cosmetic products in addition to a bank and an insurance company. Cassius praised Overton's business feat as "one of the greatest monuments of Negro Enterprises in the United States," and the picture of Overton's elaborate three-story building underscores Cassius's purpose in writing *The Third Birth of a Nation,* in part to laud the black race before a white society that consistently depicted African Americans as inept and immoral.[2]

Cassius began his first edition with an assessment of the origins of African slavery and the beginnings of the black race in America. The revision launches with a discussion of the origins of humankind and offers a rough delineation of the Book of Genesis. Cassius's emphasis on the Book of Genesis in the latter edition probably reflects his interest in Tennessee's famous Scopes Trial. John T. Scopes, a high school biology teacher, became embroiled in a controversial legal case for his teaching of evolution. The prosecution, led by three-time presidential candidate William Jennings Bryan, held tenaciously to the inerrancy of the Bible and argued vigorously that Scopes and fellow evolutionists were wrong. Like many black preachers of that era, Cassius, who had met Bryan in Philadelphia, Pennsylvania, in 1919, stayed abreast of the conflict between evolutionists and anti-evolutionists,[3] believing not only that the authenticity of the Bible was in jeopardy, but also that the humanity and dignity of black people were at stake as well.[4]

The Third Birth of a Nation exists in multiple contexts. First, Cassius wrote in a religious context, participating in the conflicting worlds of the social Gospel and fundamentalism. The former focused on addressing humans' social condition, while the latter stressed meeting their spiritual needs. On the one hand, the Race Man denounced Christians who placed too much emphasis on personal salvation and neglected social justice. When traveling east on a preaching tour in 1922, Cassius criticized black Christians in Philadelphia, Pennsylvania, for their emphasis on individual salvation. "The Colored Mission here is about fifteen years old, but, on account of a narrow, contracted method of works, is really 'drawing up.' The trouble is they believe too much in 'personal salvation.'"[5] On the other hand, Cassius unabashedly championed the fundamentalist position that accepted the veracity and divine inspiration of the Bible. He supported and admired William Jennings Bryan who, by defending the Genesis account of humans' origins, unknowingly and simultaneously became a champion for the black race.

Cassius's *Third Birth of a Nation* also had a literary context. As early as 1903, Cassius expressed his eagerness to read and rebut Charles Carroll's *The Negro a Beast*, promising that "I shall spend this winter reviewing it; and the result of my review I may publish in book form." Cassius's review scathingly denounced Carroll's racist thesis of black bestiality. Indeed, the latter's book fired Cassius's interest and determination to defend African

Americans. It "awoke in me a desire," Cassius asserted, "to be ready at all times to give a reasonable reason for any thought on those things that affected me, my race, or my religion." Cassius, as a result, had grown increasingly aware of the rise of anti-black sentiment, sensing even a Southern ploy to return the black man to slavery by depriving him of Northern and Southern friendship. He later warned, "The South is trying to create a sentiment against the negro, with the hope that when he is robbed of friendship he can be enslaved again."[6]

By 1915 Cassius began highlighting the cause of the deterioration of black-white relations more specifically. Comparing the plight of African Americans to "great ocean-going ships," he urged first that the Church of Christ heed a "signal" that was "being flashed out" to the entire country: "'S. A. N.'—'Save American Negroes,' who are out on the great ocean of religious superstition, tossed by every wind of doctrine that men can invent, and are slowly sinking beneath the waves of fanaticism and superstition." Furthermore, fondly recalling how nineteenth-century white abolitionists helped "my people rise out of the condition in which slavery had placed us," Cassius lamented the lack of white-to-black philanthropy in the twentieth century. "It has not been so long ago that the hand of the American white man was stretched out to the negro, ready and willing to aid him in every time of need." Cassius believed that regrettably racial prejudice had vitiated white compassion for black people's plight. Perhaps reflecting on the white Emancipator, Abraham Lincoln, and on his own white instructor in the nineteenth century, Frances Perkins, Cassius continued: "I firmly believe that there are thousands of men to-day who still believe this very thing, but because of a wave of prejudice that has swept over this land and nation they have halted in their effort to better the condition of my people." Cassius, who often incorrectly referred to David Wark Griffith's film *The Birth of a Nation* as a book, observed, "Such books as 'The Negro a Beast,' 'The Clansman,' and 'The Birth of a Nation' have been largely responsible for the state of affairs. I am quite sure that, as a race, we have helped it along." Certain that white incendiary literature initiated the poisoning of minds in American society, Cassius also faulted his own people for reverting to "heathenism," thereby contributing to racial tension.[7] These two points, the proliferation of inflammatory writings by white authors and the retrogression of African Americans into paganism, framed Cassius's principal arguments in *The Third Birth of a Nation.*

Near the end of World War I Cassius again noted the negative influence the writings of Carroll and Thomas Dixon, Jr., had on race relations in America. A Baptist minister who later devoted his life to writing novels, such as *The Clansman,* Dixon often portrayed black men as vicious beasts. Thus Cassius asked: "Did you ever read that book by Carroll, 'The Negro: a Beast,' and 'The Clansman,' and 'The Birth of a Nation'? If not, read them; if you do you will want to 'burn' every negro you meet; that is, if you are a white man, and if you are a black man you will want to hate every white man you meet." Such pejorative literature was divisive, degrading, and destructive, and, in the view of Cassius, "the real seed of the race problem." After scrutinizing the writings of Carroll and Dixon and after personally enduring the adverse impact they had on the racial thinking of both blacks and whites in American society, Cassius announced his plans to publish *The Third Birth of a Nation.* "It was then it came to mind to write a book that would appeal to the white race, and at the same time praise my people for the good they had done. And rebuke them for their shortcomings."[8] Having committed to the daunting tasks of attacking white racism, celebrating black achievement, and addressing black immorality, Cassius recognized as well the potential significance of such a book. "It will be the first book ever published by the Church of Christ that will appeal to my race. It will be the first book ever published that will show up the weak points in the life of my people." The author planned also to attack the fanaticism of black religion and to touch black Americans with a plea for primitive Christianity. "I will say no more, only I appeal to the Church of Christ to help put my book in the hands of the people."[9]

Chapter nine of *The Third Birth of a Nation* addresses the poisonous literature that inflamed white racism in American society. "Then came the books: 'The Octoroon,' so cunningly written that at first the near white women were pitied, but, as the tale continued, that pity was slowly changed to hate."[10] *The Octoroon or Life in Louisiana,* a play that Dion Boucicault published in book form in 1859, depicts the complexity of interracial love in the antebellum South. George Peyton, a white European who stands to inherit his uncle's estate, Terrebonne Plantation in Louisiana, falls madly in love with a beautiful and intelligent octoroon, Zoe. In a passionate scene, George pledges his unconditional love for Zoe, who knows too well the Southern proscriptions against interracial romance.

Zoe: That is the ineffaceable curse of Cain. Of the blood that feeds my heart, one drop in eight is black—bright red as the rest may be, that one drop poisons all the flood; those seven bright drops give me love like yours—hope like yours—ambition like yours—life hung with passions like dew-drops on the morning flowers; but one black drop gives me despair, for I'm an unclean thing—forbidden by the laws—I'm an Octoroon!

George: Zoe, I love none the less; this knowledge brings no revolt to my heart, and I can overcome the obstacle.[11]

Zoe's dazzling beauty and George's sincere affection bear no weight in the face of Southern customs and laws prohibiting interracial marriages. The mere love of a white man for a black woman cannot overcome the deeply entrenched Southern racist code of white superiority and black inferiority. Zoe's subhuman status as an octoroon slave places her on the auction block, and Jacob M'Closky, a wealthy scoundrel, purchases Zoe for twenty-five thousand dollars. Wrenched in the vortex of her love for a white man and her inferior standing as a black woman, Zoe commits suicide. The story reveals the degrading aspects of being a black female in antebellum America, as the mixture of black and white blood then defined a person, regardless of any other factors, as a "poisoned thing," according to the words of the play. The Octoroon could only remind Cassius of his own blighted status as a former slave in Virginia and as a second-class citizen in Progressive America.[12]

Cassius equally detested Carroll's The Negro a Beast, "with its horrific, impossible illustrations and its frightful tales of the most revolting crimes acting as a background on which to point out the revolting acts that the negro would be guilty of if they were allowed the same rights and privileges that were accorded to other men." Carroll argued against social equality and miscegenation, claiming that the white man, "the highest, and the Negro the lowest of the so-called 'five races of men,' present the strongest contrast to each other in their physical and mental characters; and in their modes of life, habits, customs, language, manners, gestures, etc."[13] Cassius deplored the detrimental effect Carroll's book had on the minds of white Americans generally and those in the Stone-Campbell Movement particularly.

Following Carroll's work was what Cassius called "that hateful book, 'The Birth of a Nation.'" Mistakenly denoting D. W. Griffith's film *The Birth of a Nation* as a book, Cassius was actually referring to Thomas Dixon's novel *The Clansman* (1905), which became the basis for Griffith's 1915 movie. Cassius could scarcely contain his outrage over both Dixon's screed and Griffith's scurrilous film. "Never in the history of the world had such a cunningly arranged compilation of falsehoods been placed before the public. Not satisfied with the story in print, it was worked out in studios and thrown upon the screen in moving picture shows, and these pictures have caused more lynchings and burnings than all other things that have been done or said." In decrying the malevolent impact of Griffith's film on race relations in America, Cassius claimed that "Men have been known to leave the show with such hatred that lynching and burning have started on the least provocation. The effect upon the mind produced by this play has proved so dangerous to the peace of the negroes, that most of the Northern cities have prohibited it to be shown; even the legislatures of most of the Northern states have passed laws forbidding 'The Birth of a Nation' being shown in the state."[14]

Many others joined Cassius's repudiation of Dixon's and Griffith's incendiary productions. A member of the Negro Protective League in Oklahoma, Cassius probably stood among black Oklahomans in Muskogee who prevented the stage performance of Dixon's *Clansman* in 1907. Despite this successful block, the Ku Klux Klan in Oklahoma used *The Birth of a Nation* as a recruitment device to enlarge its membership.[15] Many white intellectuals, however, added their voices to the clamor against the movie. Journalist Lyman Abbott wrote that "The evil in 'Birth of a Nation' lies in the fact that the play is both a denial of the power of development within the free Negro and an exaltation of race war."[16] Booker T. Washington, Cassius's hero, disapproved of the film and wrote, "Best thing would be to stop it as it can result in nothing but stirring up race prejudice."[17] W. E. B. Du Bois similarly disparaged Griffith's production and believed it contributed to mob violence.[18] While the local branch of the NAACP in Los Angeles, California, unsuccessfully sued to stop its national distribution, William Thompson, mayor of Chicago, successfully prevented the film from being shown there. The Wilmington, Delaware, city council legislated a fifty dollar fine against all who saw the controversial movie, and the Boston, Massachusetts, branch of the NAACP issued a forty-seven-page pamphlet entitled *Fighting a Vicious Film,* denouncing the motion picture.[19] Cassius's *The Third Birth of a Nation* stands among the many indictments of Griffith's infamous film, but Cassius was the only leader in Churches of Christ to repudiate the movie publicly.

Cassius's book, however, revealed a socioeconomic context. Cassius sought to expose what he called the "real cause" of the endemic white-on-black brutality in the United States of his era. He argued that the greatest fear of many white Southerners was black economic advance rather than interracial sex. The material success of American blacks was "the real cause of the prejudice the white man has for the Negro. He fears that the black man will supplant him in the matters of trade, business and profession." Because of the meteoric rise of black businessmen in Progressive America, "the Southern white man," Cassius maintained, "undertook to poison the minds of the Northern and Western white men against the negro by picturing the negro as a licentious brute that was roaming around seeking an opportunity to assault white women. No better means could have been used to inflame the minds of white men against colored men." Mind poisoning was simply a ploy, according to Cassius, which white propagandists used to derail black economic advancement.[20]

That African Americans achieved impressive economic success during the Progressive Era was indisputable. Ida B. Wells, a black anti-lynching advocate, anticipated Cassius's diagnosis of race hatred by attributing the 1892 lynching of Tom Moss in Memphis, Tennessee, to economic competition with a neighboring white grocer. The brutal affair gave Wells a new perspective: "This is what opened my eyes to what lynching really was. An excuse to get rid of Negroes who were acquiring wealth and property and thus keep the race terrorized and 'keep the nigger down.'"[21] Booker T. Washington's volume *The Negro in Business,* which Cassius studied zealously, highlighted numerous successful black farmers, caterers, hotel keepers, contractors, morticians, bankers, publishers, preachers, and inventors; and he urged other aspiring black entrepreneurs "to go forward and win success in business directions." The industry and prosperity of black Oklahomans had impressed Washington when he toured the Oklahoma Territory in 1905: "I found members of my race in Oklahoma," Washington boasted, "in competition with some of the most aggressive and progressive members of the white race in America."[22] Cassius, of course, saw and experienced firsthand the same intense economic competition between blacks and whites in Oklahoma, and so gave personal witness in *The Third Birth of a Nation.*

Black newspapers in Oklahoma, which profoundly shaped Cassius's racial outlook, regularly included references to white-black economic rivalry, and they often attributed racial conflict between African Americans and Anglo-Saxons to the avarice of the latter. "The white man," declared the *Oklahoma Guide,* "causes all the race trouble in the world. Greed is the cause." The *Muskogee Cimeter* reported in 1905 that the black man was the "only competitor the Caucasian has ever had, and as a result of this competition there is friction between the races." In addition, before the horrific 1921 Tulsa, Oklahoma, race riot, reports circulated that some black Tulsans owned assets worth more than one hundred thousand dollars, suggesting that racial tension between white and black residents in Progressive Oklahoma could have derived from economic advancement among African Americans. This was the fundamental story Cassius endeavored to tell in *The Third Birth of a Nation.*[23]

In 1920, reflecting on black people's status in America since emancipation, Cassius noted that African Americans transitioned from property to property owners. "Sixty years ago the Negro was an ignorant slave, penniless and homeless, and he himself cast off goods and chattel." Cassius continued in a vein that illustrated his grasp of the statistical information then available.

By 1875, we owned homes and towns and over three million acres of farms, and had become depositors in banks, and had begun to achieve distinction as lawyers, doctors, teachers and preachers.

By 1910 the farm holdings of the Negro had increased to twenty million acres, and their city homes had become so numerous that the white race had or thought it had, to devise some means to check the spread of their property holdings in many towns and cities of the nation.

At the present time the American Negro owns and controls five hundred thousand homes, or more than enough to make a city as large as New York City and a state as large as Texas.[24]

In Cassius's analysis, whites in the United States, alarmed at this prosperity, artfully conspired to thwart black economic growth.

Cassius also wrote from a personal context. The theme of slavery permeated *The Third Birth of a Nation,* and this emphasis unquestionably alluded to Cassius's own experiences first as a slave and then as a freedman. Cassius referred to black bondage as "the cancer of human slavery" and "the curse of slavery," and he no doubt reflected on his own turbulent transition from a chattel slave in Virginia to a "national freeman" in Oklahoma, where he and fellow African Americans gradually lost virtually all their rights. White Southerners, according to Cassius, hated to see their former property in freedom; therefore, they stripped black freedmen of their civil and political rights and did with the "ballot what they failed to do with the bullet." Cassius accordingly testified that the passage from slavery to freedom was a "long step" with "many obstacles in the way of making that step."[25]

From Cassius's perspective, black slavery profoundly affected the white man's view of ex-bondsmen. "The white man has been taught by generations of learned men, that the negro is an inferior, and only fit to be a 'hewer of wood and a drawer of water' for the white man. Therefore, when the negro attempts to assert his manhood, or stand up for his own rights, or resent a wrong, the domineering spirit of superiority in the white man will assert itself." The white-over-black relationship that existed before emancipation influenced white ex-slaveholders who hated the "negro because of the place he once held in the body of the nation."[26]

At the same time, black women and men held distorted views of true womanhood and manhood because of slavery. Cassius referred to white female slaveholders as "nervous, conceited, irresponsible, lazy, gentle-do-nothing," inappropriate traits that black women now imitated. "Most of family troubles grow out of this false idea of what a lady is and what she ought to be. True womanhood does not exist in fine clothes and a classical education, but love of home, family and strict economy are the high lights in a ladylike life." Cassius denounced the flamboyant flapper who drank in public, wore short hair and skirts, and smoked cigarettes.[27]

Like black women, black men during slavery had bad role models and were, therefore, ignorant of the "real earmarks of a gentleman." Extravagant spending of monetary resources, in the mind of Cassius, illustrated the black man's misconception of how a true gentleman should behave. "When I see a young colored man with an earning capacity of one dollar and fifty cents a day depriving himself of all the comforts of life in order to buy a fifty-dollar suit of clothes, a ten-dollar pair of shoes, a five-dollar hat and a silk shirt, simply because his employer has those things, I feel sure that that man has a mistaken idea of what it takes to be a gentleman." Cassius here reflected the wisdom of Booker T. Washington, whose mother taught him lessons of frugality and simplicity by refusing, in Washington's own words, "to go into debt for that which she did not have the money to pay for."[28]

Beyond their secular lives, the enslavement of black people in America had also vitiated their religious practices, as white slaveholders transmitted false religion to their black subjects. "We must conclude that the American slave was not converted to God through the religion that his master gave him; no man can possibly see Christ in religion that the slave brought with him out of slavery." This flawed view of God, Cassius believed, caused the black man's ostracism. "One thing that has caused the colored man more to be shunned as a social equal than any other thing is his idea of serving God." The black man's songs were too loud, his prayers too long, and his sermons too emotional and bare of meaning. "The average colored preacher is far too careless in stating the facts of religion; he is apt to make statements that are purely imagination, simply to win the sanction of his hearers; in fact, as a race we have chosen preachers with too much lungs, and too vivid imagination, and have paid too little attention to the moral, spiritual and intellectual qualifications of the man."[29]

Others shared in Cassius's critique of fellow black ministers. Booker T. Washington complained about the growing numbers of unethical black preachers. "The ministry was the profession that suffered most—on account of not only ignorant but in many cases immoral men who claimed that they were 'called to preach.'" W. E. B. Du Bois, too, criticized illiterate and immoral African American clergymen. "The paths and the higher places are choked with pretentious, ill-trained men and in far too many cases with men dishonest and otherwise immoral." Du Bois also blamed noisy black exhorters for the church's lack of relevance to their parishioners in general and their educated members in particular. "Today the church is still inveighing against dancing and theatergoing, still blaming educated people for objecting to silly and empty sermons, boasting and noise, still building churches when people need homes and schools, and persisting in crucifying critics rather than realizing the handwriting on the wall."[30]

Cassius's criticism of the emotionalism of black religionists stemmed from two sources. First, Cassius considered the religion of ex-slaves a "mixture of African heathenism and American heathenism"—the latter a hypocritical religion that slaveholders transmitted to their black bondsmen, the former marked by emotionalism and fanaticism that Africans brought to North America. Ironically, Cassius viewed the black culture of Africa as inferior to the white culture of America and argued that the "methods and practices of the colored people in religious worship" discouraged the "mixture of the races in religious worship." In Cassius's view, "meaningless prayers and unscriptural assertions" reflected the backwardness of Africa.[31]

Cassius's second criticism of black emotionalism in religion stemmed from the tendency of white members of the Stone-Campbell Movement to approach God and the Bible rationally and logically. Following this lead, Cassius and other black leaders in Churches of Christ held that when African American seekers become more informed, they become less fanatical. "As they become more enlightened they become less emotional," wrote G. P. Bowser, "and the chain of superstition that has held them so long is weakening." Marshall Keeble, preaching in Valdosta, Georgia, declared that "I am of the opinion and belief that the more of the word of God you get in you, the less emotionalism, and the more of the word of God you get in you, the less excitement. You are compelled to acknowledge that this is the quietest and least emotional service that you have ever attended in your life and this is an intelligent audience, and when you accept the gospel of Jesus Christ, it knocks all the monkey notion out." Even female educator Annie C. Tuggle cherished a religion with "no whooping and hollering." Under the influence of Campbellian rationalism, black preachers and parishioners preferred more subdued worship services.[32]

References in Cassius's *The Third Birth of a Nation* to the racial and sexual mixing of white male slave owners with their female slaves further reveals a personal context. Cassius maintained that the sexual liaisons of white men with black women morally weakened the former race in particular and Americans in general. "You may ask why the white race can not or hope to be as strong as the dark races. The answer is, three hundred years ago the white man began to mix his blood with everything that walked on two legs and bore the least resemblance to a human being, and the result is, it has become impossible to find in the most refined and virtuous home a family of children that all look alike." Cassius no doubt had in mind his own biracial background and the sexual exploitation of his mother when he commented that "It is a well known fact that the negro slave could not start the mixing of the African and the Anglo-Saxon. White men started it, because they saw in the African woman a poor, defenseless being that had no right that he need respect." Such illicit mixing, Cassius argued, led to the collapse of ancient empires.[33]

Cassius also attacked Negro minstrel shows, his animosity perhaps deriving from his experience in an all-black town in Oklahoma. He castigated black leaders who sanctioned the performance of such shows which, he believed, conveyed the "conviction that the young American colored people have no race pride." In Cassius's opinion, African Americans who degraded themselves only fueled white racism. "Now, if this had been a troupe of white people in a white town I would have thought nothing of it, because I would have known that the real purpose was to degrade the negro in the eyes of white people and thus keep alive the fact that the new addition to American freemen was too inferior to be taken seriously as a member of the family." Cassius, a conscientious race man, deeply cared about his own actions as well as those of fellow American blacks and determined never to participate in anything that showed the "worst side of the race."[34]

Cassius's grievous encounters with the evil system in Oklahoma further strengthened his indictment of segregation. "Segregation breeds crime, immorality, and vice in every form, and has proved to be the curse of every large city. All cleanliness and municipal improvement stop where segregation begins, and make slaves out of the segregated people, for their taxes help to pay for the improvements that they cannot enjoy." When the Oklahoma state legislature instituted Jim Crow legislation in 1907, Cassius, a frequent railroad traveler, suffered the humiliating effects of segregation, as mentioned earlier.[35]

In spite of the theory of black inferiority that undergirded segregation, Cassius proudly acknowledged that black soldiers during World War I "followed the flag to France." He singled out their bravery and willingness to go to war for the government. "They did not have to chase the negroes all over the United States to get them in the army; they went freely when called upon. And say, did you know that most of our colored boys did not wait to be drafted? They went freely, and learned the lesson of true manhood."[36] The phrase "our colored boys" carried personal meaning for Cassius, who gave three of his sons to the war effort. John F. Rowe Cassius served in the United States Army in France, William M. Cassius soldiered in the Philippines, and Amos Lincoln Cassius received an appointment in the army's nurses' Corp in Douglas, Arizona.[37] World War I touched Cassius's family profoundly, and he drew on such personal experiences to frame his book's arguments.

At the same time, Cassius used four specific sources in composing *The Third Birth of a Nation*. The Bible stood as Cassius's first source and his exclusive religious authority. No trained anthropologist, Cassius grounded his ethnology and anthropology in the Bible, which he unquestionably accepted as inerrant and the source of ultimate authority. Working from this base, Cassius adamantly opposed racial and sexual mixing because he believed the Bible condemned it. Relying on Genesis 11:1–10, Cassius maintained that it was not the "will of God that these nations mix or merge into one family again, and every attempt of man to undo what God has done will only bring upon the world the wrath of God, upon the children of disobedience." Reversing Matthew 19:6, Cassius asserted, "That which God has put asunder, let not man attempt to put together." Cassius then cited Proverbs 14:34: "Righteousness exalteth a nation, but sin is a reproach to any people," to argue that miscegenation caused the fall of Egypt. "The downfall of Egypt's greatness has been duplicated in nearly every nation of the world, and in every case it can be traced to the promiscuous mixing of the races." Cassius therefore took 2 Corinthians 6:17 to mean that races must not intermix. "Come out from among them, and be ye separate and I will receive you, saith the Lord."[38]

Cassius appropriated various biblical texts as well as his own reasoning to support racial equality and to repudiate racial discrimination. "A religion that does not blend all mankind in one common family is not the religion of the Bible; neither is it what God sent His son in the world to do; that one word 'Whosoever' condemns forever race favoritism in the sight of God." Cassius clearly fused his biblical understanding of race with his commitment to the Stone-Campbell principles of Scripture interpretation. "If we trust in God and do His will, can we not safely say that the negro can and will do great things during the next sixty years, if he will live a clean life, attend to his own business, stay in his own race, and throw off the yoke of man-made religion and accept God on the terms of the Bible, speaking where the Bible speaks and keeping silent where the Bible is silent?"[39] While Cassius was a unique racial and religious thinker in Churches of Christ, his exclusive doctrinal posture often prevented him from reaching the very people he yearned to touch with the Gospel.

Second, Cassius drew on William O. Blake's *The History of Slavery and the Slave Trade* as a source for his book. "This much I gleaned from a book published in England nearly 200 years ago. It was called 'The History of Slavery and the Slave Trade.' It was written by a woman. (I have forgotten her name.) The book was a present to me by an old white lady in Iowa, nearly forty years ago, and it was a present to her by her grandfather. It was burned with the rest of my library nearly twenty years ago, and the pictures in my book are as I remember them."[40] Although admittedly uncertain about the author's name and gender and other details, Cassius evidently referred to the Blake volume that first appeared in print in 1857 in Columbus, Ohio.

Cassius seemingly organized *The Third Birth of a Nation* according to four pictures he remembered from Blake's book, although the copies of Blake's work now available contain pictures unlike those Cassius recalled. The first picture, which appears in chapter 8, shows the first twenty African slaves before traders in Jamestown, Virginia. The second photograph, in chapter 9, portrays three African girls a year after arriving in Jamestown. Cassius believed these little girls, products of white-black mixing, "formed the beginning of the Negro Race in America." Chapter 11 contains both the third and fourth portraits. The former suggests that a "new race" had emerged. "If you look carefully," Cassius insisted, "you will see that there is not a full-blooded African in the bunch. Nor is there a big nosed, thick lipped, or a deformed man among them. They represent the pick of the American negro race in America at that time." The final picture, according to Cassius, portrays Abraham Lincoln and his wife, Mary Todd Lincoln, holding a "stalwart, brawny, brown skinned man, receiving from the hands of the great emancipator the freedom of the American slave."[41] Here Cassius may have recalled his own adolescent encounter with the sixteenth president of the United States.

Another nebulous source of Cassius's book was Ashley S. Johnson's 1896 *Condensed Biblical Cyclopedia*. When distinguishing between Egyptians and Ethiopians, Cassius mentioned Johnson's work, which delineated races by skin shading. "The Ethiopian was just a coarser kind of Egyptian," wrote Cassius, "and was much darker, and the Egyptian was simply a darker Hebrew, and the Hebrew a dark Anglo Saxon, and Hun." Cassius's *Third Birth of a Nation* seemingly followed Johnson's chronological arrangement by providing a historical sketch from Genesis to Exodus, but Johnson's work does not classify different ethnic groups. Thus, Cassius leaves twenty-first-century readers baffled as to whether or not he had the correct source in mind.[42]

Fourth, Cassius obviously used a cluster of unidentified sources. One of those probably was William J. Simmons's *Men of Mark.* Simmons's work, first published in 1887, furnished 157 biographical sketches of black Americans who achieved national and international prominence. Simmons, in explaining the motivation behind his book, stated, "I have faith in my people. I wish to exalt them; I want their lives snatched from obscurity to become household matter for conservation."[43] Cassius, too, admired and advocated black progress. In *The Third Birth of a Nation,* Cassius appropriated the story of Richard Allen, founder and bishop of the African Methodist Episcopal Church, to show how segregation originated in the Christian community. When white parishioners in St. George's Methodist Episcopal Church in Philadelphia "dragged" Allen and other black worshipers from their knees and expelled them, this "grave mistake," in Cassius's opinion, "gave birth to 'segregation,' and 'Jim Crowism.'" Cassius, who no doubt took this story from Simmons's work, cited the Allen episode to argue that white Christians were largely responsible for racial prejudice.[44]

With few libraries available to black researchers in Oklahoma and Cassius lacking any training in scholarly pursuits, he may have sometimes consulted inadequate sources as he compiled statistics for his book's section on the black soldiers in the Revolutionary War and the Civil War. According to Cassius, "three thousand" African Americans fought in the Revolutionary struggle, while "three hundred thousand" black men participated in the Civil War. Cassius likely resorted to William Wells Brown's two books *The Black Man, His Antecedents, His Genius, and His Achievements* (published in 1863) and *The Negro in the American Rebellion: His Heroism and His Fidelity* (published in 1867). And he no doubt possessed a copy of George Washington Williams's *History of the Negro Race in America, 1619–1880* (published in 1883). But since neither Brown nor Williams provided specific numbers for black men who fought in the Revolutionary War and the Civil War, the source of Cassius's numbers remains unclear. Recent studies place the number of black soldiers in the Revolutionary conflict at 5,000 and the black enlistment in the Union army at 186,000, so Cassius seems to have underestimated one while overstating the other.[45]

Statistical precision, of course, was not the pivot of Cassius's book, which was essentially an attempt to "trace him [the black man] from his Adamic father to his present status as an American Negro."[46] This large effort falls into six parts. Chapters 1–5 argue for the humanity and dignity of the African American as part of God's creation. Chapters 6–7 chronicle the rise and fall of the Egyptian and Ethiopian empires. "It is not my purpose to discuss the why and wherefore of the downfall of Egypt and Ethiopia, except to say that miscegenation destroyed Egypt and religious liberty destroyed Ethiopia." Cassius's opposition to racial mixing becomes the fulcrum of his book's argument. In the third section, chapters 8–11, Cassius attributes the source of America's race problem to economic competition between whites and blacks. In part four, chapters 12–17, Cassius addresses social and moral issues such as the meaning of true education, womanhood, and manhood. In keeping with his promise to rebuke fellow black Americans for their "shortcomings," Cassius chided them for "mixing that old, African superstition with the revealed gospel plan of salvation."[47]

The fifth division, chapters 18–25, perhaps comprises the core of *The Third Birth of a Nation.* In this section Cassius examines important race-laden concepts such as amalgamation, miscegenation, assimilation, Christianization, separation, extermination, and segregation. On the one hand Cassius forthrightly rejected amalgamation, miscegenation, and assimilation alike, contending that to "mix with another kind of people" contravened God's will. He further argued that racial mixing led ineluctably to extermination, just as the mixture of Hebrews and Egyptians caused the downfall of the latter. "Egypt was the most powerful nation of the earth at that time miscegenation was started in the land, and she would have continued to have been a great nation if she had not begun to mix." Cassius similarly predicted that the sexual union of blacks and whites in the United States, which white men initiated, would eventually lead to the downturn of American civilization.[48]

Furthermore, according to Cassius, the mixing of different races led to insanity. Referring to the United States as a "mongrel nation," Cassius assessed, "There is no nation except the American *'Negro'* that cannot inter-marry in the American Nation, and in some states that is done without comment. Is it any wonder then, that America has the largest lunatic asy-lums, more jails and penitentiaries, the loosest marriage laws and the most daring criminals of any nation on earth [?]" Explaining why racial mixing produced criminal and deranged behavior, Cassius asserted, "First, there are too many races in one body; second, the Bible is a book only to swear by in court, and preach from on the Lord's day, and to be disregarded as a rule of faith and practice at any time its teaching may interfere with the things a man, or even the nation, may want to do."[49] Disregard for God's Word threatened the very future of America.

On the other hand, the author of *The Third Birth of a Nation* accepted ideas such as separation and Christianization. Cassius frequently appropri-ated Old Testament texts and applied them to race relations in America. For instance, God prohibited the people of Shinar in Genesis 11:1–10 from becoming "one" nation, commanding them instead to scatter throughout the world. Cassius, consequently, championed racial separation because the "will of God" demanded that different nations be "separated" in different places. "God saw that in order that the earth should be peopled and sub-dued, that the children of men must be separated, not simply by putting them in different places, but that he must put a difference between them; he must make it so they could not understand each other, and thus force them to build up nations to fit the language that God had given them." Cassius then asked, "What is the answer?" To his own query he responded that only separation would solve the problem. "The American white man has sown in a whirlwind and he is now reaping in a storm. No nation can live by mixing, and, above all, the negro is satisfied to live his own life in his own way and among his own people."[50]

In this diagnosis Cassius stood with a number of black religious leaders in the Progressive Era who also recommended that African Americans separate from their white counterparts. Black newspapers in Oklahoma such as the *Muskogee Cimeter* advocated racial separation. Certain that the separation of the black and white people would minimize racial strife, the *Muskogee Cimeter* editor urged, "We shall stay on our side of the fence and the other fellow must stay on his or there will be h___l to pay [*sic*]." In 1909 Lucius Henry Holsey, a bishop in the Colored Methodist Episco-pal Church, argued for racial separation. "In a State to themselves, within the Federal Union, the Negro would become a free and full-fledged citizen, with all the immunities, privileges and political rights that belong to American citizens without friction, envy and jealousies. Then the Negro as a man and a race, would have a chance to develop his mental powers, his physical character, and his essential responsibilities as an American citizen."[51]

From Cassius's point of view, America had two options in solving its race problem: social and political equality or separation. "My advice, in view of all these things, is to give every people the same civil and political rights or separate them from each other and let each work out their own destiny in their own way." Pessimistic about attaining equality under white-dominated state governments, he advocated separation, but unlike Henry McNeal Turner and Marcus Garvey who urged black migration to Africa as an answer to the race question, Cassius proposed that African Americans be allowed to take up residence in Oklahoma, New Mexico, and Arizona, as these states "are more suited by climate, and in many other ways, for the use of the colored people, than they are for the whites."[52]

Cassius affirmed moreover that Christianization provided an answer to the race issue in America. "Christianity is the only force that can possibly bridge the chasm that separates man from man, because Christianity is the only means that so changes our minds that one will not think himself better than another." By "Christianization," Cassius meant his vision of primitive, apostolic Christianity, that is, taking the Bible only as the "rule of faith and practice." Cassius's understanding of the "pure religion" of the Bible excluded the "Baptist, Methodist, Presbyterian, Congregationalist, and the many other brands of religion." Christianization empowered whites and blacks to attend the "same schools," and enabled them to learn the "same lessons" from the "same Bible." Yet, it forbade interracial marrying. "Christians would not be afraid of social equality injuring their home," Cassius reassured, "because the grace of God would cast out all fear. I would not be afraid that some white man would marry my daughter; they would believe the Bible and would know that God was opposed to the mixture of the races he separated." Christianization therefore allowed followers to mingle but not mix.[53]

Intending through *The Third Birth of a Nation* to awaken a "new thought on the race problem," Cassius strove to arouse the thinking of white Christians in America about the issue of race and stir them to solve America's racism problem. In this respect Cassius's book was to a degree both influential and successful. D. T. Broadus, a white preacher in Churches of Christ, promoted *The Third Birth of a Nation* and noted that Cassius "raises the question as to whether it must be settled by Amalgamation, Miscegenation, Assimilation, Christianization, Separation or Extermination. Here you may not exactly agree with all his conclusions, but it is worth while to read and investigate it. It is anxious thought upon his part."[54] Cassius's quest for historical accuracy and biblical truth as means of settling the race problem impressed his readers and supporters.

The Third Birth of a Nation stirred racial thoughts in E. B. Grubbs, a white Christian from Paris, Texas, causing her to reflect on her own life as a white woman in the antebellum South. She recalled with fondness the care her "Black Mammy" gave her; such affection contributed to her lack of animosity toward black Americans. Writing a few days before her sixty-fifth birthday, Mrs. Grubbs stated:

> I also read Bro. Cassius' book, "The Third Birth of a Nation." I bought it for an old colored woman that lives near me, an ex-slave. There is one thing for which I am thankful, that I never had any animosity for our colored race, being left motherless at the age of five, losing my father in the Confederate army, reared by foster parents who were fine people. Being childless, they knew not how to give real parental affection, but I got that from Black Mammy, sleeping by her side many times. She was a Christian, and, of course, the cook. She would cook her dinner Sunday morning, then come to the log cabin close by, sit on the door step, where she would be given the bread and wine when the white members had been waited upon. This certainly did wound my childish heart, for she was one great mammy to me; but your books have started me to looking back, which I am prone to do sometimes too much.[55]

Such responses attested to the potency of Cassius's *Third Birth of a Nation*. It raised the racial consciousness of at least some white members in Churches of Christ, and it rekindled sentimental thoughts about their lives before and after the Civil War. In some respects, it created a sense of optimism that race relations in America could be mended and improved.

The Third Birth of a Nation also stirred thoughts about morality. In

1927, an unidentified reader from Illinois asked Cassius why he included the "unpopular" chapter "The Movie, the Soft Drink, and the Short Skirt" in his book. Cassius believed that these three things undermined the moral values of other races, so he urged black people to avoid these practices. "Therefore I thought if I could cause at least a few of my people not to adopt the habits, it would help raise them in the estimation of sober-minded men and women of other races. I do not believe that there have ever been three habits practiced in the world that have done and are doing as much harm *as soft drinks, the movies and short skirts*." Movies, Cassius believed, aroused sexual passions between boys and girls; soft drinks contained "habit-forming drugs" that destroyed "willpower," "energy," and "morality"; short skirts degraded women who, having divested themselves of the "garment of womanly modesty," exposed themselves to the "vulgar gaze of men." Cassius concluded, "Dear sister, I thank you for the two dollars you sent me, and I am glad the chapter in my book at least made you think."[56] Prompting readers to think, making white people and black people ponder race and morality, was the undergirding purpose of *The Third Birth of a Nation*. In the mind of Cassius, the two issues, race and morality, were identical.

Cassius pointedly addressed these two issues by writing his book. He had felt compelled to respond to the literary works of Charles Carroll and Thomas Dixon as well as the theatrical production of D. W. Griffith, all of which he regarded as divisive and destructive. Their effect, in Cassius's assessment, exacerbated racial tension in the Progressive Era because they poisoned the minds of whites against blacks in the United States. Cassius maintained that racial demagogues, using such works, portrayed American blacks as predatory beasts, and this would eventually deprive African Americans of support from white philanthropists in the North. Losing the financial and emotional support of their friends and becoming a despised and feared minority, American blacks—the victims of mind poisoning—would vanish as the economic competitors of white men. Samuel Robert Cassius spent his adult life spreading his chosen antidote to this poison.

But *The Third Birth of a Nation* was in many respects more than a book. It was Cassius's life. He lived it, preached it, taught it, and promoted it. He spent much of 1921 traveling, lecturing, and preaching sermons based on his new book. "At Bloomington, Ind., I was well received. Then I preached a sermon on 'Third Birth of a Nation.'" Cassius's audiences consisted of a variety of religious groups apart from Churches of Christ. "The colored Baptists opened their church for me. I preached at the colored Methodist Church in Bedford, Ind." For Cassius, not only was the pulpit a platform from which to advance the Gospel message, but it also provided an opportunity to address the issue of race. When traveling on preaching tours, the author of *The Third Birth of a Nation* often relied on proceeds from the sale of his book to reach further destinations. After conducting an evangelistic meeting in Parsons, Kansas, Cassius recognized that "If it was not for the sale of my book, 'The Third Birth of a Nation,' it would be hard for me to get home from this place."[57] Cassius's book, then, was more than an attempt to address the issue of race; it was also a source of income, which he used to propagate the Gospel, including his racial ideas.

In 1925, after relocating from Ohio to southern California to help his son Amos establish a congregation, Cassius made plans to reissue *The Third Birth of a Nation* in expanded form. Writing with a spirit of pride and with a sense of prophecy about his book, Cassius confidently predicted, "A hundred years from now your children will rise up and call you blessed, because of the thought that is put forth in that book. And the children of those who shall buy that book will say: 'How much better this country would be if our fathers had dealt with the race question along the lines laid down in S. R. Cassius' great little book.'" As with the earlier edition, Cassius determined to use funds that the book generated to disseminate the "pure Gospel" among black Californians. "I intend to use the profits from the sale of my books to enable me to preach Christ where and to the people that have not heard the pure Word of God preached. In fact, I intend to stay right here in Watts, Cal., until I see a real church of Christ in this city, which really means Los Angeles." A generous advance of three hundred dollars from Alex Lindsay of Detroit, Michigan, enabled Cassius to issue a revised version of *The Third Birth of a Nation*, an edition which, he assured prospective readers, "preaches a better sermon, right living, and primitive Christianity than I will ever be able to preach from the pulpit."[58] To Cassius, race and religion were indivisible, and his book on race afforded him monetary support to preach the Good News. And he remained confident that this proclamation of the "pure Word of God" must surely lead to racial harmony in America.

10
The Setting of a "Sun"
The Legacy of Samuel Robert Cassius

> Because for the work of Christ he was nigh unto death, not regarding
> his life, to supply your lack of service toward me.
> —Philippians 2:30

After reissuing *The Third Birth of a Nation* in 1925, Samuel Robert Cassius continued his work as a traveling evangelist, canvassing various parts of North America and Canada. In 1927 Cassius journeyed through the Northwest, preaching in Idaho, Oregon, Washington, and British Columbia. Always determined to evangelize African Americans first, Cassius lamented, "There are not as many colored people in those states as I hoped to find." But, he noted optimistically "as a rule those that are there are of a class that reflect credit on my race."[1] This comment reveals Cassius's preoccupation with the evangelization of American blacks as well as his desire to see his people present a positive image before their white counterparts. By further stressing that he ventured to preach in states where "no colored Christian preacher has ever dared to go in," Cassius implicitly criticized black evangelists for limiting themselves to the oversight of a local congregation. But more importantly, Cassius wished to indict white Churches of Christ for their lethargy in converting black Americans to "the Gospel plan of salvation as it is written in the New Testament," even while they zealously evangelized among Africans, Japanese, Chinese, and Cubans.[2]

Cassius was deeply disturbed by white believers' preoccupation with foreign missions, which he believed led to the demise of black congregations. In 1929 Cassius returned to Tulsa, Oklahoma, "to re-establish the colored loyal work in this state. While I was out of the state," Cassius explained and complained, "the United Society about killed all the colored work in Oklahoma, and if the loyal Churches of Christ that know me will help me I will stay here and try to redeem the work. Brethren, when you think of heathen, don't look beyond the United States. 'You have Africa at your door.'"[3] The following year, Cassius recalled that he had established forty-five African American congregations, but only fifteen of them remained "loyal to the 'thus saith the Lord.'" Yet all of these, Cassius pointed out, "were in places where there were white congregations that were supporting missions in every country where the 'sects' were, among red, yellow, brown and black people, yet these same people were their neighbors and were dying and going to hell, for the want of the bread of life."[4] In Cassius's judgment, the "heathen" at home demanded as much attention as the "heathen" abroad, yet the corrosive racism of white Christians blinded them to their obvious duty.

Cassius informed readers of the *Christian Leader* in 1930 that he journeyed through west Tennessee to disseminate the pure Gospel among African Americans. "I am once more out on the firing line," Cassius announced, "on a mission of love and mercy." Cassius thanked two white sisters, "Bob" Fuller of Dyer County, Tennessee, and Deemy Grady of Lake County, Tennessee, who wanted to "see the colored people have a fair show, and an equal break to hear the Gospel as it is written in the Word of God." These two women made it possible for Cassius to travel from his home in Colorado Springs, Colorado, to "preach the Word" to "my people." From west Tennessee pulpits Cassius excoriated whites in Churches of Christ who worked "overtime trying to convert Africa, China and Japan, and Cuba, and the rest of the Islands of the Sea," but neglected the "alleys and back streets of our towns and cities [which] are full of people that never have heard a real, plain, Gospel sermon." This indifference on the part of white church members prompted Cassius to demand, "Brethren, why not clean up America? While we are trying to clean the rest of the world? All the above nations are here and going to hell, and how can the Church of Christ square itself with God about my people who have been such a factor in the development of the United States?"[5]

Shortly after returning from this preaching tour, Cassius told his *Christian Leader* audience that he had visited black Churches of Christ in Tennessee, Kentucky, and Indiana. "There are congregations both white and colored in all of these towns," Cassius explained, "but they are dying for the want of the bread of life, and it don't seem to be nobody's business." Certainly Cassius made it his "business" to preach the Gospel to any who would listen, and he so committed himself to evangelizing African Americans that he frequently sacrificed his health and his family's welfare. Often referring to himself as a globe-trotter, Cassius at times left behind an ill wife to fulfill what he believed was God's call for his life. Shortly after celebrating his seventy-seventh birthday, Cassius expressed his unshakeable determination to continue preaching. "My wife is an invalid and if she should take seriously sick or pass away the Lord only knows what I would do. But brethren, I cannot and will not turn back; somebody has got to go, so please remember my wife while I hoe out my row." The overmastering passion of Cassius's life was to introduce American blacks to the "pure religion of Jesus Christ."[6]

Working toward this goal forced Cassius to rely mainly on financial assistance from white members in Churches of Christ. The Globe-trotter, consequently, lived a life of continuing frustration and disappointment because so many white believers did not share his love for the souls of black folk in America. Because he garnered such meager support from white congregations, Cassius believed that "many of our brethren regard the salvation of the negro as a joke." Cassius pointed out that white leaders of missionary societies spent large sums of money to convert Africans, Asians, Mexicans, and Europeans in foreign lands but virtually neglected African Americans. "I know that we are sending our sons and daughters to Africa, China, Japan, and the 'Isles of the Sea', but I sometimes wonder, if it is not mere 'Fad.'"[7]

Cassius did not oppose foreign missions but rather challenged his white evangelistic colleagues to place American blacks on their priority list as well. "Would it not be a blessing if the Church of Christ would wake up," Cassius wrote during the Great Depression, "and help these people [blacks in America] to see a God of Love in all these dark hours of hunger, and suffering, and thus win them back to God. Don't you think it is a shame to fool these poor ignorant Africans, and other nations across the oce[a]n by telling them that the United States is a Christian nation, and a Bible country, when the inside of the cup is full of dead men's bones."[8] Not only did the diversion of resources from domestic to foreign missions seem hypocritical, but it also meant that Cassius and other "colored preachers have to go away and leave the babes in Christ to die, or be adopted by the Christian Church."[9] Surely the black man and woman in America required as much spiritual attention as the Asian and African abroad.

Cassius, then, devoted himself to getting the Gospel to black people in America because he believed that only through the message of Christ could his race experience true moral, social, and spiritual reformation. "My people need reformation," Cassius proclaimed, "and need it bad, and they know they need it, and are ready for it, and there is none but the disciples of Christ that can supply that need." Convinced that other religious groups had forgotten about the spiritual welfare of African Americans, Cassius continued: "Every other religious body has taken a fall out of the negro but the Church of Christ, and they are like Jonah was when he went and preached to the people of Nineveh. Jonah was filled with race prejudice, and did not want the people of Nineveh to enjoy the same salvation that the Jews did."[10] Because he worked so tirelessly and diligently to meet the needs of African Americans, Cassius became easily the most recognized black preacher among Churches of Christ in the first three decades of the twentieth century. Part of this renown arose from his ubiquitous evangelistic efforts, but it stemmed mostly from his determination to keep the race problem highly visible. His enduring passion to resolve the race question in America earned him the title Race Man.

Both as an itinerant preacher and a racial reformer, Cassius profoundly impacted Churches of Christ in America during the Progressive Era, unquestionably leaving an indelible imprint on blacks and whites alike. When Cassius visited the black Church of Christ in Parsons, Kansas, W. S. Sims, minister to the congregation, reported that Cassius delivered a "great message, one that opened the eyes of many." Sims further expressed his admiration for Cassius: "We admire such men as Elder Cassius, who preaches the simple truth. We pray that God will continue to bless him in the great work he is so willingly giving his time and very life. We, the members of the Church of Christ (Colored), was glad to have him stop-over with us." Cassius noted that there were 1,200 white Christians in Parsons and that the "progressive" church comprised 1,000 members; the "loyal" church consisted of 200. When learning that the former had a budget of eight thousand dollars, Cassius chided, "Some goes to Africa, India, Japan, the Isles of the sea, but not one cent for the hell-bound negro sinners living all around their church."[11] The fact that so many white Christians remained preoccupied with foreign missions while neglecting domestic outreach disturbed Cassius throughout his ministry.

Cassius's message often resonated, nevertheless, with white members of Churches of Christ. Mattie E. Howard Coleman in Oklahoma wrote of his visit in 1902: "On Lord's day, October 12, at 11 A.M., Elder S. R. Cassius preached one of the most logical and timely sermons that we ever heard." Years later, Samuel H. Hall, a well-known white preacher in Churches of Christ, praised Cassius's missionary work in Los Angeles, California: "One of the best examples of mission work that I know of just now is the accomplishment of Bro. S. R. Cassius, at Watts, Calif." Cassius's adroitness in enlarging small-church memberships there, his ingenuity in establishing a Bible school, and his ability to erect a worship facility impressed Hall and prompted Hall to ask, "Where can you go for a better record than Bro. Cassius has made?" Because of such commendations, coupled with his passion for winning souls to Jesus Christ, Cassius carried his optimistic disposition into his declining years. In a poetically cheerful vein, Cassius wrote, "I cannot see, I cannot tell, what is before me, but my eye is not dimmed, nor is my natural force very much abated. But I do want to wind up this life of mine in a whirl-wind of glory, to the honor of God, though few and evil have the days of life been."[12]

With the passage of time, however, Cassius struggled to maintain this outlook on life, especially when he considered the spiritual plight of African Americans. In 1926 Cassius moved from California to Colorado Springs, Colorado, and established the first black Church of Christ in the state. Reflecting on the evangelistic possibilities in Colorado and neighboring states, he pledged, "I have but one thing to regret: I am too old to do much manual labor, and my wife's arm hinders her from helping me, yet we are not afraid, and are determined, with the help of God, to leave no stone unturned to plant a congregation in every available place in this state, and the Middle West." After outlining his plans of evangelism for the Midwest, Cassius again solicited monetary support from white Christians. "Brethren, if our white preachers need help, how much more must I need it here in this vast field alone."[13] Even though an aging Cassius was certain that his preaching endeavors in Colorado would accomplish great things for Christ, insufficient financial aid disappointed him. He wrote dejectedly:

> After forty-two years as a Christian minister, during which time it has been my good or bad fortune to see both sides of a Gospel preacher, I think I am safe in saying that nine out of ten of the Christian preachers of the Church of Christ live a life that is just one disappointment after another. But his greatest disappointment is to go into a new field, and labor among the unsaved until a real interest is

worked up, and then go to the Churches of Christ of that state, county or town and ask for help to continue the work, and to have the elders to tell you that *it is as much as they can do to look after their own congregations,* and turn the poor preacher away without even a "God bless you." In nine cases out of ten these very brethren have encouraged the poor preacher to sacrifice his time, neglect his family and endure hardships. But, cheered on with the belief that the great heart of the brethren is at his back, and will give him the things that he needs for his wife, children and himself, then to find that he has not a merciful friend, or a pitying foe, is worst, and the most heart-breaking disappointment that can come to a poor Gospel preacher.[14]

In many ways Cassius's lament reflected his own personal experiences as a struggling, often destitute preacher. After entering the ministry around 1883, he committed his life to changing the lives of black people with the Gospel of Christ. Even though a poverty-stricken minister who knew nothing "but hardships and disappointments," Cassius confidently declared, "I am too old to look back." Always quick to quote from the Bible, he continued, "I want to finish this life and be able to say, as Paul said, 'For I am now ready to be offered and the time of my departure is at hand. I have fought a good fight. I have finished my course. I have kept the faith. Henceforth there is laid up for me a crown of righteousness, which the Lord the Righteous Judge, shall give me at that day (II Tim. 4:6–8)." Cassius's preoccupation with the blessings of the otherworld steeled him to endure the disappointments of this world.[15]

Notwithstanding his own constant struggles, Cassius's impact on Churches of Christ broadened through his son Amos Lincoln Cassius. Frederick L. Rowe, after visiting the Cassius family in California in the winter of 1925, observed, "Bro. Cassius' son is elder of the congregation at Watts, and is a credit indeed to the cause. You don't have to talk with him long to know that he understands the Book and is able to defend it." Samuel Robert Cassius had of course given Amos biblical instruction, and Cassius's transmission of Christian character to his family moved S. H. Hall to canonize the elder Cassius with the patriarch Abraham. Hall wrote, "Another great thing about Bro. Cassius is the way he has brought his household up to fear the Lord. His son is a pillar in that church. Bro. Cassius is getting old and can not stay with us much longer, but he has trained a family to take his work where he leaves and carry it on. This is, indeed, an indication that our brother should be placed in the class with such saints as was Abraham. Speaking of Abraham, Jehovah said, 'For I know him, that he will command his children and his household after him, and they shall keep the way of the Lord, to do justice and judgment.'"[16] Hall's reference to Genesis 18:19 favorably compared Cassius and his efforts to the exceptional faith and works of the biblical character Abraham; Hall could lavish no higher praise.

Amos, the only member of the Cassius family known to have entered the preaching ministry, perpetuated his father's legacy among Churches of Christ. Like his father, Amos helped establish churches in southern California and published a short-lived journal, *Christian Counselor.* When seeking to raise money to build a church facility for the Compton Avenue Church of Christ in Los Angeles, Amos imitated his father, and pleaded with Christians to help. "My father is now in the northern part of the state trying to raise money. I decided to state our need to you in hope that you might consider some means of helping us in making this most difficult and final step." After the death of his father, Amos continued to rely on the generosity of white Christians to do missionary work throughout the country. B. C. Goodpasture, an influential leader among whites in Churches of Christ in the second half of the twentieth century, appealed to the readership of his paper, the *Gospel Advocate,* on behalf of Amos Cassius. Goodpasture recommended him as "energetic and untiring in his efforts to get the gospel to his race. He is a faithful gospel preacher." Amos counted on the philanthropy of white Churches of Christ to help him preach to American blacks, just as his father had done.[17]

While Samuel Robert Cassius earned plaudits for his dedication to biblical truths, it was as a race man that the elder Cassius had the greatest effect on the corporate mindset of Churches of Christ. Through the pages of the *Christian Leader,* Cassius as a journalist met and piqued the interest of white believers' intellects. Willard H. Morse, a New Jersey physician, wrote in 1902, "There is one correspondent of the Christian Leader who has interested me for some time, and that is S. R. Cassius. I do not know him, nor do I know any more of him than I find in these columns." A regular contributor to the *Christian Leader,* Cassius impressed Morse as an "active, consecrated negro—apt, able and aggressive. I see that man, S. R. Cassius," Morse continued, "and thousands of others of his color who have found the Lord's Christ, and are eager to push forward to highest attainments." Cassius's recurring columns addressing race matters prompted Morse to challenge indifferent fellow white Disciples. "Be honest with your hearts and admit," Morse pleaded, "that if it depended on white men and women to do the Lord's word in converting Southern negroes they would have to taste the tincture of procrastination." Morse encouraged and urged Cassius to "keep the readers of the Christian Leader informed of your faith, your hope, and your unfailing love for him who first loved us."[18]

W. Jasper Brown, a Christian from Tennessee, also read with interest Cassius's pamphlet *The Letter and Spirit of Giving and the Race Problem* and applauded the author for rebuking the improper racial practices common in white Churches of Christ. "Bro. Cassius administers a well deserved rebuke in showing the Church's attitude to the colored people. The Church of Christ is not in keeping with the Christ on this question." Conversely, Brown castigated David Lipscomb and the *Gospel Advocate* because they kept virtually silent on the race question and largely neglected the "subject of negro oppression." Brown indicted Lipscomb by exclaiming, "Talk about innovation! The worst innovation ever practiced upon man is the oppression of the negro race by the white man." Brown's comments thrilled Cassius, who replied, "If [W. Jasper Brown] had sent me $1000 it would not have caused the thanksgiving that the kind words spoken of me and my race did. Kind words don't cost much; but no man can estimate their value." Continuing his praise, Cassius concluded, "God bless you, Bro. Brown, for what you have said about myself and my race."[19]

More approbation for Cassius came from John W. Harris, a white evangelist in the Indian Territory of Oklahoma who extolled Cassius above Frederick Douglass. "No use to compare him with Fred. Douglass. Fred was what politicians made him. Bro. C. is what the gospel has made. Cassius is as a 'sun' and Fred is as a 'moon.'"[20] Cassius himself once lauded Douglass as "the greatest negro in America, if not the world,"[21] yet from Harris's religious perspective Cassius's work as a proclaimer of the Gospel lifted him above even Douglass. Personally acquainted with Cassius, Harris called him a "Christian gentleman and preacher of no mean ability. He has been before you all several years, trying to elevate his race." The commendatory remarks of Harris reveal the profound appreciation that some white Christians had for Cassius and authenticate Cassius's commitment to the spiritual elevation of his fellow blacks. Through his sermons, school, and writings, Cassius devoted himself to assisting his "race that is boycotted by the whites."[22]

While many in Churches of Christ knew and respected Cassius, the level of his reputation outside of that body of believers remains more difficult to ascertain. Perhaps Cassius's obscurity beyond the Restoration Movement as a racial reformer should be attributed to his doctrinal posture as a black preacher in Churches of Christ. His religious fellowship, many members of which made little effort toward ecumenism, tended to isolate itself from other religious bodies. Cassius endorsed this exclusivism of "loyal" white Christians, declaring in 1922 that he preached to show Methodists and Baptists that "I am right and they are wrong." Paradoxically, such legalism often shut the door in the faces of the very black people whom he yearned to uplift, thereby bringing religious bias from African Americans together with racial prejudice from white members of Churches of Christ. He certainly understood this, observing, "I have had to win my way through religious prejudice in my own race, and race prejudice among the brethren of my own faith."[23] The self-assumed restrictions of Cassius's own legalism and the unavoidable racism of some white Christians likely account for his lack of prominence outside of the Stone-Campbell Movement.

Even if little known beyond the circle of Churches of Christ in his own milieu, Cassius was widely appreciated as both an evangelist and a racial reformer who devoted his life to correcting what he understood as false religious teaching and erroneous racial views. And he courageously fought this "mind poisoning" until his health finally broke. On January 6, 1931, Cassius reported that when returning from California to Colorado, he ate "some ptomaine poison, and here I am sick, and broke." Two months later, the *Christian Leader* announced that the Race Man was critically ill and that he was "suffering great misery and that the swelling has extended from his limbs to his body." His doctor, the paper continued, "doesn't hold out any hope, but says he may live for a month or two"; Frederick L. Rowe, the journal's editor, urged readers to forward donations to Cassius's address in Colorado Springs. In April Cassius temporarily gained strength and wrote his last known extant article. He proclaimed, "I have passed through the valley and shadow of death and I am still in doubt as to whether I ever will preach another sermon." Alluding to Psalm 23, Cassius acknowledged, "But I am still trusting in the Lord, who has carried me through every trial.

Perhaps I have made mistakes, but they have been through lack of judgment."[24] Cassius's faith in a providential God and in the Bible as God's Word stood unshaken.

Reflecting on his career as an itinerant preacher, Cassius reemphasized his belief in the Bible as the divine source that must determine a person's course of life:

> This one thing I have always done. I have counted everything that was not, "Thus saith the Lord" as sin and all religions that did not have the sanction of a thus saith the Lord as just another sin that was just as bad as any other sin. That is one reason that I will go to any of the so called churches and preach; let it be Methodist, Baptist, Presbyterian or in fact any other religion because if they are not right they are wrong and are sinners in the sight of God. All sinners look alike to me, white or black, red or brown. For if you obey not the gospel o[f] our Lord and Savior, ye shall die in your sins. Therefore I have apology to make if they call me a fool. And don't you know that I don't think they are far wrong, yet I had rather be a fool ignorantly than a liar willfully. Well when it comes to the word of God; Paul sure was that same way.[25]

Thus, Cassius, after moving into the Restoration Movement as a young man, held a doctrinal posture of exclusivism throughout his life, holding no brief for religious groups who failed to adhere rigidly to New Testament tenets.

Cassius died on Monday night, August 10, 1931, leaving his wife, Selina, grief stricken, heartbroken, and impoverished as well. Mary Janes, a white Christian in Colorado Springs, wrote to the *Christian Leader* urging fellow believers to come to the financial aid of Selina Cassius. "We all know that Bro. Cassius spent his life for the cause of humanity and I think it would be a shame to let Sister Cassius suffer in her old age. There is a pretty heavy debt hanging over the only place she can call home, besides the funeral expenses." The Colorado sister continued her appeal: "I am asking every church of Christ in the United States to go to her aid. It is our Christian duty. Knowing Bro. Cassius and knowing what he stood for and how he always stood for the cause of Christ we cannot afford to let her suffer."[26]

Two months later Selina Cassius, weighed down by the Great Depression, petitioned the Pension Fund of the Disciples of Christ in Indianapolis, Indiana, for monetary relief. Her application spoke of eight children—five sons and three daughters—all grown and all common laborers, and it revealed her as plagued by poor health and bad hearing. Her house, valued at $1,200, carried a mortgage balance of $500, but she had "no income. [H]er children help her but they are all just existing themselves." Although records do not reveal whether or not the leaders of the Pension Fund acted on Selina Cassius's request, it is plain that donations trickled in from Christians throughout the country. Fidus Achates from Kansas sent eight dollars in October; a sister from West Virginia gave five dollars; J. M. Burge from Indiana contributed one dollar; a couple from Pennsylvania also sent one dollar.[27] Such gifts, although meager, attest to some Christians' concern and affection for Cassius and his family.

Cassius, throughout his ministry's span, significantly affected the lives of many white Christians in America. This black evangelist, black intellectual, and black racial reformer used his pen and his tongue to alert whites in the Restoration Movement to the plight of the black folk around them. Cassius's primary passion, however, remained the souls of American blacks. A frequent contributor to the *Christian Leader,* Cassius easily became the most visible and most vocal black man in Churches of Christ in the first few decades of the twentieth century. He used his position as a writer for this widely circulated journal to challenge unstintingly his white Christian counterparts to make the evangelization of African Americans a priority.

In Cassius's view, all too many white leaders and members of the Stone-Campbell Movement, preoccupied with providing spiritual direction for Asians, Mexicans, and Europeans, virtually neglected black Americans. Driven by this conviction, he contended that "As long as our white brethren spend all of their money, zeal, time and prayers on the Mexican, African, Japanese and Chinese and virtually say to the negro at their back doors, 'You may die and go to hell, as far as we are concerned,' our plea for 'One Lord, one faith, one baptism and one God and Father' for us all, and one hope of everlasting life will be merely a lot of hot air."[28] While many blacks and whites in Churches of Christ drew back from the issue of racism in America, Cassius refused to remain silent. Although nothing in life could stop the voice Cassius raised against religious and social injustices, death of course marked its own conclusions.

The death of Samuel Robert Cassius signaled not only the end of his influence but also the ascendancy of the influence of the redoubtable Marshall Keeble, clearly the most acclaimed black preacher in Churches of Christ in the second half of the twentieth century. Shortly after Cassius's death, B. C. Goodpasture published Keeble's sermons in book form and distributed them throughout the brotherhood of Churches of Christ. Keeble, preaching without the racial militancy of Cassius, garnered widespread financial support and regard from white Christians from the 1940s until his death in 1968. J. E. Choate has further praised him as the first black national evangelist in Churches of Christ, "the only Negro preacher to participate in the Restoration Movement on a national basis."[29] But in reality, only Cassius could lay claim to this encomium, working through a career that took him to virtually every state in the Union as well as parts of Canada.

Yet the career of Samuel Robert Cassius opened even while the nation's white masters were crafting the stifling system of segregation that they violently imposed upon the recently freed black population. Insofar as he could, Cassius refused to accept silently a pattern of life that seemed to him grossly unfair and, more importantly, completely unchristian. Such a race man could hardly expect his own fellowship, which he did not neglect to criticize on this matter, to treat him kindly in its corporate memory. And Cassius's career closed as the Great Depression lowered its deadening weight on the Republic, leaving a people with little energy for such concerns as the passing of any figure, revered or common.

So Cassius died in virtual obscurity, and the religious fellowship in which he so loyally and uniquely labored has since taken scant note of his singular career. But perhaps this would scarcely disturb Samuel Robert Cassius, for he lived his life in service to God's truth and cared little for people's recognition and even less for their approval.

Epilogue

The story of Samuel Robert Cassius played out in microcosm the broader story of black America in the decades following the Civil War. Born into slavery, Cassius was cast into freedom by the cataclysmic national war, but freedom narrowed in a nation unwilling and ill-equipped to shape the accommodations that would make this liberation something more than the mere ending of human bondage. While literacy prepared Cassius a bit more effectively to claim the advantages of emancipation than the mass of former slaves, his character provided the more essential fuel that propelled him into a life that would touch so many others, black and white, in such consequential ways.

At the same time, Cassius found that, more than anything else, the simple fact of his skin color largely dictated the courses of life open to him. His limited formal education, any lack of natural ability, the absence of monetary inheritance, and any other deficiencies paled in comparison with the certainty that Cassius was black. And perhaps the most remarkable aspect of his life was that he was able to achieve so much in the face of this fundamental and permanent reality. And as he came to recognize the arbitrary and immutable nature of his status, this understanding drove him unwillingly into the camp of the separatists, a position he felt compelled to assume in spite of his personal biracial heritage.

Yet in all this Cassius's fundamental driving force remained his commitment to his God. Drawn into a religious movement that, like much of his nation, was rent by the same dynamics that had fractured the Republic, Cassius never flagged in his devotion to his chosen cause. And he brought to this spiritual enterprise the same talents and determination that marked his efforts in the secular sphere. At the same time, he discovered in his religious community the same tensions that so disturbed and frustrated him in the other areas of his life's endeavors.

So Cassius found that in this world he could not escape the malevolent racism that dogged his every step. As he worked through the frustrations of being a black man in a nation ruled by intolerant whites, Cassius ineluctably bound up the practice of racism with that of religious sin. And throughout his life he could never accept racial discrimination as an appropriate behavior pattern for God's followers. Yet in order to preach God's Word as widely as possible, Cassius found himself forced to rely upon the inconstant support of white Christians fundamentally unwilling to accept him without the burden of prejudice. Cassius learned the grievous truth that success in religion, as in the rest of a black man's American world, hinged upon the vagaries of color. Through his long and eventful career, Samuel Robert Cassius determined never to live at peace with this bitter reality.

Notes

Introduction

1. In this book, a "race man" is one preoccupied with solving the race problem in America. See Waldo E. Martin, Jr., *The Mind of Frederick Douglass* (Chapel Hill: University of North Carolina Press, 1984), x. Concerning Douglass, Martin states: "The essential aim of his life was to resolve the problem of race." The same was true for Cassius.

2. The Stone-Campbell Movement, sometimes called the Restoration Movement, actually denotes three religious groups: Churches of Christ (which used no instruments in worship and opposed missionary societies), Disciples of Christ, and the Christian Church (the latter two both pro-instrumental and pro-missionary societies). These three groups trace their origin back to four principal leaders: Barton W. Stone (1772–1844), Thomas Campbell (1763–1854), Alexander Campbell (1788–1866), and Walter Scott (1796–1861). These men sought to "restore" primitive or apostolic Christianity in the modern world. Three of the best sources on the history of the Stone-Campbell Movement include David Edwin Harrell, Jr.'s two volumes of *A Social History of the Disciples of Christ, Quest for a Christian America: The Disciples of Christ and American Society to 1866* (Nashville, TN: The Disciples of Christ Historical Society, 1966) and *The Social Sources of Division of the Disciples of Christ, 1865–1900* (Atlanta, GA: Publishing Systems, 1973); and Richard T. Hughes's *Reviving the Ancient Faith: The Story of Churches of Christ in America* (Grand Rapids, MI: Eerdmans, 1996). For other useful studies, see Earl I. West, *The Search for the Ancient Order: A History of the Restoration Movement, 1849–1906* (Nashville, TN: Gospel Advocate Company, 1986 [1950]); James DeForest Murch, *Christians Only: A History of the Restoration Movement* (Cincinnati: Standard Publishing, 1962); Leroy Garrett, *The Stone-Campbell Movement: An Anecdotal History of Three Churches* (Joplin, MO: College Press Publishing Company,

1987); and Henry E. Webb, *In Search of Christian Unity: A History of the Restoration Movement* (Abilene, TX: Abilene Christian University Press, 2003).

Before 1906, the terms "Churches of Christ" and "Disciples of Christ" are used interchangeably. After this date, "Disciples of Christ" denotes the group that used instrumental music in worship, while "Churches of Christ" refers to the group that sang a cappella in worship and opposed missionary societies. Cassius eventually sided with the latter group.

3. Cassius believed that as an evangelist in Churches of Christ he was obligated to preach the "pure Gospel" just as the apostles of Jesus did in the first century. In essence, terminology such as "pure Gospel," "pure worship," "pure Word of God," "pure religion of Jesus Christ," and "New Testament Christianity" was used interchangeably by Cassius and other pioneer black preachers in the Stone-Campbell Movement to denote worshiping without instruments, partaking of the Lord's Supper every Sunday, and evangelizing without missionary societies. The notions of "rejecting human opinions," speaking where the Scriptures speak, and remaining silent where Scriptures are silent date back to Thomas Campbell's "Declaration and Address." For Campbell's address, see Charles Alexander Young, ed., *Historical Documents Advocating Christian Union* (1904; repr., Joplin, MO: College Press Publishing Company, 1985); and Robert Richardson, *Memoirs of Alexander Campbell, Embracing a View of the Origin, Progress and Principles of the Religious Reformation Which He Advocated* (Indianapolis: Religious Book Service, 1897).

4. Thomas H. Kirkman, "Scattered Thoughts," *Christian Leader* 34 (March 2, 1920): 9. Henceforth, *Christian Leader* will be abbreviated as *CL*.

5. Cassius, "Field Reports," *CL* 34 (June 8, 1920): 12; Kirkman, "Acknowledgments," *CL* 34 (June 8, 1920): 13. Cassius resided in Oklahoma from 1891 to 1922. But he traversed the country spreading what he understood was the "pure Gospel."

6. Cassius, "The Gallipolis Meeting," *CL* 34 (June 22, 1920): 13. Because of their emphasis on "baptism for the remission of sins," Churches of Christ have tended to measure their evangelistic success by the number of people they baptize.

7. Cassius, "Going Home," *CL* 34 (July 27, 1920): 16; *Gallipolis Daily Tribune* (June 12, 1920): 1; *Gallipolis Daily Tribune* (July 15, 1920): 1; *Gallipolis Daily Tribune* (July 24, 1920): 1.

8. Cassius, "Going Home," *CL* 34 (July 27, 1920): 16.

9. Cassius, "Save the American Negro," *Gospel Advocate* 57 (December 2, 1915): 1227.

10. Cassius, "Going Home," *CL* 34 (July 27, 1920): 16.

11. Cassius, "Going Home," *CL* 34 (July 27, 1920): 16.

12. W. E. B. Du Bois, *The Souls of Black Folk* (1903; repr., Boston: Bedford / St. Martin's, 1997), 38.

13. C. Eric Lincoln and Lawrence H. Mamiya, *The Black Church in the African American Experience* (Durham, NC: Duke University Press, 1990), 12–15.

14. August Meier, *Negro Thought in America, 1880–1915: Racial Ideologies in the Age of Booker T. Washington* (Ann Arbor: University of Michigan Press, 1963), 160.

15. The author is keenly aware that many other African American leaders in the Stone-Campbell Movement, such as G. P. Bowser (1874–1950), Marshall Keeble (1878–1968), and Annie C. Tuggle (1890–1976), were admirers of Booker T. Washington. But none of these people were ex-slaves from Virginia, as Cassius and Washington were. Hence, Cassius's identification with Washington was more complete and more significant. "We were born in the same State, both of slave mothers, and both were the sons of white men. The only difference is, I know the year of my birth and the name of my white father" (Cassius, "Looking Backward," *CL* 29 [December 14, 1915]: 4).

16. J. E. Choate, *Roll Jordan Roll: A Biography of Marshall Keeble* (Nashville, TN: Gospel Advocate Company, 1974), 84; West 3:185; Calvin H. Bowers, *Realizing the California Dream: The Story of Black Churches of Christ in Los Angeles* (Calvin Bowers, 2001), 30.

17. Cassius, "The Annual Meeting of the Oklahoma Colored Disciples," *Christian Leader and the Way* 23 (August 24, 1909): 13. In 1904, the *Christian Leader* merged with James A. Harding's paper *The Way* and changed its name to *Christian Leader and the Way.*

18. Cassius, "Among Our Colored Disciples," *CL* 18 (April 5, 1904): 12–13.

19. Cassius, "The American Negro," *CL* 34 (February 24, 1920): 6.

20. Cassius, "The American Negro," *CL* 34 (February 24, 1920): 6.

21. Cassius, "It Pays to Be a Man," *CL* 34 (April 16, 1920): 13.

22. Cassius, "It Pays to Be a Man," *CL* 34 (April 16, 1920): 13.

Chapter 1

1. Unless noted otherwise, all scriptural references are taken from the King James Version published in 1611. This was Samuel Robert Cassius's Bible.

2. *Prince William and Virginia Advertiser* (May 2, 1857): 3. See also *Slave Inhabitants for Prince William County* (August 31, 1850), 781, 783.

3. Samuel Robert Cassius referred to Macrae as a "drunkard." See Samuel Robert Cassius, *The Third Birth of a Nation* 2nd ed. (Cincinnati: F. L. Rowe, 1925), 5. Even though Cassius never explicitly identified his white father, his derogatory statement about Macrae appears to have been an indirect reference to his biological father. See also John C. Inscoe, "Carolina Slave Names: An Index to Acculturation," *Journal of Southern History* 44 (November 1983): 544.

4. Joel Williamson, *New People: Miscegenation and Mulattoes in the United*

States (New York: New York University Press, 1984). It is likely that young Samuel attached "Robert" and "Cassius" to his first name after freedom, just as his heroes Frederick Augustus Washington Bailey changed his name to Frederick Douglass after escaping from slavery and Booker Burroughs added Taliaferro Washington to his name when slavery ended. See Frederick Douglass, *Narrative of the Life of Frederick Douglass, an American Slave Written by Himself* (1845; repr., New York: W. W. Norton, 1997), 71–72; and Booker T. Washington, *Up from Slavery* (1901; repr., New York: Oxford University Press, 1995), 20–21. It is possible, then, that Cassius meant "Robert" to commemorate Robert E. Lee's alleged act of kindness in purchasing him and his mother to prevent them from being sold to the Deep South, and perhaps he intended "Cassius" to honor the ancient Roman general. It was not uncommon for slaves to adopt famous names from classical antiquity. See Willard H. Morse, "S. R. Cassius" *CL* (February 4, 1902): 9. For an example of a slave mother who named her son Cicero because she liked the sound of the three-syllable name, see John W. Blassingame, ed., *Slave Testimony: Two Centuries of Letters, Speeches, Interviews, and Autobiographies* (1977; repr., Baton Rouge: Louisiana State University Press, 2002), 580–81. See also Eugene D. Genovese, *Roll Jordan Roll: The World the Slaves Made* (1972; repr., New York: Pantheon Books, 1974), 443–50; and Peter Kolchin, *American Slavery, 1619–1877* (New York: Hill and Wang, 1993), 45–46.

5. Cassius, *Third Birth* (2nd ed.) 5. See also Margaret Sanborn, *Robert E. Lee: The Complete Man, 1861–1870* (Philadelphia: J. B. Lippincott Company, 1967), 162–63; and Gary W. Gallagher, ed., *Lee, the Soldier* (Lincoln: University of Nebraska Press, 1996), 20.

6. An analysis of birth records for that time actually sets the precise day of his birth as May 15, 1853. For documentation of Cassius's birth, see "Registers of Birth, Deaths, and Marriages" (reel 32), in the Prince William Public Library System, Manassas, Virginia. See also Ronald Ray Turner, *Prince William County Virginia Birth Records* (Manassas, VA, 1994), 122; and Cassius, *Third Birth* (2nd ed.) 5.

7. It is possible that Cassius, a lover of poetry, authored this poem. Samuel Robert Cassius, "I Am the Queen of May" *CL* 40 (May 11, 1926): 11.

8. Cassius, *Third Birth* (2nd ed.) 5.

Chapter 2

1. Samuel Robert Cassius, "'Behold, I Make All Things New,'" *Christian Leader* 33 (January 7, 1919): 8; Constance McLaughlin Green, *The Secret City: A History of Race Relations in the Nation's Capital* (Princeton, NJ: Princeton University Press, 1967), 57.

2. Green 119–54.

3. *The Negro in Virginia* (1940; repr., Winston-Salem, NC: John F. Blair, 1994), 211; Lillian G. Dabney, "The History of Schools for Negroes in the District of Columbia, 1807–1947" (PhD diss., The Catholic University of America, 1949), 23–24; Green 62; and James M. McPherson, *Battle Cry of Freedom: The Civil War Era* (New York: Ballantine Books, 1988), 355–57.

4. Cassius, "Looking Backward," *CL* 29 (December 14, 1915): 4.

5. "Miss Carter's Report," *Freedmen's Record* 2 (October 1866): 176; Dabney 53–54; Dorothy Sterling, ed., *We Are Your Sisters: Black Women in the Nineteenth Century* (New York: W. W. Norton, 1997), 286. On white Northern instructors who came south with "the Gospel and the Primer" to educate black freedmen, see Leon F. Litwack, *Been in the Storm So Long: The Aftermath of Slavery* (New York: Alfred A. Knopf, 1979), 450–51; and Robert C. Morris, *Reading, 'Riting, and Reconstruction: The Education of Freedmen in the South, 1861–1870* (1976; repr., Chicago: University of Chicago Press, 1981), 54–84.

6. Horatio T. Strother, *The Underground Railroad in Connecticut* (Middletown, CT: Wesleyan University Press, 1962), 117–18.

7. Emma V. Brown to Miss Stevenson, the *Freedmen's Journal* (January 1865): 8.

8. *Extracts from Letters of Teachers and Superintendents of the New-England Freedmen's Aid Society* (Boston: John Wilson and Son, 1864), 18.

9. Frances W. Perkins, "West-Roxbury Branch Society," *Freedmen's Record* (February 1865): 20.

10. *American Freedmen* 1 (May 1866): 29.

11. Cassius, "Looking Backward," *CL* 29 (December 14, 1915): 4.

12. Perkins, "West-Roxbury Branch Society," 20.

13. Cassius, "Looking Backward," *CL* 29 (December 14, 1915): 4.

14. Cassius, "The Race Problem," *CL* 17 (March 10, 1903): 9. For more on the six thousand people who attended President Abraham Lincoln's second inaugural reception, see Carl Sandburg, *Abraham Lincoln: The Prairie Years and the War Years* (1954; repr., New York: Galahad Books, 1993), 665. For black freedmen who venerated Abraham Lincoln as "Father Abraham" and as messiah, see *The Negro in Virginia,* 236; and Eric Foner, *Reconstruction: America's Unfinished Revolution, 1863–1877* (New York: Harper and Row Publishers, 1988), 73.

15. Norman R. Yetman, ed., *Life under the "Peculiar Institution": Selections from the Slave Narrative Collection* (New York: Holt, Rinehart and Winston, 1970), 220.

16. Yetman 234.

17. Cassius, "The Race Problem," *CL* 17 (March 10, 1903): 9.

18. Cassius, "Looking Backward," *CL* 29 (December 14, 1915): 4. The passage of the Thirteenth Amendment (which abolished slavery), the Fourteenth Amendment (which granted African Americans citizenship rights), and the Fifteenth Amendment (which granted American blacks voting rights) was largely responsible for the presence of black legislators in state and national governments during

the Reconstruction era. See Foner as well as Emma Lou Thornbrough, ed., *Black Reconstructionists* (Englewood Cliffs, NJ: Prentice-Hall, 1972).

19. Cassius, *The Letter and Spirit of Giving and the Race Problem* (n.p., n.d.), 29. For an insightful examination of Frederick Douglass's integrationist philosophy, see Mia Bay, *The White Image in the Black Mind: African-American Ideas about White People, 1830–1925* (New York: Oxford University Press, 2000), 66–71.

20. The statement that Cassius was the first black male to graduate from a high school in Washington, D.C., was extracted from Cassius's obituary. The composer of the obituary was either Cassius's son, Amos Lincoln Cassius, or Cassius's friend, Frederick L. Rowe. See "Obituary" *CL* 45 (September 29, 1931): 13–14. See also Mary Church Terrell, "History of the High School for Negroes in Washington," *Journal of Negro History* 2 (July 1917): 253–54.

21. Chapter 6 contains more information about Cassius's family.

22. Cassius, "Behold, I Make All Things New" *CL* 33 (January 7, 1919): 8.

Chapter 3

1. Cassius, "Looking Backward and Forward," *CL* 41 (December 27, 1927): 3. According to Joseph E. Cain, Cassius converted to the Stone-Campbell Movement in 1883 under the preaching of "Bro. Brown." See Cain, "Among Our Colored Disciples," *CL* 10 (October 27, 1896): 5. For an insightful discussion of race relations in post–Civil War Washington, D.C., see Green 119–54.

2. Cassius, "Looking Backward and Forward," *CL* 41 (December 27, 1927): 3; Cassius, "Looking Backward and Forward," *Gospel Advocate* (January 16, 1930): 16.

3. Cassius, *Third Birth* (2nd ed.) 84–85. Unfortunately, Cassius never revealed which religious group, if any, he aligned himself with before moving into the Stone-Campbell Movement. Cassius's disdain for his owner, James W. F. Macrae, a member of the Episcopal Church, likely pushed him into either the Baptist or Methodist camp. For a thorough and insightful discussion of black religion in antebellum Virginia, see Luther P. Jackson, "Religious Development of the Negro in Virginia from 1760 to 1860," *Journal of Negro History* 16 (January 1931): 169–239. For an excellent treatment of post–Civil War separations in the three major denominations in America, see Kenneth K. Bailey, "The Post–Civil War Racial Separations in Southern Protestantism: Another Look" *Church History* 46 (December 1977): 453–73.

4. On the significance of the Campbell-Purcell debate, see both Harrell, *Quest,* 215–17 and Hughes 35–37.

5. Cassius, *Negro Evangelization and the Tohee Industrial School* (Cincinnati, OH: Christian Leader Print, 1898), 10.

6. Cassius, "The Condenser," *CL* 15 (September 24, 1901): 5.

7. In 1899, after chiding black members of his congregation in Oklahoma for mingling too freely with Methodists, Cassius stated, "What we need now is a few Campbells, Stones and Rowes—men that are broad enough to allow for men's shortcomings without making a sacrifice of the truth" (Cassius, "Among Our Colored Disciples," *CL* 13 [September 5, 1899]: 5). John F. Rowe (1827–97), a close friend and mentor of Cassius, established the *Christian Leader* in 1886. Rowe invited Cassius to write for the *CL* in 1895.

8. Cassius, "A Trip to the Golden Gate," *CL* 16 (August 12, 1902): 13.

9. Cassius, "Where Are We?" *CL* 24 (April 19, 1910): 4.

10. Cassius, "The Right Man in the Right Place," *Christian Companion* 23 (September 14, 1916): 2.

11. Cassius, "I Wonder," *CL* 33 (December 30, 1919): 9.

12. Hughes 24–25. Alexander Campbell published the *Christian Baptist* from 1823 to 1830, and the *Millennial Harbinger* from 1830 to 1866. The *Millennial Harbinger* continued until 1870.

13. Cassius, "The Condenser," *CL* 15 (October 15, 1901): 5. For biographical data on Frederick A. Wagner as well as his work in Japan, see West 3:313–16.

14. Examples of Wagner's anti-Catholic writings appear in F. A. Wagner, "A Reply to 'A Catholic,'" *CL* 6 (February 23, 1892): 3–4.

15. Cassius, "Bro. Cain is Dead," *CL* 32 (August 27, 1918): 5.

16. Cassius, "Several Things," *Christian Leader and the Way* 23 (April 13, 1909): 13; Cain, "The Condenser," *Christian Leader and the Way* 23 (May 18, 1909): 5.

17. Cain, "The Condenser," *Christian Leader and the Way* 23 (May 18, 1909): 5.

18. Cassius, "Is Christianity Losing Ground?" *CL* 17 (May 19, 1903): 13.

19. Hughes 131.

20. Cassius, "Is Christianity Losing Ground?" *CL* 17 (May 19, 1903): 13.

21. The quotes from the *Savannah Tribune* and the *Washington Bee* appear in Cassius, "The Race Problem," *CL* 15 (September 3, 1901): 9. The *Savannah Tribune* aptly captured what black newspapers meant to Cassius and other African Americans in an editorial that stated, "The Negro press shapes and molds sentiment in the Negro's behalf, and every family should consider it indispensable. Better do without some of the necessaries of life than to be without a Negro paper" (*Savannah Tribune* [July 18, 1903]: 2).

22. Cassius, "The Race Problem," *CL* 15 (September 3, 1901): 9. Cassius here had in mind advocates of animal rights such as Henry Salt (1851–1939), who founded the Humanitarian League in England in 1891 and sought to rescue animals from barbarous treatment. Anticruelty-to-animal societies also flourished in America during the Progressive Era. See Henry S. Salt, *Animals' Rights: Considered in Relation to Social Progress* (1892; repr., Clarks Summit, PA: Society for Animal Rights, 1980), 15.

23. For Abernethy's speech, see "To Expel the Negro from the South," *Literary Digest* (March 23, 1901): 342–43. For Cassius's response, see "The Race Problem," *CL* 15 (April 30, 1901): 13.

24. For Vardaman's speech, see "Gov. Vardaman's Inaugural Address," *Greenwood Enterprise* (January 22, 1904): 2–3. For Cassius's response to the Mississippi governor, see Cassius, "The Race Problem," *Christian Leader and the Way* 18 (March 15, 1904): 2. The best biography on Vardaman remains William F. Holmes, *The White Chief: James Kimble Vardaman* (Baton Rouge: Louisiana State University Press, 1970).

25. Cassius, "The Race Problem," *Christian Leader and the Way* 18 (March 15, 1904): 2.

26. J. S. De Jarnette, "An Oklahoma Protest," *Christian Leader and the Way* 18 (April 12, 1904): 12.

27. John D. Baird and Charles Ryskamp, eds., *The Poems of William Cowper* (Oxford: Clarendon Press, 1995), 3:13–14, 283–85.

28. For places where Cassius cited in its entirety "The Negro's Complaint," see both Cassius, *The Letter and Spirit* 30–31; and Cassius, *Negro Evangelization* 8. Cassius erroneously stated that a "white lady in England" wrote the poem (Cassius, "The Ethiopian's Complaint," *CL* 37 [April 17, 1923]: 8). For other references by Cassius to this poem, see "The Great Commission," *CL* 44 (December 2, 1930): 3.

29. Cassius, "Among Our Colored Disciples," *CL* 16 (October 14, 1902): 4.

30. Cassius, "Among Our Colored Disciples," *CL* 16 (October 14, 1902): 4.

31. Cassius, "The Southern Christian Institute," *CL* 36 (October 17, 1922): 3.

32. Cassius, "The Southern Christian Institute," *CL* 36 (October 17, 1922): 3.

33. Cassius, "Looking Backward and Forward," *CL* 41 (December 27, 1927): 3. For a complete rendering of the poem, see "The Old Preacher," *CL* 50 (February 19, 1936): 6.

34. Cassius, "Among Our Colored Disciples," *CL* 17 (May 5, 1903): 2.

35. Cassius, "Among Our Colored Disciples," *CL* 17 (May 5, 1903): 2. See also Jon Michael Spencer, *Black Hymnody: A Hymnological History of the African-American Church* (Knoxville: University of Tennessee Press, 1992), 66–67.

36. Cassius, "Thanksgiving," *CL* 36 (December 5, 1922): 16. See also Eileen Southern, *The Music of Black Americans: A History* (1971; repr., New York: W. W. Norton, 1983), 450–51; and Gwendolin Sims Warren, *Ev'ry Time I Feel the Spirit: 101 Best-Loved Psalms, Gospel Hymns, and Spiritual Songs of the African-American Church* (1997; repr., New York: Henry Holt and Company, 1999), 106–7.

37. Cassius, "Watch Him Go," *CL* 41 (April 26, 1927): 16.

38. Cassius, "Lord, I Done Done," *CL* 43 (November 19, 1929): 16.

39. Cassius, "Lord, I Done Done," *CL* 43 (November 19, 1929): 16.

40. William J. Simmons, *Men of Mark: Eminent, Progressive, and Rising* (1887; repr., Chicago: Johnson Publishing Company, 1970), 3.

41. Cassius, *The Letter and Spirit* 30.

Chapter 4

1. Cassius, "Let Him Be unto Thee as a Heathen Man," *CL* 26 (April 9, 1912): 3.

2. Cassius, "It Pays to Be a Man," *CL* 34 (April 6, 1920): 13.

3. Harrell, *Quest* 26–27; Hughes 275. For more details, see M. Eugene Boring, *Disciples and the Bible: A History of Disciples Biblical Interpretation in North America* (St. Louis, MO: Chalice Press, 1997); and Michael W. Casey, *The Battle over Hermeneutics in the Stone-Campbell Movement, 1800–1870* (Lewiston, NY: Edwin Mellen Press, 1998).

4. Hughes 287; Boring 69–79.

5. Cassius, "A Trip to the Golden Gate," *CL* 16 (August 12, 1902): 13.

6. Cassius, "A Trip to the Golden Gate," *CL* 16 (August 12, 1902): 13.

7. Cassius, "Among Our Colored Disciples," *CL* 17 (October 13, 1903): 13.

8. Cassius, *The Letter and Spirit* 28.

9. Cassius, "The Race Problem," *CL* 15 (March 19, 1901): 4.

10. Cassius, "The Race Problem," *CL* 15 (March 19, 1901): 4.

11. Cassius, "The Race Problem," *CL* 15 (February 12, 1901): 9.

12. Cassius, "The Race Problem," *CL* 15 (February 12, 1901): 4.

13. Cassius, "The Race Problem," *CL* 15 (February 12, 1901): 4.

14. Cain Hope Felder, ed., *Stony the Road We Trod: African American Biblical Interpretation* (Minneapolis, MN: Fortress Press, 1991), 27. For white exegetes' use of the Ruth narrative, see G. B. F. Hallock, "A Happy Choice," *CL* 34 (April 20, 1920): 3; and "Lessons from the Book of Ruth," *CL* 35 (August 16, 1921): 3. It is noteworthy that in 1930 the *Christian Leader* did make racial applications from the Book of Ruth. See "Lesson 5—Third Quarter: Naomi and Ruth (A Study in Racial Relationship)," *CL* 44 (July 15, 1930): 14–15. But its use was not Cassius-like.

15. Cassius, *The Letter and Spirit* 9.

16. Cassius, *The Letter and Spirit* 16–18; D. L. Ammons, "Field Reports," *CL* 15 (March 5, 1901): 12.

17. Cassius, "The Negro a Beast," *CL* 16 (January 7, 1902): 9. Cassius is referring to Charles Darwin's *On the Origin of Species*.

18. Cassius, *Third Birth* (2nd ed.) 72–74.

19. "Editorial," *Muskogee Cimeter* (May 4, 1905): 4; "Race Separation Helps," *Western Age* (May 28, 1909): 2; Lucius Henry Holsey, "Race Segregation," in

Stephen W. Angell and Anthony B. Pinn, eds., *Social Protest Thought in the African Methodist Episcopal Church, 1862–1939* (Knoxville: University of Tennessee Press, 2000): 69.

20. Compare Cassius, *Third Birth* (2nd ed.) 73, with Stuart O. Landry, "Rebuilding the Tower of Babel: A Study of Christianity and Segregation," Special Collections, Mitchell Memorial Library, Mississippi State University, 12. See also Carey Daniel's 1955 sermon "God: The Original Segregationist," which refers to the narrative in Genesis 11 (Center for Restoration Studies, Abilene Christian University, Abilene, Texas).

21. Cassius, *Third Birth* (2nd ed.) 72–74.

22. For Acts 20:35, see Cassius, "Among Our Colored Disciples," *CL* 16 (November 25, 1902): 3. For Ecclesiastes 11:1, see Cassius, "Cast Thy Bread upon the Waters," *CL* 16 (November 18, 1902): 4. For Galatians 6:7, see Cassius, "The Race Problem," *CL* 18 (March 15, 1904): 2.

23. Cassius, "The Race Problem," *CL* 15 (April 30, 1901): 13. The notion that God used natural catastrophes to chasten white oppressors in America was prevalent in black racial thought. In 1907, the *Oklahoma Guide* noted, "The people of Norman got gay and said no Negro should stop in Norman over night, and the Lord got on the wind and clouds, passed through Norman dealing out destruction." White inhabitants of Snyder, Oklahoma Territory, similarly expelled African Americans from its community; thus, "the Lord sent a cyclone which dealt death and the destruction to Snyder and her Inhabitancies [*sic*]" (*Oklahoma Guide* [May 23, 1907]: 2).

24. Cassius, "Additional Acknowledgments," *CL* (December 17, 1901): 13.

25. Cassius, "Among Our Colored Disciples," *CL* 17 (December 8, 1903): 13.

26. Cassius, "Lonesome," *CL* 21 (June 4, 1907): 12.

27. Cassius, "Thankfulness," *CL* 31 (November 20, 1917): 4.

28. Cassius, "Giving Thanks," *CL* 35 (November 15, 1921): 8.

29. Cassius, "Negro Evangelization," in J. J. Limerick, ed., *The Gospel in Chart and Sermon* (Cincinnati, OH: John F. Rowe, 1897), 203–4.

30. Cassius, "Negro Evangelization," in J. J. Limerick, ed., *The Gospel in Chart and Sermon* (Cincinnati, OH: John F. Rowe, 1897), 206.

31. D. M. Oliser and P. W. Adams, "What the People Think of the Book, 'Gospel in Chart and Sermon,'" *CL* 11 (September 7, 1897): 10.

32. Douglass 75.

33. Cassius, "Behold I Make All Things New," *CL* 15 (April 9, 1901): 9.

34. Cassius, "Among Our Colored Disciples," *CL* 17 (October 6, 1903): 13.

35. Cassius, "Unity," in F. L. Rowe, *Our Savior's Prayer for Unity: A Symposium on the Seventeenth Chapter of John* (Cincinnati, OH: F. L. Rowe, 1918), 29–30.

36. Hughes 173. Stone-Campbell devotees inherited and modified the "five

finger exercise" from Walter Scott, who used a six-point plan to attract people to his meetings in the Western Reserve.

37. Cassius, "Among Our Colored Disciples," *CL* 15 (April 9, 1901): 9.

38. Cassius, "God and Water," *CL* 17 (November 10, 1903): 4. There are no known extant copies of Cassius's pamphlet "Faith, Repentance, Confession and Baptism."

39. J. H. D. Tomson, "Queries," *Christian Leader and the Way* 26 (May 21, 1912): 2–3. The term "loyal" referred to people in the Stone-Campbell Movement who sided with noninstrumental Churches of Christ; the terms "disloyal" and "digressive" referred to people who sided with pro–missionary society and pro–instrumental music Disciples of Christ and/or Christian Church.

40. The quotations in this paragraph are from Cassius, "The Seventh Day, the Lord's Day, Rest and Worship," *Christian Leader and the Way* 27 (April 29, 1913): 3. See also Francis M. Turner, "A Chat with a Seventh-Day Adventist," *Christian Leader and the Way* 27 (January 28, 1913): 1.

41. Cassius, "No Room in the Inn," *CL* 36 (December 19, 1922): 6.

42. Cassius, "No Room in the Inn," *CL* 36 (December 19, 1922): 6.

43. Cassius, "No Room in the Inn," *CL* 36 (December 19, 1922): 6.

44. Theo Delong, "No Room in the Inn," *CL* 37 (January 9, 1923): 16.

45. Frederick L. Rowe, "No Room in the Inn," *CL* 37 (January 9, 1923): 16.

46. Cassius, "No Room in the Inn," *CL* 37 (January 23, 1923): 10.

47. Margaret Sanger, *Margaret Sanger: An Autobiography* (New York: W. W. Norton, 1938), 106–20.

48. Margaret Sanger, *Happiness in Marriage* (1926; repr., New York: Blue Ribbon Books, 1940), 194.

49. Cassius, "No Room in the Inn," *CL* 37 (January 23, 1923): 10; Homer H. Adamson, "Babes and Negroes," *CL* 37 (January 16, 1923): 2.

50. Cassius, "The Seventh Day," *CL* 27 (April 29, 1913): 3; Cassius, "The Church of Christ and the Negro," *CL* 33 (February 8, 1916): 7.

51. Cassius, "The Great Commission," *CL* 44 (December 2, 1930): 3.

52. In 1868, the white-controlled Georgia state legislature expelled Henry M. Turner and other black members. In response to their expulsion, Turner gave an impassioned address. See Edwin S. Redkey, ed., *Respect Black: The Writings and Speeches of Henry McNeal Turner* (New York: Arno Press, 1971), 14–28. Cassius raised similar questions in "Thanksgiving," *CL* 36 (December 5, 1922): 16.

Chapter 5

1. Cassius, "The Race Problem," *CL* 15 (April 30, 1901): 13; Cassius, "The Race Problem," *CL* 15 (September 3, 1901): 15.

2. Joel Williamson, *A Rage for Order: Black/White Relations in the American South since Emancipation* (New York: Oxford University Press, 1986), 70–80. See also C. Vann Woodward's useful chapter 2 in *The Strange Career of Jim Crow* (1955; repr., New York: Oxford University Press, 1966), 31–65.

3. David Lipscomb, "The Freedmen—Their Condition," *Gospel Advocate* 10 (1868): 199. Lipscomb's racial thought of black retrogression into barbarianism was consistent with other prevailing racial theories. Philip A. Bruce (1856–1933), a Southern intellectual aristocrat in Virginia and a racial radical, similarly argued that the emancipation of slaves led to their moral deterioration (Bruce, *The Plantation Negro as a Freeman: Observations on His Character, Condition, and Prospects in Virginia* [1889; repr., Williamstown, MA: Corner House Publishers, 1970], 129, 165). Social Darwinists further propounded a similar notion of black extinction because of emancipation. See Frederick L. Hoffman, *Race Traits and Tendencies of the American Negro* (New York: Macmillan Company, 1896); and George M. Fredrickson, *The Black Image in the White Mind: The Debate on Afro-American Character and Destiny, 1817–1914* (New York: Harper and Row, 1971).

4. William K. Pendleton, "The Great Want of the Colored People," *Millennial Harbinger* 40 (1869): 171.

5. David Lipscomb, "Race Prejudice," *Gospel Advocate* 20 (1878): 120–21.

6. David Lipscomb, "The Negro in the Worship—A Correspondence," *Gospel Advocate* 49 (July 4, 1907): 425; Robert E. Hooper, *Crying in the Wilderness: A Biography of David Lipscomb* (Nashville, TN: David Lipscomb College, 1979), 11, 104.

7. E. A. Elam, "The Negro in the Worship," *Gospel Advocate* 49 (July 4, 1907): 424.

8. Lipscomb, "The Negro in the Worship," *Gospel Advocate* 49 (July 4, 1907): 425. See also Lipscomb, "Teaching the Colored People," *Gospel Advocate* 16 (1874): 283.

9. Cassius, "A Colored Brother's Protest," *Christian Evangelist* (November 14, 1889): 726. For more on J. W. Jenkins's appointment to superintendent of the Board of Negro Education and Evangelization, see Clayton Cheyney Smith, "Our Work among the Colored People," *Christian Evangelist* 36 (April 20, 1899): 490; and Harrell, *Social Sources* 177.

10. Cassius, "A Colored Brother's Protest," 726. Garrison replied to Cassius in the same article.

11. Clayton Cheyney Smith, "What Claim Has the Negro upon Us?" *Christian Evangelist* 30 (January 5, 1893): 12.

12. Clayton Cheyney Smith, "What Claim Has the Negro upon Us?" *Christian Evangelist* 30 (January 5, 1893): 12.

13. Cassius, "Our Colored Disciples," *CL* 10 (January 21, 1896): 13.

14. John M. McCaleb, "Japan Letter—A Plea for the Colored Man," *Christian Leader and the Way* 21 (January 1, 1907): 2.

15. John M. McCaleb, "Japan Letter—How to Reach the Colored Man," *Christian Leader and the Way* 21 (September 3, 1907): 3.

16. John M. McCaleb, "Japan Letter—How to Reach the Colored Man," *Christian Leader and the Way* 21 (September 3, 1907): 3.

17. John M. McCaleb, "Japan Letter—How to Reach the Colored Man," *Christian Leader and the Way* 21 (September 3, 1907): 3; Leon F. Litwack, *Trouble in Mind: Black Southerners in the Age of Jim Crow* (New York: Vintage Books, 1998), 198.

18. John M. McCaleb, "Japan Letter—How to Reach the Colored Man," *Christian Leader and the Way* 21 (September 3, 1907): 2.

19. W. J. Cash, *The Mind of the South* (New York: Alfred A. Knopf, 1941), 114–17. The occasion of Booker T. Washington dining in the White House with President Theodore Roosevelt in 1901 offers an instructive example of how pervasive the "Southern rape complex" was in the New South. White Southerners interpreted the Washington-Roosevelt meeting as black advancement against white womanhood, the perpetuator of white supremacy. "The President," the *Richmond Times* decried, "is willing that negroes shall mingle freely with whites in the social circle—that white women may receive attentions from negro men; it means that there is no racial reason in his opinion why whites and blacks may not marry and intermarry, why the Anglo-Saxon may not mix negro blood with his blood" (quoted in H. W. Brands, *T. R.: The Last Romantic* [New York: Basic Books, 1997], 423). The *Greenwood Commonwealth* published a derisive poem entitled "Niggers in the White House." A stanza of the poem went:

I see a way to settle it,
Just as clear as water—
Let Mr. Booker T. Washington
Marry Teddy's daughter. ("Niggers in the White House," *Greenwood Commonwealth* [January 31, 1903]: 2)

See also Willard B. Gatewood, Jr., *Theodore Roosevelt and the Art of Controversy: Episodes of the White House Years* (Baton Rouge: Louisiana State University Press, 1970), 32–61.

20. Cassius, "The Great Commission," *CL* 44 (December 2, 1930): 3. David Edwin Harrell has brilliantly shown that white leaders in the Stone-Campbell Movement vigorously opposed "social equality" (*Social Sources* 204–5). Furthermore, "Banco's Ghost" is a reference to the ghost of Banquo in William Shakespeare's *Macbeth,* which Cassius likely read. Macbeth and Banquo, servants of

the king of Scotland, became bitter rivals for the king's throne. The former conspired and murdered the latter. After the slaughter of Banquo, his ghost appeared before Macbeth at the banquet table and struck fear and guilt in Macbeth's heart. In similar fashion, Banquo's ghost of social equality frightened white Christians away from the black man in the United States. For rhetorical uses of Banquo's ghost contemporary with Cassius, see "Springfield Boy Lead[s] Mob," *Boley Progress* (April 16, 1906): 1; and Henry N. Paul, *The Royal Play of Macbeth: When, Why, and How It Was Written by Shakespeare* (New York: Octagon Books, 1971), 410.

21. Cassius, "Acknowledgments," *CL* 13 (May 16, 1899): 5. See also Litwack, *Trouble in Mind* 280–81. A detailed examination of the brutal execution of Sam Hose is offered by Mary Louise Ellis, "'Rain Down Fire': The Lynching of Sam Hose" (PhD diss., Florida State University, 1992).

22. David Lipscomb, "The Negro—His Crimes and Treatment," *Gospel Advocate* (1901): 600.

23. David Lipscomb, "The Negro—His Crimes and Treatment," *Gospel Advocate* (1901): 600.

24. Cassius, "The Negro a Beast," *CL* 16 (January 7, 1902): 9. Jonah 3:8 was one of the biblical references used by the unidentified woman.

25. Cassius, *The Letter and Spirit* 28.

26. D. L. Ammons, "Field Reports," *CL* 15 (March 5, 1901): 12.

27. Harrell, *Social Sources* 204–5.

28. Cassius, "Our Colored Disciples," *CL* 10 (January 21, 1896): 13.

29. Cassius, "Negro Evangelization," *CL* 10 (May 5, 1896): 7; Cassius, "Our Colored Disciples," *CL* 10 (May 19, 1896): 12.

30. Cassius, "Negro Evangelization," *CL* 10 (June 23, 1896): 12–13.

31. Cassius, "Our Opportunity," *CL* 11 (March 23, 1897): 4.

32. Cassius, "Acknowledgments," *CL* 11 (June 15, 1897): 5.

33. Cassius, "My Position on All Questions of Fellowship," *CL* 11 (September 21, 1897): 4.

34. Homer E. Moore, "Moore vs. Cassius," *CL* 11 (October 19, 1897): 12–13.

35. Cassius, "Moore vs. Cassius," *CL* 11 (October 19, 1897): 12–13.

36. Cassius, "Among Our Colored Disciples," *CL* 16 (November 25, 1902): 3.

37. Cassius, "Adrift," *CL* 16 (December 30, 1902): 4–5.

38. Cassius, "Adrift," *CL* 16 (December 30, 1902): 4–5.

39. Cassius, "Adrift," *CL* 16 (December 30, 1902): 4–5.

40. Cassius, "The Annual Meeting of the Oklahoma Colored Disciples," *Christian Leader and the Way* 23 (August 24, 1909): 13.

41. Cassius, "Negro Evangelization," *Christian Standard* (January 15, 1916): 30–31. For a good and thorough treatment of the missionary society controversy

in the nineteenth century, see Bill Humble, "The Missionary Society Controversy in the Restoration Movement, 1823–1875" (PhD diss., University of Iowa, 1964).

42. Cassius, "The Right Man in the Right Place," *Christian Companion* 23 (September 14, 1916): 2.

43. Cassius, "The Right Man in the Right Place," *Christian Companion* 23 (September 14, 1916): 2.

44. Cassius, "Among Our Colored Disciples," *Christian Companion* 22 (October 7, 1915): 4–5; Harrell, *Social Sources* 207.

45. Harrell, *Social Sources* 207; Cassius, "A Colored Brother's Tribute," *Gospel Advocate* 59 (December 6, 1917): 1189.

Chapter 6

1. Cassius, "Among Our Colored Disciples," *Christian Leader and the Way* 23 (January 19, 1909): 12.

2. Cassius, "Among Our Colored Disciples," *CL* 10 (October 27, 1896): 5. Theodore Roosevelt, alarmed by the declining birthrate among white college-trained women who limited the number of children they had, popularized the terminology "race suicide" in 1905. See Roosevelt, "The Woman and the Home" [March 13, 1905] in Roosevelt, vol. 16 of *The Works of Theodore Roosevelt* (New York: Charles Scribner's Sons, 1926), 164.

3. Cassius often reported that he had twenty-three children. "I have never received a salary and have raised a family of 23 children, 12 of whom have obeyed the gospel" ("Bro. Cassius Queen Again," *CL* 44 [April 1, 1930]: 16). See also "Obituary," *CL* 45 (September 29, 1931): 13–14.

4. United States Census of Oklahoma, 1900, 1910, 1920, Guthrie, Oklahoma, County Clerk's Office, Logan County, Oklahoma. I am thankful to Bob Chada and Don Haymes for helping me unearth this data. For a record of the death of Cassius's son, see Cassius, "Among Our Colored Disciples," *CL* 15 (August 20, 1901): 12–13.

5. Cassius, "After Thirty-Two Years," *CL* 36 (September 19, 1922): 8.

6. *Western Age* (May 15, 1908): 2.

7. Cassius, "Among Our Colored Disciples," *CL* 28 (October 6, 1914): 13; Cassius, "Among Our Colored Disciples," *CL* 30 (November 14, 1916): 13.

8. Cassius, "Among Our Colored Disciples," *CL* 32 (July 16, 1918): 8; Cassius, "The Race Problem and the War," *CL* 32 (August 13, 1918): 8.

9. William T. Milligan, "In Memory of A. L. Cassius," *Christian Echo* (April 19, 1983): 4. For record of Amos Lincoln Cassius's matriculation at Tuskegee Institute, see Student Records, 1909–10, Office of the Registrar, Tuskegee Institute, Tuskegee, Alabama.

10. Linda O. McMurry, *George Washington Carver: Scientist and Symbol* (New York: Oxford University Press, 1981), 90.

11. Milligan, "In Memory of A. L. Cassius," *Christian Echo* (April 19, 1983): 4. For more biographical information on Amos Lincoln Cassius, see Bowers 129–37 and Frank Pack, "Amos Lincoln Cassius: Pioneer Black Leader," *Discipliana* 43 (summer 1983): 29.

12. Cassius, "Among Our Colored Disciples," *CL* 32 (May 7, 1918): 13; Cassius, "Looking Backward," *CL* 44 (January 28, 1930): 16.

13. Cassius, "Among Our Colored Disciples," *CL* 11 (December 14, 1897): 12.

14. Cassius, "Among Our Colored Disciples," *CL* 16 (October 14, 1902): 4.

15. Cassius, "Acknowledgments," *CL* 17 (August 18, 1903): 5; Cassius, "Field Reports," *Christian Leader and the Way* 18 (May 3, 1904): 12; Cassius, "Field Reports," *Christian Leader and the Way* 20 (January 9, 1906): 12–13; Cassius, "Acknowledgments," *Christian Leader and the Way* 21 (March 19, 1907): 13.

16. Cassius, "Lonesome," *Christian Leader and the Way* 21 (June 4, 1907): 12; Cassius, "There Is Nothing to It," *Christian Leader and the Way* 24 (May 31, 1910): 13; Cassius, "Among Our Colored Disciples," *Christian Leader and the Way* 24 (December 6, 1910): 13.

17. Cassius, "Among Our Colored Disciples," *Christian Leader and the Way* 18 (April 5, 1904): 12–13; Cassius, "Among Our Colored Disciples," *Christian Leader and the Way* (October 24, 1905): 13; Cassius, "Acknowledgments," *Christian Leader and the Way* 27 (February 18, 1913): 13; Cassius, "Field Reports," *CL* 32 (February 12, 1918): 12; Cassius, "Acknowledgments," *CL* 32 (March 19, 1918): 13.

18. Cassius, "Among Our Colored Disciples," *Firm Foundation* 33 (March 21, 1916): 7; W. W. Thornberry, "Field Reports," *CL* 35 (September 27, 1921): 13; Cassius, "My Mission," *CL* 35 (November 22, 1921): 13; Cassius, "Field Reports," *CL* 37 (May 1, 1923): 11.

19. Cassius, "I Have Kept the Faith," *CL* 36 (October 31, 1922): 7.

20. Cassius, "Horse Neck," *CL* 34 (July 20, 1920): 13.

21. Cassius, "A Storm in Guthrie," *CL* 36 (June 6, 1922): 11.

22. Cassius, "What I Am Doing," *CL* 36 (June 13, 1922): 8.

23. Cassius, "Thanksgiving," *CL* 36 (December 5, 1922): 16.

24. Cassius, "Field Reports," *CL* 37 (May 8, 1923): 11; Cassius, "An Unusual Sight," *CL* 37 (May 15, 1923): 16.

25. Cassius, "Field Reports," *CL* 37 (May 22, 1923): 11; Cassius, "My Meeting at No. 7 Coal Mine," *CL* 37 (May 29, 1923): 12; Cassius, "The World, the Flesh and the Devil," *CL* 37 (June 19, 1923): 3; Cassius, "Bro. Cassius Is Thankful," *CL* 41 (October 4, 1927): 16.

26. Cassius, "I Have Wondered," *CL* 30 (September 19, 1916): 6; Cassius, "Acknowledgments," *CL* (February 27, 1917): 16.

27. Cassius, "Being Led of the Spirit," *CL* 38 (October 14, 1924): 12.

28. Cassius, "The Church of Christ in Oakland," *CL* 38 (October 21, 1924): 12.

29. Cassius, "I Have Kept the Faith," *CL* 36 (January 31, 1922): 3; Cassius, "Bro. Cassius Is Thankful," *CL* (October 4, 1927): 16.

30. Cassius, "My Trip to the East," *CL* 36 (June 20, 1922): 16. West correctly observes that evangelists realized that "not to give these [detailed financial reports] would cast suspicion on their integrity and damage their support" (3:309).

31. Cassius, "Do We Know, or Do We Care," *CL* 38 (February 26, 1924): 16.

32. Cassius, "Among Our Colored Disciples," *Christian Leader and the Way* 21 (September 24, 1907): 13; Cassius, "There Is Nothing to It," *Christian Leader and the Way* 24 (May 31, 1910): 13; Cassius, "Thanksgiving," *CL* 36 (December 5, 1922): 16; Cassius, "What Will the Harvest Be?" *CL* 44 (April 15, 1930): 16.

33. M. D. B., "Clippings and Comments," *CL* 35 (February 22, 1921): 5; West 3:48.

Chapter 7

1. James H. Garrison, "Indianapolis Convention," *Christian Evangelist* 34 (October 28, 1897): 674. See also Harrell, *Social Sources* 179.

2. Joel Williamson, *Crucible of Race: Black/White Relations in the American South since Emancipation* (New York: Oxford University Press, 1984), 71. James H. Garrison, "Our Budget," *Christian Evangelist* 34 (December 16, 1897): 788.

Other Stone-Campbell Movement journals lavished praise on Booker T. Washington. In 1899, J. W. Shepherd highly commended Washington's book *The Future of the American Negro*. Shepherd applauded Washington, who emphasized that black Americans should be trained in the industrial arts. "The author is doing a good work for his people," Shepherd explained, "and certainly should have the sympathy and support of all right-thinking people of all sections" (Shepherd, "Book Reviews," *Gospel Advocate* 41 [December 14, 1899]: 798). The *Christian Leader* often published Sunday-evening talks Washington gave to Tuskegee students, and it sometimes delineated the impressive growth of the school in Alabama. See Booker T. Washington, "Look Ahead!" *CL* 16 (January 21, 1902): 7; "General News," *CL* 17 (January 13, 1903): 16; and "The Modern Washington," *CL* 17 (February 17, 1903): 10.

3. Quoted in Choate 21; Tuggle, *Another World Wonder* (n.p., n.d.), 104; R. Vernon Boyd, *Undying Dedication: The Story of G. P. Bowser* (Nashville: Gospel Advocate Company, 1985).

4. Cassius, "Looking Backward," *CL* 29 (December 14, 1915): 4.

5. Cassius, *Negro Evangelization* 8. Washington received an honorary master's degree from Harvard University in 1896.

6. Reproduced in Booker T. Washington, *Up from Slavery* 128. For Wells's brief tenure as leader of African Americans after the death of Douglass, see Linda O. McMurry, *To Keep the Waters Troubled: The Life of Ida B. Wells* (New York: Oxford University Press, 1998), 233.

7. Quoted in Washington, *Up from Slavery* 129, 131; C. Vann Woodward, *Origins of the New South, 1877–1913* (1951; repr., Baton Rouge: Louisiana State University Press, 1997), 356. For more on the significance of Washington's racial views, see Rayford W. Logan, *The Betrayal of the Negro: From Rutherford B. Hayes to Woodrow Wilson* (1965; repr., New York: Da Capo Press, 1997), 280; and Williamson 63.

8. Cassius, "An Appreciation of Booker T. Washington," *Gospel Advocate* (December 23, 1915): 1302.

9. Booker T. Washington, "Boley, A Negro Town in the West," *Outlook* 88 (January 4, 1907): 31.

10. Cassius, "An Appreciation of Booker T. Washington," *Gospel Advocate* (December 23, 1915): 1302.

11. Cassius, "The Race Problem," *CL* 17 (March 10, 1903): 9.

12. Cassius, "Save the American Negro," *Gospel Advocate* 57 (December 2, 1915): 1226.

13. Cassius, "The Great Commission," *CL* 45 (December 2, 1930): 3.

14. Cassius, "The Race Problem," *CL* 17 (March 10, 1903): 9.

15. Cassius, "The Great Commission," *CL* 45 (December 2, 1930): 3.

16. For Cassius's announcement about his Tohee Industrial School, see Cassius, *Negro Evangelization* 15–16. For more information, see Joseph E. Cain, "Occasional Notes," *CL* 14 (August 28, 1900): 8–9.

17. Cassius, *Negro Evangelization* 14.

18. For Washington's speech in Guthrie, Oklahoma, see "Dr. Washington's Address," *Boley Progress* (November 30, 1905): 6; see also "Extracts from Booker T. Washington's Speech," *Western Age* (November 24, 1905): 1.

19. Cassius, "Catholicism or Christ," *CL* 10 (May 26, 1896): 13.

20. Cassius, "Catholicism or Christ," *CL* 11 (August 3, 1897): 15.

21. Cassius, "Catholicism or Christ," *CL* 11 (August 3, 1897): 5. For a good treatment of the Catholic presence in Oklahoma, see Thomas Elton Brown, "Bible-Belt Catholicism: A History of the Roman Catholic Church in Oklahoma, 1905–1945" (PhD diss., Oklahoma State University, 1974), 36–37. Brown's study shows that by 1916, Catholics in Oklahoma had established approximately fifty-one private and parochial schools and educated approximately 5,500 students. In the same year, more children were enrolled in Catholic schools than in all other religious and private schools in Oklahoma. Hence, Cassius's concerns about Catholic hegemony in Oklahoma were legitimate.

22. Cassius, "Catholicism or Christ," *CL* 10 (May 26, 1896): 15; Cassius, *Negro*

Evangelization 15. One of the more influential Catholic bishops in the Twin Territories of Oklahoma was Theophile Meerschaert (1847–1924). "Appointed in 1891 at the age of forty-four, he was Oklahoma's Catholic bishop until his death in 1924. In this thirty-two year period the number of parishes with resident pastors grew from 11 statewide to 71; churches and chapels from 21 to 169; schools from 11 to 54; diocesan priests from 2 to 68; and Catholic laity from about 5,000 to over 57,000" (James D. White, "Destined for Duty: The Life and Diary of Bishop Theophile Meerschaert," *Chronicles of Oklahoma* 71 (spring 1993): 5.

23. "Negro Nuns of New Orleans," *Western Age* (October 27, 1905): 1.

24. "The Catholic Church and the Negro," *Western Age* (April 20, 1906): 4.

25. "The Catholic Church," *Western Age* (May 11, 1906): 1. For more references of black newspapers in Oklahoma to the Catholic Church, see "Catholic Church Invited Negro Members," *Oklahoma Guide* (January 3, 1907): 1; "A Negro Priest," *Western Age* (October 4, 1907): 4; and "Boston Negro Catholics," *Western Age* (March 27, 1908): 2.

26. Cassius, "The Use and Abuse of the Religious Press," *CL* 11 (April 27, 1897): 13.

27. Cassius, "Among Our Colored Disciples," *CL* 11 (October 28, 1897): 13. For Cassius's attempt to sell vegetable seeds, see Cassius, "The Tohee Industrial School," *CL* 13 (February 28, 1899): 13. Regrettably, no known extant copies of Cassius's paper, the *Industrial Christian,* exist.

28. Cassius, "S. R. Cassius and the Industrial School," *CL* 11 (July 20, 1897): 12.

29. Cassius, "Among Our Colored Disciples," *CL* 11 (December 14, 1897): 12.

30. For Etta Duke's letter to Cassius, see Cassius, "Tohee Industrial School," *CL* 12 (August 23, 1898): 5.

31. Joseph E. Cain, "Occasional Notes," *CL* 11 (January 12, 1897): 5.

32. Cassius, "Among Our Colored Disciples," *CL* 11 (December 14, 1897): 12.

33. Cassius, "Acknowledgments," *CL* 13 (May 23, 1899): 12.

34. Cassius, "Acknowledgments," *CL* 13 (August 15, 1899): 5.

35. Quoted in Cassius, "The Tohee Industrial School," *CL* 13 (August 15, 1899): 13.

36. Quoted in Cassius, "The Tohee Industrial School," *CL* 13 (August 15, 1899): 13.

37. Cassius, "Monthly Report of the Tohee Industrial School," *CL* 13 (September 12, 1899): 12; Cassius, "Second Monthly Report of the Tohee Industrial School," *CL* 13 (October 17, 1899): 13.

38. Cassius, "Looking Backward," *CL* 14 (January 9, 1900): 13; Cassius, "Field Reports," *CL* 15 (June 4, 1901): 12–13.

39. Cassius, "Behold I Make All Things New," *CL* 15 (April 9, 1901): 8–9.

40. Cassius, "Among Our Colored Disciples," *CL* 17 (December 8, 1903): 13.

There is no evidence that Cassius's school and paper influenced the emergence of Langston University.

41. Cassius, "Acknowledgments," *CL* 16 (April 15, 1902): 5. See also Hannibal B. Johnson, *Acres of Aspiration: The All-Black Towns in Oklahoma* (Austin, TX: Eakin Press, 2002), 111–12.

42. Louis R. Harlan, "The Secret Life of Booker T. Washington," *Journal of Southern History* 37 (August 1971): 393–416. See also Harlan, *Booker T. Washington: The Wizard of Tuskegee, 1901–1915* (New York: Oxford University Press, 1983), 248.

43. Cassius, "Among Our Colored Disciples," *CL* 17 (October 27, 1903): 5. Cassius was angry when he made this statement. He was upset that his congregation at Springvale gave the visiting preacher "more in one or two weeks than we had received in all these years."

44. Cassius, "An Appreciation of Booker T. Washington," *Gospel Advocate* (December 23, 1915): 1303; Cassius, "Looking Backward," *CL* 14 (January 9, 1900): 4.

45. Cassius, "Looking Backward," *CL* 14 (January 9, 1900): 4.

Chapter 8

1. For Cassius's statement, see Cassius, "Behold I Make All Things New," *Christian Leader* 15 (April 9, 1901): 8. For advertisements about the Oklahoma Territory, see *Langston City Herald* (December 19, 1891): 1–2; *Langston City Herald* (February 6, 1892): 3; *Langston City Herald* (October 8, 1892): 1. For more insight into the black experience in Oklahoma, see also Kaye M. Teall, *Black History in Oklahoma: A Resource Book* (Oklahoma City: Oklahoma City Public Schools, 1971), 150–58; and Jimmie Lewis Franklin, *Journey toward Hope: A History of Blacks in Oklahoma* (Norman: University of Oklahoma Press, 1982).

2. "To Make a Negro State," *New York Times* (February 28, 1890): 1. In 1973, Jere W. Roberson questioned whether Edward P. McCabe really intended to create a separate state for blacks in Oklahoma: "It seems doubtful that McCabe planned to create a black state out of the Oklahoma Territory. There simply was no way to move enough black votes into the area." See Roberson, "Edward P. McCabe and the Langston Experiment," *Chronicles of Oklahoma* (fall 1973): 355.

3. Joseph Taylor, "The Rise and Decline of a Utopian Community, Boley, Oklahoma," *Negro History Bulletin* (April 1940): 92–93; Mozell C. Hill, "The All-Negro Society in Oklahoma" (PhD diss., University of Chicago, 1946), 28, 160; Meier 63; John Hope Franklin and John Whittington Franklin, eds., *My Life and an Era: The Autobiography of Buck Colbert Franklin* (Baton Rouge: Louisiana State University Press, 1997), xviii.

4. Arthur L. Tolson, *The Black Oklahomans: A History, 1541–1972* (1966; repr., New Orleans, LA: Edwards Printing Company, 1974), 68–89; Edwin S. Redkey,

Black Exodus: Black Nationalist and Back-to-Africa Movements, 1890–1910 (New Haven, CT: Yale University Press, 1969), 100; William Loren Katz, *The Black West* (New York: Doubleday and Company, 1971), 249–50.

5. Booker T. Washington, "Boley, A Negro Town in the West," *Outlook* (January 4, 1908): 31. For sources that attribute Oklahoma's black influx to a host of different issues, see Kenneth Marvin Hamilton, "Black Town Promotion and Development on the Middle Border, 1877–1914" (PhD diss., Washington University, 1978), 202; Norman L. Crockett, *The Black Towns* (Lawrence: Regents Press of Kansas, 1979), 47; and Johnson 33–75.

6. Cassius, "Colored Missions in Oklahoma," *Christian Evangelist* (December 7, 1893): 772; Cassius, "Among Our Colored Disciples," *CL* 10 (September 29, 1896): 12; Cassius, "Among Our Colored Disciples," *CL* 10 (October 27, 1896): 5. Formerly known as Jackson in Logan County, Oklahoma, Tohee was named for a renowned Iowa Indian chief. See George H. Shirk, *Oklahoma Place Names* (Norman: University of Oklahoma Press, 1965), 207.

7. Cassius, "Among Our Colored Disciples," *CL* 10 (September 1, 1896): 12. The quotation by Booker T. Washington is from Washington, *Up from Slavery* 131.

8. Cassius, "The Recent Race Riots," *CL* 12 (December 13, 1898): 9; Cassius, "Boley, I. T.," *Christian Leader and the Way* 21 (October 15, 1907): 5.

9. Cassius, "Among Our Colored Disciples," *CL* 11 (October 26, 1897): 13.

10. Johnson 79.

11. Cassius, "Among Our Colored Disciples," *CL* 13 (December 12, 1899): 12.

12. Cassius, "Acknowledgments," *CL* 15 (May 14, 1901): 5; Cassius, "Among Our Colored Disciples," *CL* 17 (January 27, 1903): 5.

13. Cassius, "Apostolic Missions," *CL* 17 (November 24, 1903): 5.

14. Cassius, "Acknowledgments," *CL* 17 (December 15, 1903): 13.

15. Cassius, "Acknowledgments," *Christian Leader and the Way* 19 (March 14, 1905): 13.

16. Cassius, "Among Our Colored Disciples," *Christian Leader and the Way* 21 (September 24, 1907): 13.

17. Cassius, "I Had to Do It," *CL* 33 (May 20, 1919): 12.

18. For information on the creation of the Negro Protective League, see George N. Perkins, "Single Statehood," *Oklahoma Guide* (August 31, 1905): 1. For Cassius's involvement in the Negro Protective League, see Stephen D. Russell, "Langston Notes," *Western Age* (June 21, 1907): 3. In 1904, Stephen D. Russell organized the *Western Age* in Langston, an early all-black town in Oklahoma. Similarly, George N. Perkins purchased the *Oklahoma Guide* in the early 1900s to promote civil rights for African Americans. Cassius knew and worked with both of these black leaders. For biographical sketches on Russell and Perkins, see Nudie E. Williams, "They Fought for Votes: The White Politician and the Black Editor,"

Chronicles of Oklahoma 64 (spring 1986): 19–35; and Nudie E. Williams, "The African Lion: George Napier Perkins, Lawyer, Politician, Editor," *Chronicles of Oklahoma* 70 (winter 1993): 450–65.

19. George N. Perkins, "Against Statehood," *Oklahoma Guide* (October 6, 1904): 1; George N. Perkins, "Editorial," *Oklahoma Guide* (October 10, 1907): 2. For the creation of the Blaine County Colored Protective League, see *Muskogee Cimeter* (May 10, 1907): 1; and *Oklahoma Guide* (October 10, 1907): 2.

20. James R. Scales and Danney Goble, *Oklahoma Politics: A History* (Norman: University of Oklahoma Press, 1982), 36. For expressions of black Oklahomans' worries about the passage of Jim Crow legislation, see "The Political Issues," *Oklahoma Safeguard* (December 20, 1906): 1. Historian Charles A. Beard has rendered the best contemporary exposition of the Oklahoma constitution (Beard, "The Constitution of Oklahoma," *Political Science Quarterly* 24 [1909]: 104). Scholar Irvin Hurst has insightfully noted that all of the 112 framers of Oklahoma's constitution were white males, most of them were Democrats, and 75 of them came from Southern states and transported their Southern racial views to the newest state (Hurst, *The 46th Star: A History of Oklahoma's Constitutional Convention and Early Statehood* [Oklahoma City, OK: Semco Color Press, 1957], 8). See also Philip Mellinger, "Discrimination and Statehood in Oklahoma," *Chronicles of Oklahoma* 49 (1971): 367.

21. Cassius, "Jim Crow as I Saw It," *Western Age* (February 28, 1908): 4.

22. Cassius, "Jim Crow as I Saw It," *Western Age* (February 28, 1908): 4.

23. Cassius, *Third Birth* (2nd ed.) 96–103.

24. Cassius, "Out on the Firing Line Again," *Christian Leader and the Way* 22 (September 1, 1908): 12.

25. Cassius, "Oklahoma City," *CL* 35 (December 13, 1921): 13.

26. Cassius, "Among Our Colored Disciples," *Christian Leader and the Way* 24 (August 30, 1910): 13.

27. "The Grandfather Clause in Oklahoma," *Outlook* (August 1910): 853–54.

28. Cassius, "Among Our Colored Disciples," *CL* 15 (August 20, 1901): 12.

29. Cassius, "An Urgent Case," *CL* 10 (May 12, 1896): 13; Cassius, "Among Our Colored Disciples," *CL* 17 (August 25, 1903): 12; and Cassius, "Acknowledgments," *Christian Leader and the Way* 18 (May 3, 1904): 12.

30. Cassius, "Acknowledgments," *CL* 15 (July 30, 1901): 5.

31. Cassius, "Acknowledgments," *Christian Leader and the Way* 19 (July 11, 1905): 13.

32. Cassius, "The Great Storm in Oklahoma," *Christian Leader and the Way* 22 (June 23, 1908): 13.

33. Cassius, "Among Our Colored Disciples," *CL* 15 (August 20, 1901): 13.

34. Cassius, "The Stafford Meeting," *CL* 35 (June 28, 1921): 13.

35. Cassius, "Bro. Cassius Burned Out," *CL* 19 (January 24, 1905): 5.

36. Cassius, "Bro. Cassius Burned Out," *CL* 19 (January 24, 1905): 5.

37. Cassius, "Acknowledgments," *Christian Leader and the Way* 19 (February 14, 1905): 13.

38. Cassius, "Tried in the Fire," *Christian Leader and the Way* 19 (February 28, 1905): 5.

39. Cassius, "Tried in the Fire," *Christian Leader and the Way* 19 (February 28, 1905): 5. For other references to prairie fires in Oklahoma and New Mexico, see "Prairie Fires in Oklahoma," *Mulhall Enterprises* (April 13, 1895): 4; John W. Harris, "Oklahoma," *CL* 10 (November 24, 1896): 13; and S. L. Barker, "Bro. Barker's Loss," *CL* 19 (March 28, 1905): 5. For a definition of "White Capping," see Williamson, *Rage for Order* 81–82.

40. Cassius, "Tried in the Fire," *Christian Leader and the Way* 19 (February 28, 1905): 5; J. C. Glover, "Jots," *Christian Leader and the Way* 19 (February 7, 1905): 5; H. A. Stigers, "Let Us Take Care of the Stuff at Home," *Christian Leader and the Way* 19 (March 7, 1905): 3. Interestingly, Stigers continued to display interest in assisting black evangelists as she generously contributed to the work of Richard N. Hogan (1902–97) in the 1940s (James L. Lovell, "Mrs. H. A. Stigers Never Fails to Preach Christ," *West Coast Christian* 4 [November 1941]: 3).

41. Stigers, "Let Us Take Care of the Stuff at Home," *Christian Leader and the Way* 19 (March 7, 1905): 3.

42. Cassius, "Tried in the Fire," *Christian Leader and the Way* 19 (March 21, 1905): 13.

43. Cassius, "A Statement from S. R. Cassius," *Christian Leader and the Way* 19 (May 2, 1905): 12.

44. Cassius, "Acknowledgments," *Christian Leader and the Way* 19 (May 16, 1905): 13.

45. Cassius, "Negro Arrested," *Christian Leader and the Way* 19 (July 25, 1905): 13. See also "Negro Pooh-Bah Arrested," *Kansas City [Weekly] Journal* (June 15, 1905): 1. This paper derisively referred to Cassius as a "Pooh-Bah" (one holding many public or private offices), stating, "Sheriff Murphy tonight arrested Jess Corsius [Samuel Robert Cassius], the negro postmaster at Tohee, who is charged with disposing of mortgaged property. Corsious is town trustee, township committeeman and a minister of the gospel." It is unclear whether Cassius was actually arrested.

46. Cassius, "A Storm in Guthrie," *CL* 36 (June 6, 1922): 11.

47. Cassius, "Acknowledgments," *CL* 13 (January 17, 1899): 5; Cassius, "The Passing of Tohee," *Christian Leader and the Way* 19 (December 25, 1905): 12. Cassius subsequently relocated from Tohee to Meridian, Oklahoma, where he lived from 1906 to 1916. From Meridian, Cassius moved to Guthrie until he left the state

in 1922. For documentation of Cassius's earnings as postmaster of Tohee, Oklahoma Territory, see *Official Registers of the United States, Record of Appointment of Postmasters*, National Archives, Washington, D.C.

48. Cassius, "Report of the Colored Mission Work," *CL* 37 (January 2, 1923): 2. For documentation of Cassius's property holdings, see Public Records in Logan County, Oklahoma [Guthrie, Oklahoma].

49. George N. Perkins, "Reign of Terror Exists," *Oklahoma Guide* (May 5, 1904): 1; *Oklahoma Guide* (July 7, 1904): 2; Cassius, "Among Our Colored Disciples," *Christian Leader and the Way* 18 (September 6, 1904): 13. In 1907, white citizens in Snyder ordered all African Americans "to leave Snyder and it is feared that a race war will result if the Negroes do not obey" ("Negroes Ordered out of Snyder," *Oklahoma Guide* [May 23, 1907]: 2). In 1910, the *Boley Progress* reported that blacks "are being driven from Dawson, after the shooting of a deputy sheriff by a negro" ("Oklahoma Happenings," *Boley Progress* [October 27, 1910]: 2).

50. Cassius, "Among Our Colored Disciples," *CL* 15 (October 8, 1901): 5.

51. Cassius, "Among Our Colored Disciples," *CL* 15 (November 19, 1901): 13.

52. Franklin, *Journey toward Hope* 33.

53. Cassius, "Acknowledgments," *CL* 17 (August 18, 1903): 5.

54. Cassius, "Guthrie, Oklahoma," *CL* 35 (February 15, 1921): 16. Cassius announced that he would leave Oklahoma in 1921, but he did not leave the state until 1922.

Chapter 9

1. It seems that Cassius actually produced three editions of *The Third Birth of a Nation:* first as a pamphlet (date unknown), second as a book (in 1920), third as a longer book (in 1925). For purposes of clarity, this chapter focuses on the 1925 publication. Cassius called his book *The Third Birth of a Nation* because the first birth of the nation took place in 1776 with the signing of the Declaration of Independence and the Revolutionary War. The second birth occurred on January 1, 1864 (or 1863), when Abraham Lincoln issued the Emancipation Proclamation. The third birth took place in 1915 when D. W. Griffith produced his controversial movie *Birth of a Nation.* In Cassius's mind, these three events had dramatic and devastating effects on race relations in the United States (Cassius, *Third Birth* [2nd ed.] 2, 7, 31, 34).

2. Cassius, *Third Birth* (2nd ed.) 3. For reference to Anthony Overton's impressive business enterprises, see Allan H. Spear, *Black Chicago: The Making of a Negro Ghetto, 1890–1920* (Chicago: University of Chicago Press, 1967), 113.

3. Jeffery P. Moran, "Reading Race into the Scopes Trial: African American Elites, Science, and Fundamentalism," *Journal of American History* 90 (December

2003): 891–911. For a thorough treatment of the Scopes Trial, see Edward J. Larson, *Summer for the Gods: The Scopes Trial and America's Continuing Debate over Science and Religion* (New York: Basic Books, 1997).

4. Cassius, "Among the Churches of Christ," *CL* 33 (October 14, 1919): 16.

5. Cassius, "The Colored Mission in Philadelphia," *CL* 36 (July 11, 1922): 8.

6. Cassius, "The Negro a Beast or in the Image of God," *CL* 17 (February 4, 1903): 5; Cassius, "The Race Problem," *CL* 18 (March 15, 1904): 2. See also Cassius, "A Colored Brother's Tribute," *Gospel Advocate* 59 (December 6, 1917): 1189.

7. Cassius, "Save the American Negro," *Gospel Advocate* (December 2, 1915): 1226–27.

8. Cassius, "The Race Problem and the War," *CL* 32 (August 13, 1918): 8.

9. Cassius, "The Third Birth of a Nation," *CL* 34 (May 11, 1920): 16.

10. Cassius, *Third Birth* (2nd ed.) 38–39.

11. Dion Boucicault, *The Octoroon or Life in Louisiana,* in Arthur Hobson Quinn, ed., *Representative American Plays* (New York: Century Company, 1919), 443. An "octoroon" was a woman with one-eighth of black blood in her veins.

12. Boucicault 443.

13. Cassius, *Third Birth* (2nd ed.) 39. Charles Carroll, *The Negro a Beast, or, in the Image of God* (1900; repr., Miami, FL: Mnemosyne Publishing Company, 1969), 45.

14. Cassius, *Third Birth* (2nd ed.) 39.

15. Carter Blue Clark, "A History of the Ku Klux Klan in Oklahoma" (PhD diss., University of Oklahoma, 1976), 37.

16. Lyman Abbott, "The Birth of a Nation," *Outlook* (April 14, 1915): 854.

17. Harlan, *Booker T. Washington: The Wizard* 431–35.

18. David Levering Lewis, *W. E. B. Du Bois: The Fight for Equality and the American Century, 1919–1963* (New York: Henry Holt and Company, 2000), 86–87.

19. Thomas R. Cripps, "The Reaction of the Negro to the Motion Picture Birth of a Nation," *Historian* 25 (February 1963): 344–62; Robert L. Zangrando, *The NAACP Crusade against Lynching, 1909–1950* (Philadelphia, PA: Temple University Press, 1980), 34–35. For significant biographical information on Thomas Dixon, Jr., a Baptist minister-turned-novelist, see Raymond Allen Cook, *Fire from the Flint: The Amazing Careers of Thomas Dixon* (Winston-Salem, NC: John F. Blair, 1968).

20. Cassius, *Third Birth* (2nd ed.) 38. It is noteworthy that Kelly Miller (1863–1939), an African American educator at Howard University in Washington, D.C., presaged Cassius's assessment of Dixon's inflammatory literature by fifteen years, stating, "You [Thomas Dixon, Jr.] poison the mind and pollute the imagination through the subtle influence of literature." "Race hatred," Miller asserted, "is the most malignant poison that can afflict the mind" (Miller, "As to the Leopard's

Spots: An Open Letter to Thomas Dixon, Jr.," in *Race Adjustment: Essays on the Negro in America* [1905; repr., New York, NY: Neale Publishing Company, 1910], 55, 57).

21. Wells, *Crusade for Justice: The Autobiography of Ida B. Wells,* ed. Alfreda M. Duster (Chicago: University of Chicago Press, 1970), 64. As early as 1898, Cassius had detected that many white Americans plotted to impede the material, political, and social progress of their black counterparts. "The only desire that possesses the white man's mind is to keep the negro down. Therefore everyone killed leaves one less to control" (Cassius, "The Recent Race Riots," *CL* 35 [December 13, 1898]: 5). Cassius's words "to keep the negro down" strikingly mirror those of Ida B. Wells, who used a similar phrase in response to the lynching of her close friend Tom Moss. Black newspapers in Oklahoma regularly published Wells's statements against lynching; thus, it is possible that Cassius borrowed the phrase from her. For Wells's assessment of Moss's lynching, see McMurry, *To Keep the Waters Troubled* 143.

22. Washington, *The Negro in Business* (1907; repr., New York: AMS Press, 1971), 3, 206. See also Washington, "Boley, A Negro Town in the West," *Outlook* 88 (January 4, 1907): 31. For African Americans' economic and cultural growth in the Progressive Era, see John Hope Franklin and Alfred A. Moss, Jr., *From Slavery to Freedom: A History of African Americans* (1947; repr., Boston: McGraw-Hill, 2000), 312–13.

23. George N. Perkins, "Town Without Law," *Oklahoma Guide* (September 22, 1904): 1; *Muskogee Cimeter* (March 9, 1904): 4; Scott Ellsworth, *Death in a Promised Land: The Tulsa Race Riot of 1921* (Baton Rouge: Louisiana State University Press, 1982), 16.

24. Cassius, "The American Negro," *CL* 34 (February 24, 1920): 6. For more on African American economic advancement, see "Advancing People," *CL* 34 (March 23, 1920): 7.

25. Cassius, *Third Birth* (2nd ed.) 34, 85, 91.

26. Cassius, *Third Birth* (2nd ed.) 89.

27. Cassius, *Third Birth* (2nd ed.) 56.

28. Cassius, *Third Birth* (2nd ed.) 57–58; Washington, *Up from Slavery* 20.

29. Cassius, *Third Birth* (2nd ed.) 64–65.

30. Washington, *Up from Slavery* 48. For Du Bois's statements, see Du Bois, *Du Bois on Religion,* ed. Phil Zuckerman (New York: Rowan and Littlefield Publishers, 2000), 46.

31. Cassius, *Third Birth* (2nd ed.) 66.

32. G. P. Bowser, "Better Outlook for the Colored People," *Gospel Advocate* 70 (August 30, 1928): 836; quoted in B.C. Goodpasture, *Marshall Keeble: Biography and Sermons* (1931; repr., Nashville, TN: Gospel Advocate Company, 1966), 38;

Tuggle, *Another World Wonder* 12. For a reference to the influence of "Campbellian rationalism" on African American Churches of Christ, see Hughes 287.

33. Cassius, *Third Birth* (2nd ed.) 79.

34. Cassius, *Third Birth* (2nd ed.) 49–50.

35. Cassius, *Third Birth* (2nd ed.) 103. See Cassius's article "Jim Crow as I Saw It," in *Western Age* (1908).

36. Cassius, *Third Birth* (2nd ed.) 109.

37. For explicit references to Cassius's sons participating in World War I, see Cassius, "Among Our Colored Disciples," *CL* 32 (July 16, 1918): 8; and Cassius, "The Race Problem and the War," *CL* 32 (August 13, 1918): 8.

38. Cassius, *Third Birth* (2nd ed.) 73–74, 79–80.

39. Cassius, *Third Birth* (2nd ed.) 64, 110.

40. Cassius, *Third Birth* (2nd ed.) 40–41.

41. Cassius, *Third Birth* (2nd ed.) 28, 40, 52, 67. As early as 1898, Cassius had argued that a "new race" had emerged as a result of the racial and sexual mixing of white slave owners and black slaves. The black American "is a straight cross between the original African and the Anglo-Saxon, having almost an equal proportion of both races. He is the embodiment of the most peaceful, hopeful, forgiving and joyous disposition in America" (Cassius, *Negro Evangelization* 10). See also William O. Blake, *The History of Slavery and the Slave Trade, Ancient and Modern* (Columbus, OH: J. and H. Miller, 1857).

42. Compare Cassius, *Third Birth* (2nd ed.) 21 with Ashley S. Johnson, *Condensed Biblical Cyclopedia: Designed for Those Who Have But Little Time for Study* (Louisville, KY: Guide Printing and Publishing Company, 1896).

43. William J. Simmons, *Men of Mark: Eminent, Progressive and Rising* (Chicago: Johnson Publishing Company, 1896), 3.

44. Cassius, *Third Birth* (2nd ed.) 99.

45. Cassius, *Third Birth* (2nd ed.) 108. For more accurate numbers on the black men who fought in the American Revolution and the Civil War, see Franklin and Moss 88, 238; and Benjamin Quarles, *The Negro in the Civil War* (Boston: Little, Brown and Company, 1953), xii.

46. Cassius, "The Third Birth of a Nation," *CL* 37 (March 27, 1923): 12.

47. Cassius, *Third Birth* (2nd ed.) 28, 66.

48. Cassius, *Third Birth* (2nd ed.) 74.

49. Cassius, *Third Birth* (2nd ed.) 25–26.

50. Cassius, *Third Birth* (2nd ed.) 83.

51. *Muskogee Cimeter* (May 4, 1905): 4. For other blacks who held racial separatist views, see "Race Separation Helps," *Western Age* (May 28, 1909): 2; and Lucius Henry Holsey 69.

52. Cassius, *Third Birth* (2nd ed.) 94.

53. Cassius, *Third Birth* (2nd ed.) 83.

54. Cassius, *Third Birth* (2nd ed.) 4; D. T. Broadus, *Christian Worker* 6 (December 16, 1920): 3.

55. E. B. Grubbs, "An Appreciative Sister," *CL* 35 (January 11, 1921): 8.

56. For the chapter on "The Movie, the Soft Drink, and the Short Skirt," see Cassius, *Third Birth* 61–63; for Cassius's response, see Cassius, "The Movie, the Soft Drink, and the Short Skirt," *CL* 41 (August 30, 1927): 8.

57. Cassius, "The Stafford, Ohio Meeting," *CL* 35 (May 17, 1921): 9; Cassius, "Traveling About," *CL* 35 (August 2, 1921): 13; Cassius, "The Meeting at Parsons," *CL* 36 (January 17, 1922): 16.

58. Cassius, "The Third Birth of a Nation," *CL* 39 (January 27, 1925): 10; Cassius, "Field Reports," *CL* 39 (October 6, 1925): 11; Cassius, "Twelve Months' Work," *CL* 39 (October 27, 1925): 16.

Chapter 10

1. Cassius, "My Trip to the Northwest," *CL* 41 (June 21, 1927): 12–13. As early as 1923, Cassius had visited and preached in both New York and Canada. See Cassius, "Field Reports," *CL* 37 (March 13, 1923): 10–11.

2. Cassius, "Report of Work Done in 1927," *CL* 42 (January 17, 1928): 10.

3. Cassius, "Field Reports," *CL* 43 (April 23, 1929): 13.

4. Cassius, "The Negro Question in the Church of Christ," *CL* 44 (March 4, 1930): 16.

5. Cassius, "Out on the Firing Line," *Gospel Advocate* 72 (July 10, 1930): 671.

6. Cassius, "A Failure," *CL* 44 (August 26, 1930): 13. Cassius accepted the designation of globe-trotter as a compliment, observing, "They call me a globe trotter, and I thank God that I am, and I am only sorry that there are not more globe trotters and less stationary preachers" (Cassius, "The Heathen at Home," *CL* 42 [March 20, 1928]: 14).

7. Cassius, "The Negro Question in the Church of Christ," *CL* 44 (March 4, 1930): 16.

8. Cassius, "Ain't It the Truth," *CL* 44 (October 28, 1930): 14.

9. Cassius, "He's Gone Again," *CL* 44 (November 18, 1930): 13.

10. Cassius, "In Behalf of the Colored," *Christian Leader and the Way* 25 (May 16, 1911): 5.

11. Cassius, "The Meeting at Parsons," *CL* 36 (January 17, 1922): 16; W. S. Sims, "Bro. Cassius Commended," *CL* 36 (March 28, 1922): 16.

12. Mattie E. Howard Coleman, "A Grand Success," *CL* 16 (November 11, 1902): 12; S. H. Hall, "Bro. S. R. Cassius and His Work," *CL* 39 (September 29,

1925): 8; Cassius, "Still Optimistic in His Age," *Christian Evangelist* LXII (January 14, 1926): 59.

13. Cassius, "The First Colored Church of Christ in Colorado," *CL* 40 (December 21, 1926): 13.

14. Cassius, "The Preacher's Disappointments in Life," *CL* 41 (January 11, 1927): 16.

15. Cassius, "The Preacher's Disappointments in Life," *CL* 41 (January 11, 1927): 16.

16. Frederick L. Rowe, "In California," *CL* 39 (February 17, 1925): 10; Hall, "Bro. S. R. Cassius and His Work," *CL* 39 (September 29, 1925): 8.

17. A. L. Cassius, "Help Needed," *CL* 39 (May 26, 1925): 11; B. C. Goodpasture, "Help Brother Cassius," *Gospel Advocate* 88 (December 5, 1948): 2.

18. Willard H. Morse, "S. R. Cassius," *CL* 16 (February 4, 1902): 9.

19. W. Jasper Brown, "The Brother in Black," *CL* 16 (November 4, 1902): 4; Cassius, "Cast Thy Bread upon the Waters," *CL* 16 (November 18, 1902): 4.

20. John W. Harris, "An Open Letter to Leader Readers," *CL* 15 (May 14, 1901): 12.

21. Cassius, *The Letter and Spirit* 29.

22. John W. Harris, "An Open Letter to Leader Readers," *CL* 15 (May 14, 1901): 12.

23. Cassius, "My Trip to the East," *CL* 36 (June 20, 1922): 12.

24. Cassius, "Behold I Make All Things New," *CL* 45 (January 6, 1931): 16; Frederick L. Rowe, "Bro. Cassius Is Very Sick," *CL* 45 (March 10, 1931): 9; Cassius, "Brother Cassius Improves," *CL* 45 (April 28, 1931): 16.

25. Cassius, "Brother Cassius Improves," *CL* 45 (April 28, 1931): 16.

26. Mary Janes, "Sister Cassius' Needs," *CL* 45 (September 8, 1931): 7.

27. For references to donations Selina Cassius received after her husband's death, see Frederick L. Rowe, "Missionary Receipts," *CL* 45 (September 22, 1931): 9; Frederick L. Rowe, "Missionary Receipts," *CL* 45 (October 27, 1931): 9; and Frederick L. Rowe, "Leader Fund," *CL* 46 (February 9, 1932): 9.

28. Cassius, "Can One Hundred Thousand Ministers Be Wrong?" *CL* 43 (May 28, 1929): 9.

29. Choate ix.

Bibliography

Primary Sources

Manuscript Collections

Cassius, Samuel Robert. *Negro Evangelization and the Tohee Industrial School.* Cincinnati, OH: Christian Leader Print, 1898.
———. *The Letter and Spirit of Giving and the Race Problem.* n.p., n.d.
Daniel, Carey. "God: The Original Segregationist." Dallas, Texas. 1955. Center for Restoration Studies. Abilene Christian University. Abilene, Texas.
Landry, Stuart O. "Rebuilding the Tower of Babel: A Study of Christianity and Segregation." Special Collections. Mitchell Memorial Library. Mississippi State University. Starkville, Mississippi.

Government Documents

Census Records for Prince William County, 1850, 1853, 1860. Manassas, Virginia.
Official Registers of the United States. Record of Appointment of Postmasters. National Archives. Washington, D.C.
Public Records. Logan County, Oklahoma. Guthrie, Oklahoma.
"Registers of Birth, Deaths, and Marriages." Reel 32. Prince William Public Library System. Manassas, Virginia.
Slave Inhabitants for Prince William County, 1850. Census Records (August 31, 1850).
Student Records, 1909–10. Office of the Registrar. Tuskegee University. Tuskegee, Alabama.
United States Census of Oklahoma, 1900, 1910, 1920. Guthrie, Oklahoma. County Clerk's Office, Logan County, Oklahoma.

Newspapers

American Freedmen (Washington, D.C.), 1866.
Atlanta Constitution (Atlanta, GA), 1900.

Boley Progress (Indian Territory, OK), 1905, 1906–10.
Freedmen's Record (Boston, MA), 1865.
Gallipolis Daily Tribune (Gallipolis, OH), 1920.
Greenwood Enterprise (Greenwood, MS), 1904.
Kansas City [Weekly] Journal (Kansas City, MO), 1905.
Langston City Herald (Langston City, OK), 1890–93.
Literary Digest, 1901.
Mulhall Enterprises (Oklahoma), 1895.
Muskogee Cimeter (Muskogee, OK), 1905–8.
New York Times 1890–91, 1900.
Oklahoma Guide (Guthrie, OK), 1904–7.
Oklahoma Safeguard (Oklahoma), 1906.
Outlook, 1907, 1910, 1915.
Prince William and Virginia Advertiser (Manassas, VA), 1857.
Richmond Enquirer (Richmond, VA), 1844.
Savannah Tribune (Savannah, GA), 1903.
Washington Bee (Washington, D.C.), 1901.
Western Age (Langston, Logan County, OK), 1905–9.

Religious Newspapers

Christian Companion (Wichita, KS), 1916.
Christian Evangelist (St. Louis, MO), 1889, 1893, 1897.
Christian Leader (Cincinnati, OH), 1893–1931.
Christian Leader (Cincinnati, OH), 1904.
Christian Standard (Cincinnati, OH), 1916.
Christian Worker (Wichita, KS), 1920.
Firm Foundation (Fort Worth, TX), 1915–16.
Gospel Advocate (Nashville, TN), 1899, 1901, 1915, 1917, 1920, 1930.
Millennial Harbinger (Bethany, WV), 1869.
West Coast Christian (Los Angeles, CA), 1941.

Books

Baird, John D., and Charles Ryskamp, eds. *The Poems of William Cowper.* Oxford: Clarendon Press, 1995.
Blake, William O. *The History of Slavery and the Slave Trade, Ancient and Modern.* Columbus, OH: J. and H. Miller, 1857.
Blassingame, John W., ed. *Slave Testimony: Two Centuries of Letters, Speeches, Interviews, and Autobiographies.* 1977. Baton Rouge: Louisiana State University Press, 2002.

Boucicault, Dion. *The Octoroon or Life in Louisiana.* 1859. In *Representative American Plays,* ed. Arthur Hobson Quinn. New York: Century Company, 1919.

Bruce, Philip A. *The Plantation Negro as a Freeman: Observations on His Character, Condition, and Prospects in Virginia.* 1889. Williamstown, MA: Corner House Publishers, 1970.

Carroll, Charles. *The Negro a Beast, or, in the Image of God.* 1900. Miami, FL: Mnemosyne Publishing Company, 1969.

Cassius, Samuel Robert. *The Third Birth of a Nation.* 1st ed. Cincinnati, OH: F. L. Rowe, 1920.

———. *The Third Birth of a Nation.* 2nd ed. Cincinnati, OH: F. L. Rowe, 1925.

Darwin, Charles. *On the Origin of Species.* 1859. Cambridge, MA: Harvard University Press, 1966.

Douglass, Frederick. *Narrative of the Life of Frederick Douglass, An American Slave.* 1845. New York: W. W. Norton, 1997.

Du Bois, W. E. B. *Du Bois on Religion.* Ed. Phil Zuckerman. New York: Rowan and Littlefield Publishers, 2000.

———. *The Souls of Black Folk.* 1903. Boston: Bedford/St. Martin's, 1997.

Extracts from Letters of Teachers and Superintendents of the New-England Freedmen's Aid Society. Boston: John Wilson and Son, 1864.

Goodpasture, B. C. *Marshall Keeble: Biography and Sermons.* 1931. Nashville, TN: Gospel Advocate Company, 1966.

Holsey, Lucius Henry. "Race Segregation." *A. M. E. Church Review* 26 (October 1909): 109–23. In *Social Protest Thought in the African Methodist Episcopal Church, 1862–1939,* ed. Stephen W. Angell and Anthony B. Pinn. Knoxville: University of Tennessee Press, 2000.

Irving, Washington. *A History of New York.* New York: Inskeep and Bradford, 1809.

Limerick, J. J., ed. *The Gospel in Chart and Sermon.* Cincinnati, OH: John F. Rowe, 1897.

Miller, Kelly. "As to the Leopard's Spots: An Open Letter to Thomas Dixon, Jr." In *Race Adjustment: Essays on the Negro in America.* 1905. New York: Neale Publishing Company, 1910.

Redkey, Edwin S., ed. *Respect Black: The Writings and Speeches of Henry McNeal Turner.* New York: Arno Press, 1971.

Richardson, Robert. *Memoirs of Alexander Campbell, Embracing a View of the Origin, Progress and Principles of the Religious Reformation Which He Advocated.* 2 vols. Indianapolis, IN: Religious Book Service, 1897.

Roosevelt, Theodore. Vol. 16 of *The Works of Theodore Roosevelt.* New York: Charles Scribner's Sons, 1926.

Rowe, F. L., ed. *Our Savior's Prayer for Unity: A Symposium on the Seventeenth Chapter of John.* Cincinnati, OH: F. L. Rowe, 1918.

Salt, Henry S. *Animals' Rights: Considered in Relation to Social Progress*. 1892. Clarks Summit, PA: Society for Animal Rights, 1980.

Sanger, Margaret. *Happiness in Marriage*. 1926. New York: Blue Ribbon Books, 1940.

———. *Margaret Sanger: An Autobiography*. New York: W. W. Norton, 1938.

Simmons, William J. *Men of Mark: Eminent, Progressive and Rising*. Chicago: Johnson Publishing Company, 1896.

Thornbrough, Emma Lou, ed. *Black Reconstructionists*. Englewood Cliffs, NJ: Prentice-Hall, 1972.

Tuggle, Annie C. *Another World Wonder*. n.p., n.d.

Washington, Booker T. *The Negro in Business*. New York: AMS Press, 1971 [1907].

———. *Up from Slavery*. 1901. New York: Oxford University Press, 1995.

Wells, Ida B. *Crusade for Justice: The Autobiography of Ida B. Wells*. Ed. Alfreda M. Duster. Chicago: University of Chicago Press, 1970.

Young, Charles Alexander. ed. *Historical Documents Advocating Christian Union*. Joplin, MO: College Press Publishing Company, 1985.

Secondary Sources

Bailey, Kenneth K. "The Post–Civil War Racial Separations in Southern Protestantism: Another Look." *Church History* 46 (December 1977): 453–73.

Bay, Mia. *The White Image in the Black Mind: African-American Ideas about White People, 1830–1925*. New York: Oxford University Press, 2000.

Beard, Charles A. "The Constitution of Oklahoma," *Political Science Quarterly* 24 (1909): 95–104.

Boring, M. Eugene. *Disciples and the Bible: A History of Disciples Biblical Interpretation in North America*. St. Louis, MO: Chalice Press, 1997.

Bowers, Calvin H. *Realizing the California Dream: The Story of Black Churches of Christ in Los Angeles*. Calvin Bowers, 2001.

Boyd, R. Vernon. *Undying Dedication: The Story of G. P. Bowser*. Nashville, TN: Gospel Advocate Company, 1985.

Brands, H. W. *T. R.: The Last Romantic*. New York: Basic Books, 1997.

Brown, Thomas Elton. "Bible-Belt Catholicism: A History of the Roman Catholic Church in Oklahoma, 1905–1945." PhD diss., Oklahoma State University, 1974.

Cash, W. J. *The Mind of the South*. New York: Alfred A. Knopf, 1941.

Choate, J. E. *Roll Jordan Roll: A Biography of Marshall Keeble*. Nashville, TN: Gospel Advocate Company, 1974.

Clark, Carter Blue. "A History of the Ku Klux Klan in Oklahoma." PhD diss., University of Oklahoma, 1976.

Cook, Raymond Allen. *Fire from the Flint: The Amazing Careers of Thomas Dixon*. Winston-Salem, NC: John F. Blair, 1968.

Cripps, Thomas R. "The Reaction of the Negro to the Motion Picture Birth of a Nation." *Historian* (February 1963): 344–62.

Crockett, Norman L. *The Black Towns.* Lawrence: Regents Press of Kansas, 1979.

Dabney, Lillian G. "The History of Schools for Negroes in the District of Columbia, 1807–1947." PhD diss., The Catholic University of America, 1949.

Ellis, Mary Louise. "'Rain Down Fire': The Lynching of Sam Hose." PhD diss., Florida State University, 1992.

Ellsworth, Scott. *Death in a Promised Land: The Tulsa Race Riot of 1921.* Baton Rouge: Louisiana State University Press, 1982.

Felder, Cain Hope, ed. *Stony the Road We Trod: African American Biblical Interpretation.* Minneapolis, MN: Fortress Press, 1991.

Foner, Eric. *Reconstruction: America's Unfinished Revolution, 1863–1877.* New York: Harper and Row Publishers, 1988.

Franklin, Jimmie Lewis. *Journey toward Hope: A History of Blacks in Oklahoma.* Norman: University of Oklahoma Press, 1982.

Franklin, John Hope, and John Whittington Franklin, eds. *My Life and an Era: The Autobiography of Buck Colbert Franklin.* Baton Rouge: Louisiana State University Press, 1997.

Franklin, John Hope, and Alfred A. Moss, Jr. *From Slavery to Freedom: A History of African Americans.* 1947. Boston: McGraw-Hill, 2000.

Fredrickson, George M. *The Black Image in the White Mind: The Debate on Afro-American Character and Destiny, 1817–1914.* New York: Harper and Row, 1971.

Gallagher, Gary W., ed. *Lee, the Soldier.* Lincoln: University of Nebraska Press, 1996.

Garrett, Leroy. *The Stone-Campbell Movement: An Anecdotal History of Three Churches.* Joplin, MO: College Press Publishing Company, 1987.

Gatewood, Willard B., Jr. *Theodore Roosevelt and the Art of Controversy: Episodes of the White House Years.* Baton Rouge: Louisiana State University Press, 1970.

Genovese, Eugene D. *Roll Jordan Roll: The World the Slaves Made.* 1972. New York: Pantheon Books, 1974.

Green, Constance McLaughlin. *The Secret City: A History of Race Relations in the Nation's Capital.* Princeton, NJ: Princeton University Press, 1967.

Hamilton, Kenneth Marvin. "Black Town Promotion and Development on the Middle Border, 1877–1914." PhD diss., Washington University, 1978.

Harlan, Louis. *Booker T. Washington: The Making of a Black Leader, 1856–1901.* New York: Oxford University Press, 1972.

———. *Booker T. Washington: The Wizard of Tuskegee, 1901–1915.* New York: Oxford University Press, 1983.

———. "The Secret Life of Booker T. Washington." *Journal of Southern History* 37 (August 1971).

Harrell, David Edwin, Jr. *Quest for a Christian America: The Disciples of Christ and*

American Society to 1866. Vol. 1 of *A Social History of the Disciples of Christ*. Nashville, TN: Disciples of Christ Historical Society, 1966.

————. *The Social Sources of Division of the Disciples of Christ, 1865–1900*. Vol. 2 of *A Social History of the Disciples of Christ*. Atlanta, GA: Publishing Systems, 1973.

Hill, Mozell C. "The All-Negro Society in Oklahoma." PhD diss., University of Chicago, 1946.

Holmes, William F. *The White Chief: James Kimble Vardaman*. Baton Rouge: Louisiana State University Press, 1970.

Hooper, Robert E. *Crying in the Wilderness: A Biography of David Lipscomb*. Nashville, TN: David Lipscomb College, 1979.

Hughes, Richard T. *Reviving the Ancient Faith: The Story of Churches of Christ in America*. Grand Rapids, MI: Eerdmans, 1996.

Humble, Bill. "The Missionary Society Controversy in the Restoration Movement, 1823–1875." PhD diss., University of Iowa, 1964.

Hurst, Irvin. *The 46th Star: A History of Oklahoma's Constitutional Convention and Early Statehood*. Oklahoma City, OK: Semco Color Press, 1957.

Inscoe, John C. "Carolina Slave Names: An Index to Acculturation." *Journal of Southern History* 44 (November 1983): 544.

Jackson, Luther P. "Religious Development of the Negro in Virginia from 1760 to 1860." *Journal of Negro History* 16 (January 1931): 169–239.

Johnson, Hannibal B. *Acres of Aspiration: The All-Black Towns in Oklahoma*. Austin, TX: Eakin Press, 2002.

Katz, William Loren. *The Black West*. New York: Doubleday and Company, 1971.

Kolchin, Peter. *American Slavery, 1619–1877*. New York: Hill and Wang, 1993.

Larson, Edward J. *Summer for the Gods: The Scopes Trial and America's Continuing Debate over Science and Religion*. New York: Basic Books, 1997.

Lewis, David Levering. *W. E. B. Du Bois: The Fight for Equality and the American Century, 1919–1963*. New York: Henry Holt and Company, 2000.

Lincoln, C. Eric, and Lawrence H. Mamiya. *The Black Church in the African-American Experience*. Durham, NC: Duke University Press, 1990.

Litwack, Leon F. *Been in the Storm So Long: The Aftermath of Slavery*. New York: Alfred A. Knopf, 1979.

————. *Trouble in Mind: Black Southerners in the Age of Jim Crow*. New York: Vintage Books, 1998.

Logan, Rayford W. *The Betrayal of the Negro: From Rutherford B. Hayes to Woodrow Wilson*. 1965. New York: Da Capo Press, 1997.

Martin, Waldo E., Jr. *The Mind of Frederick Douglass*. Chapel Hill: University of North Carolina Press, 1984.

McMurry, Linda O. *George Washington Carver: Scientist and Symbol*. New York: Oxford University Press, 1981.

————. *To Keep the Waters Troubled: The Life of Ida B. Wells.* New York: Oxford University Press, 1998.

McPherson, James M. *Battle Cry of Freedom: The Civil War Era.* New York: Ballantine Books, 1988.

Meier, August. *Negro Thought in America, 1880–1915: Racial Ideologies in the Age of Booker T. Washington.* Ann Arbor: University of Michigan Press, 1963.

Mellinger, Philip. "Discrimination and Statehood in Oklahoma." *Chronicles of Oklahoma* 49 (1971): 340–78.

Moran, Jeffrey P. "Reading Race into the Scopes Trial: African American Elites, Science, and Fundamentalism." *Journal of American History* 90 (December 2003): 891–911.

Morris, Robert C. *Reading, 'Riting, and Reconstruction: The Education of Freedmen in the South, 1861–1870.* 1976. Chicago: University of Chicago Press, 1981.

Murch, James DeForest, *Christians Only: A History of the Restoration Movement.* Cincinnati, OH: Standard Publishing, 1962.

The Negro in Virginia. 1940. Winston-Salem, NC: John F. Blair, 1994.

Paul, Henry N. *The Royal Play of Macbeth: When, Why, and How It Was Written by Shakespeare.* New York: Octagon Books, 1971.

Quarles, Benjamin. *The Negro in the Civil War.* Boston: Little, Brown and Company, 1953.

Redkey, Edwin S. *Black Exodus: Black Nationalist and Back-to-Africa Movements.* New Haven, CT: Yale University Press, 1969.

Roberson, Jere W. "Edward P. McCabe and the Langston Experiment." *Chronicles of Oklahoma* (fall 1973): 343–55.

Sanborn, Margaret. *Robert E. Lee: The Complete Man, 1861–1870.* Philadelphia: J. B. Lippincott Company, 1967.

Sandburg, Carl. *Abraham Lincoln: The Prairie Years and the War Years.* 1954. New York: Galahad Books, 1993.

Scales, James R., and Danney Goble. *Oklahoma Politics: A History.* Norman: University of Oklahoma Press, 1982.

Shirk, George H. *Oklahoma Place Names.* Norman: University of Oklahoma Press, 1965.

Simmons, William J. *Men of Mark: Eminent, Progressive, and Rising.* 1887. Chicago: Johnson Publishing Company, 1970.

Southern, Eileen. *The Music of Black Americans: A History.* 1971. New York: W. W. Norton, 1983.

Spear, Allan H. *Black Chicago: The Making of a Negro Ghetto, 1890–1920.* Chicago: University of Chicago Press, 1967.

Spencer, Jon Michael. *Black Hymnody: A Hymnological History of the African-American Church.* Knoxville: University of Tennessee Press, 1992.

Sterling, Dorothy, ed. *We Are Your Sisters: Black Women in the Nineteenth Century.* New York: W. W. Norton, 1997.

Strother, Horatio T. *The Underground Railroad in Connecticut.* Middletown, CT: Wesleyan University Press, 1962.

Taylor, Joseph. "The Rise and Decline of a Utopian Community, Boley, Oklahoma." *Negro History Bulletin* (April 1940): 92–93.

Teall, Kaye M. *Black History in Oklahoma: A Resource Book.* Oklahoma City Public Schools, 1971.

Terrell, Mary Church. "History of the High School for Negroes in Washington." *Journal of Negro History* 2 (July 1917): 252–66.

Tolson, Arthur L. *The Black Oklahomans: A History, 1541–1972.* 1966. New Orleans, LA: Edwards Printing Company, 1974.

Warren, Gwendolin Sims. *Ev'ry Time I Feel the Spirit: 101 Best-Loved Psalms, Gospel Hymns, and Spiritual Songs of the African-American Church.* 1997. New York: Henry Holt and Company, 1999.

Webb, Henry E. *In Search of Christian Unity: A History of the Restoration Movement.* 2nd ed. Abilene, TX: Abilene Christian University Press, 2003.

West, Earl I. *The Search for the Ancient Order: A History of the Restoration Movement, 1849–1906.* 1950. Nashville, TN: Gospel Advocate Company, 1986. 4 volumes.

White, James D. "Destined for Duty: The Life and Diary of Bishop Theophile Meerschaert." *Chronicles of Oklahoma* 71 (spring 1993): 4–41.

Williamson, Joel. *Crucible of Race: Black/White Relations in the American South since Emancipation.* New York: Oxford University Press, 1984.

———. *New People: Miscegenation and Mulattoes in the United States.* New York: New York University Press, 1984.

———. *A Rage for Order: Black/White Relations in the American South since Emancipation.* New York: Oxford University Press, 1986.

Woodward, C. Vann. *Origins of the New South, 1877–1913.* 1951. Baton Rouge: Louisiana State University Press, 1997.

———. *The Strange Career of Jim Crow.* 1955. New York: Oxford University Press, 1966.

Yetman, Norman R., ed. *Life under the "Peculiar Institution": Selections from the Slave Narrative Collection.* New York: Holt, Rinehart and Winston, 1970.

Zangrando, Robert L. *The NAACP Crusade against Lynching, 1909–1950.* (Philadelphia, PA: Temple University Press, 1980.

Index